KU-485-096

Russian Political Institutions

BY

DEREK J. R. SCOTT

GEORGE ALLEN & UNWIN LTD
Ruskin House
Museum Street London

FIRST PUBLISHED IN 1958
SECOND EDITION 1961
THIRD EDITION 1965
FOURTH EDITION 1969

This book is copyright under the Berne Convention. All rights are reserved. Apart from any fair dealing for the purpose of private study, research, criticism or review, as permitted under the Copyright Act, 1956, no part of this publication may be reproduced, stored in a retrieval system, or transmitted, in any form or by any means, electronic, electrical, chemical, mechanical, optical, photocopying, recording or otherwise, without the prior permission of the copyright owner. Enquiries should be addressed to the Publishers.

This fourth edition © Derek J. R. Scott, 1969

Cloth Edition SBN 04 320061 3
Paper Edition SBN 04 320062 1

This book has been set in Linotype Times New Roman type and printed in Great Britain by Western Printing Services Ltd, Bristol

6 00 019799 4

TELEPEN

MINERVA SERIES OF STUDENTS' HANDBOOKS

NO. 2

General Editor

PROFESSOR

BRIAN CHAPMAN

M.A., D.PHIL. (*Oxon*)

Russian Political Institutions

In the same series

1. INTERNATIONAL INSTITUTIONS *by Professor Paul Reuter*

3. FREE ELECTIONS *by Professor W. J. M. Mackenzie*

4. MODERN FORMS OF GOVERNMENT: *A Comparative Study by the Rt. Hon. Michael Stewart, M.P.*

5. THE USE OF ECONOMIC STATISTICS *by C. A. Blyth*

6. THE SOVIET ECONOMY *by Professor Alex Nove*

7. BRITISH FOREIGN POLICY *The Process of Readjustment 1945–1961 by F. S. Northedge*

8. PUBLIC FINANCE AND BUDGETARY POLICY *by Professor Alan Willams*

9. MACRO-ECONOMICS *by F. S. Brooman*

10. INTRODUCTION TO THE SOCIAL SCIENCES *by Professor Maurice Duverger Translated by M. Anderson*

11. TRANSPORT AND PUBLIC POLICY *by Professor K. M. Gwilliam*

12. INFLATION AND THE THEORY OF MONEY *by Professor R. J. Ball*

13. READINGS FROM LIBERAL WRITERS *by John Plamenatz*

14. A HISTORY OF POST-WAR RUSSIA *by R. W. Pethybridge*

15. THE WORKS OF JOSEPH DE MAISTRE *by Jack Lively*

16. PLANNING AND GROWTH IN RICH AND POOR COUNTRIES *Edited by A. G. Ford and W. Birmingham*

17. THEORIES OF ECONOMIC DEVELOPMENT AND GROWTH *by Y. S. Brenner*

18. SAMPLING *by Freda Conway*

19. THE SCIENCE OF SOCIETY *by Professor Stephen Cotgrove*

20. THE BRITISH SYSTEM OF GOVERNMENT *by Professor A. H. Birch*

21. COMPARATIVE SOCIAL ADMINISTRATION *by Barbara N. Rodgers, John Greve and John S. Morgan*

22. INTERNATIONAL ECONOMICS *by Professor Sidney Wells*

23. CONSTITUTIONAL BUREAUCRACY: *The Development of British Central Administration Since the Eighteenth Century by Henry Parris*

PREFACE TO THE FOURTH EDITION

Since the appearance of the third edition in 1965 the rejection of the innovations of Mr. Krushchov which was then apparent has been consolidated and confirmed in a reversion to some of the forms and terminology of the Stalin tradition, apparently informed by the same nostalgia for a securer past which has latterly manifested itself in Stalinist ways of argument with misliked opinions at home or within the Soviet power abroad. The present edition takes account of such reversions and variants as documented to the middle of 1968, and has been so extensively revised that it is entirely reset, but it records no significant change in the character and style of the system, since at present the author sees none. In the expectation that continued aspirations towards manners of operation generally acceptable as economically rational and more respectful than hitherto of human dignity and uncoerced co-operation, still seeking expression within assumptions of the possibility of some form of systematic control of the totality of the national life, are likely to lead to repeated further manipulation of the indigenously evolved institutions, to which the external world offers no obvious alternatives, this edition pretends to no more than a transient accuracy. Since the author learns from his Soviet reader (a Mr. Marat N. Perfiljev, in his *Kritika burzhuaznyh teori o sovetskoi politicheskoi sisteme*, Leningrad 1968) that he is an ideologist of capitalism he suspects that some more inspiring message would be in order, and since the British *Glavlit* has failed to provide correction must await guidance from the British *Agitprop*.

D.J.R.S.
Glasgow, 1968

Acknowledgements

This book could hardly have been published without the advice given in the course of its evolution by Professor W. J. M. Mackenzie, Professor P. W. Campbell and the late Professor D. P. Costello, then all of the University of Manchester, and the typing skill and patience of my aunt Mrs. W. Pevalin. None of these bears any responsibility for anything which has happened since the first edition.

CONTENTS

PREFACE   *page* 5

INTRODUCTION: SCOPE OF THE ATTEMPT   15

Difficulties of Russian Studies   15

Method and Plan   17

I. WHAT RUSSIAN POLITICS ARE ABOUT

Material Inheritance   21

    Territory and natural endowment
    Foreign contacts and expansion of the Russians
    Late development

Administrative Tradition   23

    Absence of representative institutions
    Absence of local self-government
    Peasant emancipation and the rural commune
    Alexander II's local-government reform
    Judicial reform
    A country of poor peasants

Attitudes   29

    Peasant discontent, rural and urban
    Lack of firm body of support for the regime
    Disruptive force of the intelligentsia
    What is national character?
    Russian national character before the revolution
    Military defeat precipitates revolt of 1905
    First acceptance of liberal democracy

Doctrinal Equipment   33

    Why Marxism appealed to the Russians
    Difficulties and organisation of the early Russian Marxists
    Lenin's Russification of Marxist doctrine
    What belief in Marxism has changed in Russia

The Manner of Seizing Power   41

    The prepared 'October' revolution of 1917
    The issues remaining to be solved
    The lessons to the ambitious

The Issues   42

    Who shall rule?
    Economic priorities?
    The frontiers and security
    Particularism
    Local alliances in the centralised state

The Periods   *page* **45**

      War communism and anti-bolshevik threats
      The N.E.P. and the succession to Lenin
      Planning and the consolidation of Stalin's power
      Unbridled Stalinism
      Unstable oligarchy

The Participants   **53**

      Citizens
      Followers of politics
      The political society
      The sovereign decision-making body

II. SOVIETS, UNION AND CONSTITUTIONAL STATE

The Invention of the Soviets   **56**

      Marx on the Paris commune
      The soviets of 1905
      Lenin builds them into the Marxist state
      His attitude between 'February' and 'October'
      Congresses of soviets and executive committees
      Addition of a government of conventional type
      By-passing the soviets ('dual subordination')
      Purging the soviets
      Absence of a legal formulation of sovietism

The Union   **63**

      Nationalist demands and Russian bolshevik response
      Bolshevik acceptance of 'federalism' ('autonomy')
      Its content
      The People's Commissariat for Nationalities
      The formation of the U.S.S.R.
      The Union legislature
      The types of ministries
      Sense in which this is 'not federalism'
      Federal powers over federated units
      A matter of 'subordination', not of limitation
      Utility of Soviet autonomy-federalism
      Promotion to the status of a federated unit
      Autonomous units
      How secure is federal and autonomous status?

Administrative Areas   **72**

      Economic motive of division, and mutability
      The invention of new areas (1920's)
      The problem of the intermediate level (1930's)
      The Stalinist trend to fragmentation and its reversal
      Consolidation of 'village' and district areas—motive
      What it means in terms of population
      Manifestation of urbanisation
      Why keep the 'village' soviet?

Collective Administration *page* 77

    'Collegiality'
    The collective head of state
    The ministry 'collegium'
    'Collegiality' and 'one-man headship' in industrial
        management
    Collective management of national economy replaced
        by ministerial management

The Function of Soviet Constitutionalism 79

    Why constitutions are made
    Soviet Union's lack of pressing motive to adopt a written
        constitution
    The occasions of the three constitutions
    The manner of making of the 1936 constitution

Contents of the Constitution 82

    The chapter headings
    Declarations of faith (Chapters I and X)
    Rights of federating units
    Excess of detail in political structure and machinery
    Apparent return to the separation of powers
    Amendment and interpretation of the constitution
    Uniformity of constitutions of federated and autonomous
        units

Utility of the Constitution 87

    The constitution as record
    Supplementary evidence
    The constitution as ideology

What Remains? 88

III. CONVENTIONAL STATE MACHINERY

The Representative Bodies—What They Are 89

    Size and basis of election of U.S.S.R. Supreme Soviet
    Supreme Soviets of union and autonomous republics
    Local soviets
    Soviets no longer 'political foundation' of the U.S.S.R.

How They are Formed 92

    Unequal representation before 1936
    Franchise under 1936 constitution
    Method of voting
    Electoral commissions
    Registration
    Nomination and constituency conferences
    Practice of open voting
    Cases and causes of failure to secure election
    Some functions of Soviet elections
    Product of the elections (party membership, etc.)
    Pattern of composition of 1954 Supreme Soviet

What They Do   *page* 99

    Rules and practice on frequency of meetings
    Verification of mandates
    Officers of the Supreme Soviet
    Standing commissions of Supreme Soviet
    Local standing commissions
    Separate and joint sessions of houses of Supreme Soviet
    Nature of discussion
    Official categorisation of Supreme Soviet business
    Business performed by 1954 Supreme Soviet
    Business of a local soviet
    Soviets as vehicle of criticism of local administration
    Lobbying in the soviet system
    Soviets as briefing conferences
    Soviets as schools of government
    Why people attend soviets

The Inner Bodies—How They are Formed   111

    Nature of executive committees, praesidia, bureaux
    Praesidium of a Supreme Soviet
    Executive committee of a local soviet
    Selection of members of an executive committee
    Type of person selected
    Councils of ministers
    Quality of the ministers
    Other members of the Council of Ministers
    Presidium of the Council of Ministers
    Ministers and Supreme Soviet
    Councils of ministers of union republics

What They Do   119

    Acts of the councils of ministers
    Acts of the Praesidium of the Supreme Soviet
    Meetings of the councils of ministers and praesidia
    Their part in the system of hierarchic supervision
    Work of a local soviet executive committee
    An urban local soviet executive committee
    Acts of executive committees
    Meetings of executive committees
    Supervision over supervision
    Reconciliation of myth and practical needs

The Ministries and Departments   125

    The ministries at federal level
    The ministries at union-republic level
    Ministries and administrations of autonomous republics
    Departments and administrations of local executive
        committees
    Internal structure of the ministries
    Ministerial acts and authority
    The minister and his collegium

IV. THE PARTY
Structure   *page* 136

Relations of the party structure to the state structure
Party rules and designations
Structure of primary organisations of the party
Representative machinery of the party
Committees and central committees
Bureaux and secretaries
Congresses of the C.P.S.U.
Central Committee of the C.P.S.U.
Plenary meetings of the Central Committee
Former bureaux of the Central Committee
Praesidium of the Central Committee
Bureaux of republican party central committees
Secretariat of the party
The First Secretaryship since Stalin
The junior secretaries
Central checking ('revision') commission
Committee of party control
Advancement at the top

Staff   153

Changing principles of organisation of party staff
Party schools

Work in the Forces and with Youth   155

Party groups; party work in ministries and armed forces
Party work with youth

Membership   158

Principles of recruitment
Party strength in 1917
Recruiting drives
Exclusions and restrictions
The party in the period of purges
Recruitment rules and practice from 1939
The post-war membership policy
Composition by nationality
Composition by sex
Composition by occupation
The party and its allies in the state machinery
Interlocking of party and state deliberative bodies

What Membership Means   168

Duties of membership
Rights of membership
Financial and social burdens of membership
Dangers of membership
Incentives to seek membership
Influence of members
Influence and obligations of office-holders
Paid officials
Advancement in the party

12   CONTENTS

The Party as Administrative Machinery   *page* 176

    The task set the party
    How the party works in the administration
    Party oversight
    Party responsibility for agriculture
    Party responsibility for staffing ('cadres')
    The 'nomenklatura' in party staffing work
    Principle of abstention from detail
    Shortcomings of party officials
    The cost of party oversight

The Party as Organised Faith   184

    Ideology
    The utility of ideology
    The cost of ideology
    Party self-education and propaganda
    Distinction of propaganda and agitation
    The Central Committee department of propaganda and
        agitation
    Party control of the press
    Members' neglect of ideological work

The Party as Symbol   190

    Embodiment of the revolutionary tradition
    Embodiment of internationalism

V. THE WEB OF MANAGEMENT

Organisation in Industry   191

    'Subordination' of industrial enterprises
    The links with the ministry

Agriculture   196

    The ministerial pattern
    The constitution of collective farms
    The management of collective farms
    Checks upon the management
    State farms and collective farms
    The collective-farm members' incentives
    Machine-tractor stations
    Disposal of produce

Organs of Detection and Regulation   203

    The banking system
    Audit
    State control
    Police
    The procuracy

Organs of Adjudication   208

    Arbitration
    The judicial system
    Civil business of the courts

Criminal business of the courts   *page*
Other punitive jurisdictions
Pressures on the judges
The quality of Soviet judicial work

Other Lines of Control   216

Trade unions
The press
Specialised societies, churches, etc.

The Men in the Machine   220

Recruitment and establishments in industry
Posting
Powers of the manager
Unauthorised managerial methods

Education and the Educated   223

The general education system
Higher education
The content of Soviet education
The learned institutions and their task
Assignments, incentives and limitations of the Soviet
    educated
The scholar and politics

The Armed Forces   231

The citizen's experience of the forces
The officers
Political influence of the military

VI. DECISION AND PERFORMANCE

Top-level Decisions   234

What is the sovereign decision-taking body?
What sort of matters does it decide?

Planning and Budgeting   236

The economic plan—a general order
The instruments of planning
Their preparation
Budgets
The process of budgeting
Heads of revenue
The revenue of local soviets
Responsibility for expenditure

Low-level Decisions   242

Occasions for general consultation of the public
How to get things done from below
The field for private agreement and initiative

Securing Performance—Economic   *page* 244

>   Financial incentives to plan-fulfilment
>   Negative side to emphasis on plan-fulfilment

Securing Performance—General   246

>   Absence of freedom from supervision—its results
>   Penal system
>   Economic motive in penal system
>   Incentives to the ambitious
>   The stimulus of general well-being
>   The sense of national danger
>   The sense of national power
>   The fiction of the enemy
>   Consequences of absence of party conflict

BIBLIOGRAPHY   253

INDEX   257

reasonable or it would be imposed by force. This is so with the transfer of any political system from one country to another, and a system forcibly imposed is bad whatever its origin. We study Russian political institutions as we study any institutions of any society, as part of the study of man, in order to understand what it feels like to be another person in other circumstances—to know, as far as we may, the reasons others see for acting as they do. We cannot hope to refrain entirely from judgment, since it is in human nature to judge. It is therefore well to have reasons for our judgment. This book rests on the assumption that a judgment is acceptable only in so far as its standards are Russian, a reasonable estimate of what Russians, in Russian circumstances, would find more or less satisfactory. Placed as we are in respect of access to detailed information, we can hardly assess any particular institution. Even for better documented countries it is difficult to say how far any part of the system can be changed without changing the whole. On the system as a whole it is possible to comment without being entirely unscientific.

The documentary means of access to the experience of the Russians are the daily and periodical press, published texts of legal instruments and commentaries upon them, and the official textbooks intended for the use of various classes of students and officials. The legal texts are defective. The gazette of the acts of the Supreme Soviet (*Vedomosti Verhovnogo Soveta*),[1] or, in fact, since the Supreme Soviet meets rarely, mainly of its Praesidium, now appears weekly, but contains little but honours and awards, changes of administrative areas, agencies and ministers, and posting of ambassadors. The union republics' similarly named gazettes are now often available and can be more informative. The acts of the

---

[1] The principles of transliteration followed in this book are: to avoid it wherever possible, to use as few letters as possible, and to respect generally accepted conventional spellings of proper names in frequent use where consistency would produce an unfamiliar form. The letter 'y' is always a vowel, the letter 'j' is used to represent the consonantal 'y' sound. After the vowels 'i' and 'y' at the ends of words it is omitted. The hard sign (separating two sounds) is represented by an apostrophe. The letter 'e' is to be understood always to have a consonantal 'y' sound before it without any indication (one exception will worry only those who already know the Russian form). The Russian 'h' sound is represented by the letter 'h' (the exception for proper names preserves the now familiar initial of Mr. Khrushchov's surname). 'Zh' has its conventional sound. The Russian 'e' as in Mr. Khrushchov's name is transliterated according to sound; the adjectival ending in 'go' (as here) according to sight. Terms quoted in parentheses in the text are always given in the singular if capable of being so used. Where used in the plural in the text they are given the English form of plural in 's', however badly it fits.

INTRODUCTION

Scope of the Attempt

Difficulties of Russian Studies

It is difficult to approach the study of anything Russian in the same frame of mind as we are accustomed to bring to the understanding of other societies. The Russian authorities present the experience of their country as of universal application, and the foreign observer is apt, in the same spirit, to take it as an example, good or bad. Moreover, the world is now much involved in Russian affairs, and its ability to see them dispassionately is affected by a reasonable desire to know what Russia is going to do next. But both polemic and prophecy, particularly tempting in the field of politics, are remote from the study of political institutions. These are the more or less conventionalised processes by which the divergent wills of individuals in a society are, in fact, reconciled into acceptance of courses of action taken in the name of the society as a whole or of recognised associations within it. We seek in this book to understand the process where the individuals involved are Russians, as we are already accustomed to do where they are Americans or Frenchmen. Our concern is with the very recent period of history which we call the present, though this is not to be understood without some reference to the remoter past.

We have to face at the outset the problem of the terms in which to discuss Russian politics. Many of the institutions which we traditionally accept as keys to the nature of political systems—the legislature, elections or the head of state—exist, but are of little significance in the real process of politics as we define it. Others—the government or the party—although important, are something very different from the institutions similarly designated in the systems with which people in this country are more familiar. Other terms useful in political discourse—the civil service or central and local government, and the different balances between them—are inapplicable because of the virtual absence in the Russian system of the distinctions which they imply. The total field of study is itself different. If we decide (as to make his subject manageable the political scientist must) to consider as politics only such adjustment of wills as is effected by means of some formal machinery, such as meetings in particular places, established and obligatory procedures and a systematic apparatus of coercion, we find ourselves obliged to take account of many activities in Russia which in lands of liberal tradition are not politics. What crops the cultivator is to plant, how much of his resources the factory manager is to put to investment, what research projects are to be undertaken in the universities, are all not merely relevant questions. Without them much of the system has no purpose.

We are also notably less well supplied with detailed and reliable information than in the study of most other countries. The motives of individuals' actions are the stuff of our studies, and we cannot reach the individuals. Russia produces few memoirs and only the personages of approved national legend have biographies. The examples of Soviet citizens presented by Russian sources are improbably uniform if one considers that theirs is a very large country with still imperfect communications. Lack of personal contacts makes it difficult to know the relative reliability of different sources of information and to fill in any missing detail so as to complete a picture which will satisfy our standards of realism. The view is obscured by a systematic secretiveness maintained by severe penalties for disclosure of information not elsewhere considered as of vital importance. The official picture is black and white. There is a clamour of self-praise; there is also much denunciation of faults, though these are normally either past or exceptional and always individual or tactical rather than consequent upon the grand strategy of the system; but the normal, the adequate performance, the reasonable settlement, are rarely shown, since they teach no lessons. There is little which looks like objective assessment from within. Outside there are no witnesses or commentators whom all, friends or opponents of the regime, are prepared to accept as factual and unbiased. Eyewitnesses are either visitors on an official conducted tour or refugees with a sense of grievance. Their bona fides is certain to be questioned, however unjustly; it was usually questioned even in the days of the Tsars. Finally, despite recurrent waves of official advocacy of collective leadership, more rests upon a few individual personalities than perhaps in any other country, and these are largely unknown.

The system neither claims to be, nor is, permanent. According to the official creed, political as well as other social institutions are a superstructure of which the foundations are economic forces, the ultimate result of which is determined beyond human power to alter it and in face of which there is scope for wisdom only in knowing how to conform to and assist them and to avoid the stresses of wrestling with the inevitable. The superstructure is determined by

the foundations, though only the initiates know how, and even i it seems, can rarely explain before the event. Whatever the theo cal background, it proves in practice very hard to be sure that v we think we know of the position in the Soviet Union yesterda true of today. Administrative areas, the system of government off and their competence, the departmental structure within them, legislation for the time being in force, even the identity of the par pants in the central counsels of the system, are in a state of petual flux.

All this is distinctive of Russia only in degree. The political in tutions of any major power are habitually discussed with refere to their supposed magical properties as secrets of greatness; this l been true of British practices and still evidently affects assessment those of the United States. No administrative corps can resist t temptation to preserve its mysteries from the vulgar eye of t observer, and that of the United Kingdom perhaps less than mo Russia differs only in that the administration is more comprehe sive. There are countries with which, for geographical and oth reasons, direct contact is as difficult. But probably in no country comparable general interest, except China, are the obstacles in th way of understanding so many.

Method and Plan

Recognising these limitations, we may nevertheless seek so to arrange the information which we have as to form a picture more o less corresponding to that which presents itself to the Soviet Citizen when he takes a decision on his relations with his fellow-citizens. In so doing we must recognise that the decisions are taken on the basis of material circumstances and traditions which can never be fully described. The context differs for each individual engaged in the process, for Russians, like other people, lead lives of their own. At best we can give a rough sketch of an aspect of the whole which needs to be filled in with knowledge of the geography, history, literature and other aspects of the life of the country.

Also, as with other countries, but, for the reasons suggested, especially in the case of Russia, we must in our capacity of political scientists beware of passing avoidable judgments. It is not a question relevant to our work, whether we should like to live under such a system. In our personal capacities as residents in the same world we may be concerned, lest the tendencies of the system be such that we might have to. But communism as developed in Russia would, upon transfer to this or any other country, either be further modified to accord with the recipients' associations and ideas of what is

Councils of Ministers, containing mainly administrative instructions, and the greatest in volume of the classes of rules which Soviet citizens have to obey, are now more generously published than before in various specialised collections and handbooks, and the annual collection for party workers of the major policy-setting measures, *Spravochnik Partinogo Rabotnika* is a valuable source, but apparently much still fails to come to public attention. In any case, decisions and decrees not themselves divulged have consequences which must be divulged, and we can read much of the legislation in this indirect fashion in the press. The press is itself an imperfect source. Apart from material of a Court-circular character and international news consisting largely of formal exchanges of messages between governments, it is concerned primarily with exhortation, self-congratulation and the denunciation of shortcomings. Much of this praise and blame is evidently justified. In the statements of fact there is probably little falsification, though there is much suppression. The textbooks are mostly highly legalistic and give little indication of the practice of politics, but they are useful as indications of the official approach. In addition, among the works published outside Russia we get a fair volume of memoirs and travellers' tales which, though subject to the bias which we have mentioned, contain much information which fits in with what we already know. A knowledge of human nature enables us to spot the more notably tall stories.

Since to write about Russia is to be suspected of bias, certain assumptions must be admitted at the outset. It is assumed that though revolution and Marxist indoctrination have modified the motivation of the Russians, the change has not been so far-reaching as to render inapplicable what we think we know of human nature elsewhere, or of Russia before the revolution. It is assumed that the answers which post-revolutionary experience together with approved pre-revolutionary thought provide to the problems of life are not so complete as to obviate the necessity for drawing upon the experience accumulated from the centuries of the nation's life. Also, lest value judgments be detected, the author must admit to holding that while all government is bad in that through its operation the individual feels frustrated by forces outside himself, that is least bad in which the occasions of such frustration are fewest. Another assumption is that, in general, efficiency is good, that a political system should be operated with the expenditure of the least amount of time of the smallest number of people, and that the achievement of any of its purposes should not render more difficult the achievement of the rest.

Chapter I is intended to suggest some of the experience, practical and theoretical, upon which Soviet politics draw, and the nature of the purposes which it is their function to reconcile. Chapter II treats of the manner of the invention of the institutions claimed to be distinctive of the Soviet state—the soviets, the Union and collective administration—and of the place in this original creation of the highly unoriginal instrument formerly known as the Stalin constitution. Chapter III examines the organisation and functions of machinery familiar in liberal states but functioning there to rather different purpose; elected bodies, the inner bodies elected by them, and the administrative departments headed by members of some of the latter. Chapter IV concerns the party, its organisation, membership and manner of operation. Chapter V examines the structure which under the ministries discharges their main function, the operative management of the fully nationalised economy, and other systems of control, including the judicial system and the armed forces, which with the party and Soviet system make up the intricate web of Russian administration. In Chapter VI a brief attempt is made to explain how priorities of tasks are decided upon, obligations determined and performance of them secured.

CHAPTER I

What Russian Politics are About

Politics, in the Soviet Union as in any other country, are the complex of activities by which the circumstances of a country—its inheritance both of material conditions and of traditionally accepted attitudes—are shaped into a tolerable life for its people—tolerable in the sense that they will in fact tolerate it.

Material Inheritance

The territory of the U.S.S.R. in itself has sufficed to make the political experience of its people very different from that of western Europe. The area of the country is 8,512,000 square miles. No part of this vast area extends into latitudes farther south than those of the continent of Europe, and part of the mainland extends some eight hundred miles north of the Arctic circle. Moscow has four or five months of frost in the year, and even the northern parts of the Crimea have three or four. In some 47 per cent of the territory the soil below the surface to varying depths remains permanently frozen. Distance from the sea produces an extreme range of temperature, extending in part of eastern Siberia from a monthly mean of $-60°F$. in January to $60°F$. in July, and in exceptional seasons more than half as much again in either direction. Over large parts of the territory summer is extremely short and winter conditions such as to prevent agricultural work. Only parts of the Crimean and Baltic coasts enjoy a temperate climate. The soil includes, in the black-earth belt, extending from the Ukraine south-eastward, some of the best grain-growing land in the world, and some well-watered valleys in the Caucasus and central Asia are fertile, but in general the country is poorly endowed for agriculture. Much of the Asian south is desert, and more than half the country to the north has poor soil added to an unfavourable climate. In most parts the rainfall is poor or unreliable. The mineral resources, rich in the country as a whole, are scarce in European Russia. Mountains defend most of the southern frontier but present little obstacle to internal movement, though forest, frost and flood make for poor overland communication across the Siberian plain. Rivers provide better natural

21

routes, but few in any part of the country are naturally navigable by
vessels of economic size or provide an outlet to an ice-free sea. In
the south the east-west communications by land are good. To the
north-west the land frontier in its natural state was blocked by
forest and marsh, and the extent of northern coastal waters navigable for any considerable part of the year was, until recently, narrowly limited. The best communications with Europe lay down the
rivers running south to the Black Sea.

The first Russian state, centred on Kiev, on this southern river
system, derived its Christianity, in the Greek form, and its considerable early civilisation from the Eastern Roman Empire of Constantinople, thus adding cultural to physical isolation from western
Europe. The open plains to the south-east brought invasion by the
Tatars, which in 1240 put an end to Kiev as the Russian capital, and
for some five centuries cut Russia off from the Black Sea as well.
It was left to the principalities of the northern forests, among which
Moscow took the lead, to reassemble, resettle and expand the country. In 1547 the Prince of Moscow was crowned Tsar (Caesar), and
in 1589 the Metropolitan of the Russian Church, who had settled
there in 1326, was at the Tsar's instance raised to the status of
Patriarch, the two titles implying a claim to the succession to the
Roman-Byzantine inheritance, vacant since the fall of Constantinople to the Turks in 1485. At the accession of Peter the Great
(1682 as joint Tsar under a regency and 1689 as effective ruler)
Russia was still without an outlet by sea to Europe either to the
north—otherwise than round the North Cape—or to the south.
During his reign, however, both routes were opened, and the former
was safeguarded by the foundation of St. Petersburg, to which the
capital was transferred; the route to the south was again lost. The
move to the east into northern Siberia, which may be dated from
1578, met with very little resistance from the scattered tribes, and
by the middle of the seventeenth century it brough the Russians to
the Pacific. The land acquired, however, was not inviting to the
voluntary settler, and the expansion was a venture of the Tsars for
the sake of the tribute in furs paid by the native tribes. Another
motive was early found in the utilisation of the territory as a penal
colony, and this continued, with subsequent differentiation between
convicts and exiles—the latter usually quite leniently treated—
almost without interruption up to the revolution. Free settlement
was early encouraged but not very successfully, and reliance was put
mainly upon plantation of crown serfs and cossacks. In the south,
where resistance was stronger, systematic garrisoning and settlement led the way and slowly gained ground against Tatar resistance.
The progress culminated in 1783 in the conquest of the Khanate of

INTRODUCTION

Scope of the Attempt

Difficulties of Russian Studies

It is difficult to approach the study of anything Russian in the same frame of mind as we are accustomed to bring to the understanding of other societies. The Russian authorities present the experience of their country as of universal application, and the foreign observer is apt, in the same spirit, to take it as an example, good or bad. Moreover, the world is now much involved in Russian affairs, and its ability to see them dispassionately is affected by a reasonable desire to know what Russia is going to do next. But both polemic and prophecy, particularly tempting in the field of politics, are remote from the study of political institutions. These are the more or less conventionalised processes by which the divergent wills of individuals in a society are, in fact, reconciled into acceptance of courses of action taken in the name of the society as a whole or of recognised associations within it. We seek in this book to understand the process where the individuals involved are Russians, as we are already accustomed to do where they are Americans or Frenchmen. Our concern is with the very recent period of history which we call the present, though this is not to be understood without some reference to the remoter past.

We have to face at the outset the problem of the terms in which to discuss Russian politics. Many of the institutions which we traditionally accept as keys to the nature of political systems—the legislature, elections or the head of state—exist, but are of little significance in the real process of politics as we define it. Others—the government or the party—although important, are something very different from the institutions similarly designated in the systems with which people in this country are more familiar. Other terms useful in political discourse—the civil service or central and local government, and the different balances between them—are inapplicable because of the virtual absence in the Russian system of the distinctions which they imply. The total field of study is itself different. If we decide (as to make his subject manageable the political scientist must) to consider as politics only such adjustment of wills as is effected by means of some formal machinery, such as meetings in

15

particular places, established and obligatory procedures and a systematic apparatus of coercion, we find ourselves obliged to take account of many activities in Russia which in lands of liberal tradition are not politics. What crops the cultivator is to plant, how much of his resources the factory manager is to put to investment, what research projects are to be undertaken in the universities, are all not merely relevant questions. Without them much of the system has no purpose.

We are also notably less well supplied with detailed and reliable information than in the study of most other countries. The motives of individuals' actions are the stuff of our studies, and we cannot reach the individuals. Russia produces few memoirs and only the personages of approved national legend have biographies. The examples of Soviet citizens presented by Russian sources are improbably uniform if one considers that theirs is a very large country with still imperfect communications. Lack of personal contacts makes it difficult to know the relative reliability of different sources of information and to fill in any missing detail so as to complete a picture which will satisfy our standards of realism. The view is obscured by a systematic secretiveness maintained by severe penalties for disclosure of information not elsewhere considered as of vital importance. The official picture is black and white. There is a clamour of self-praise; there is also much denunciation of faults, though these are normally either past or exceptional and always individual or tactical rather than consequent upon the grand strategy of the system; but the normal, the adequate performance, the reasonable settlement, are rarely shown, since they teach no lessons. There is little which looks like objective assessment from within. Outside there are no witnesses or commentators whom all, friends or opponents of the regime, are prepared to accept as factual and unbiased. Eyewitnesses are either visitors on an official conducted tour or refugees with a sense of grievance. Their bona fides is certain to be questioned, however unjustly; it was usually questioned even in the days of the Tsars. Finally, despite recurrent waves of official advocacy of collective leadership, more rests upon a few individual personalities than perhaps in any other country, and these are largely unknown.

The system neither claims to be, nor is, permanent. According to the official creed, political as well as other social institutions are a superstructure of which the foundations are economic forces, the ultimate result of which is determined beyond human power to alter it and in face of which there is scope for wisdom only in knowing how to conform to and assist them and to avoid the stresses of wrestling with the inevitable. The superstructure is determined by the foundations, though only the initiates know how, and even they, it seems, can rarely explain before the event. Whatever the theoretical background, it proves in practice very hard to be sure that what we think we know of the position in the Soviet Union yesterday is true of today. Administrative areas, the system of government offices and their competence, the departmental structure within them, the legislation for the time being in force, even the identity of the participants in the central counsels of the system, are in a state of perpetual flux.

All this is distinctive of Russia only in degree. The political institutions of any major power are habitually discussed with reference to their supposed magical properties as secrets of greatness; this has been true of British practices and still evidently affects assessment of those of the United States. No administrative corps can resist the temptation to preserve its mysteries from the vulgar eye of the observer, and that of the United Kingdom perhaps less than most. Russia differs only in that the administration is more comprehensive. There are countries with which, for geographical and other reasons, direct contact is as difficult. But probably in no country of comparable general interest, except China, are the obstacles in the way of understanding so many.

Method and Plan

Recognising these limitations, we may nevertheless seek so to arrange the information which we have as to form a picture more or less corresponding to that which presents itself to the Soviet Citizen when he takes a decision on his relations with his fellow-citizens. In so doing we must recognise that the decisions are taken on the basis of material circumstances and traditions which can never be fully described. The context differs for each individual engaged in the process, for Russians, like other people, lead lives of their own. At best we can give a rough sketch of an aspect of the whole which needs to be filled in with knowledge of the geography, history, literature and other aspects of the life of the country.

Also, as with other countries, but, for the reasons suggested, especially in the case of Russia, we must in our capacity of political scientists beware of passing avoidable judgments. It is not a question relevant to our work, whether we should like to live under such a system. In our personal capacities as residents in the same world we may be concerned, lest the tendencies of the system be such that we might have to. But communism as developed in Russia would, upon transfer to this or any other country, either be further modified to accord with the recipients' associations and ideas of what is reasonable or it would be imposed by force. This is so with the transfer of any political system from one country to another, and a system forcibly imposed is bad whatever its origin. We study Russian political institutions as we study any institutions of any society, as part of the study of man, in order to understand what it feels like to be another person in other circumstances—to know, as far as we may, the reasons others see for acting as they do. We cannot hope to refrain entirely from judgment, since it is in human nature to judge. It is therefore well to have reasons for our judgment. This book rests on the assumption that a judgment is acceptable only in so far as its standards are Russian, a reasonable estimate of what Russians, in Russian circumstances, would find more or less satisfactory. Placed as we are in respect of access to detailed information, we can hardly assess any particular institution. Even for better documented countries it is difficult to say how far any part of the system can be changed without changing the whole. On the system as a whole it is possible to comment without being entirely unscientific.

The documentary means of access to the experience of the Russians are the daily and periodical press, published texts of legal instruments and commentaries upon them, and the official textbooks intended for the use of various classes of students and officials. The legal texts are defective. The gazette of the acts of the Supreme Soviet (*Vedomosti Verhovnogo Soveta*),[1] or, in fact, since the Supreme Soviet meets rarely, mainly of its Praesidium, now appears weekly, but contains little but honours and awards, changes of administrative areas, agencies and ministers, and posting of ambassadors. The union republics' similarly named gazettes are now often available and can be more informative. The acts of the

---

[1] The principles of transliteration followed in this book are: to avoid it wherever possible, to use as few letters as possible, and to respect generally accepted conventional spellings of proper names in frequent use where consistency would produce an unfamiliar form. The letter 'y' is always a vowel, the letter 'j' is used to represent the consonantal 'y' sound. After the vowels 'i' and 'y' at the ends of words it is omitted. The hard sign (separating two sounds) is represented by an apostrophe. The letter 'e' is to be understood always to have a consonantal 'y' sound before it without any indication (one exception will worry only those who already know the Russian form). The Russian 'h' sound is represented by the letter 'h' (the exception for proper names preserves the now familiar initial of Mr. Khrushchov's surname). 'Zh' has its conventional sound. The Russian 'e' as in Mr. Khrushchov's name is transliterated according to sound; the adjectival ending in 'go' (as here) according to sight. Terms quoted in parentheses in the text are always given in the singular if capable of being so used. Where used in the plural in the text they are given the English form of plural in 's', however badly it fits.

Councils of Ministers, containing mainly administrative instructions, and the greatest in volume of the classes of rules which Soviet
citizens have to obey, are now more generously published than
before in various specialised collections and handbooks, and the
annual collection for party workers of the major policy-setting
measures, *Spravochnik Partinogo Rabotnika* is a valuable source,
but apparently much still fails to come to public attention. In any
case, decisions and decrees not themselves divulged have consequences which must be divulged, and we can read much of the
legislation in this indirect fashion in the press. The press is itself an
imperfect source. Apart from material of a Court-circular character
and international news consisting largely of formal exchanges of
messages between governments, it is concerned primarily with exhortation, self-congratulation and the denunciation of shortcomings.
Much of this praise and blame is evidently justified. In the statements of fact there is probably little falsification, though there is
much suppression. The textbooks are mostly highly legalistic and
give little indication of the practice of politics, but they are useful
as indications of the official approach. In addition, among the works
published outside Russia we get a fair volume of memoirs and
travellers' tales which, though subject to the bias which we have
mentioned, contain much information which fits in with what we
already know. A knowledge of human nature enables us to spot the
more notably tall stories.

Since to write about Russia is to be suspected of bias, certain
assumptions must be admitted at the outset. It is assumed that
though revolution and Marxist indoctrination have modified the
motivation of the Russians, the change has not been so far-reaching
as to render inapplicable what we think we know of human nature
elsewhere, or of Russia before the revolution. It is assumed that
the answers which post-revolutionary experience together with
approved pre-revolutionary thought provide to the problems of life
are not so complete as to obviate the necessity for drawing upon
the experience accumulated from the centuries of the nation's life.
Also, lest value judgments be detected, the author must admit to
holding that while all government is bad in that through its operation the individual feels frustrated by forces outside himself, that is
least bad in which the occasions of such frustration are fewest.
Another assumption is that, in general, efficiency is good, that a
political system should be operated with the expenditure of the least
amount of time of the smallest number of people, and that the
achievement of any of its purposes should not render more difficult
the achievement of the rest.

Chapter I is intended to suggest some of the experience, practical and theoretical, upon which Soviet politics draw, and the nature of the purposes which it is their function to reconcile. Chapter II treats of the manner of the invention of the institutions claimed to be distinctive of the Soviet state—the soviets, the Union and collective administration—and of the place in this original creation of the highly unoriginal instrument formerly known as the Stalin constitution. Chapter III examines the organisation and functions of machinery familiar in liberal states but functioning there to rather different purpose; elected bodies, the inner bodies elected by them, and the administrative departments headed by members of some of the latter. Chapter IV concerns the party, its organisation, membership and manner of operation. Chapter V examines the structure which under the ministries discharges their main function, the operative management of the fully nationalised economy, and other systems of control, including the judicial system and the armed forces, which with the party and Soviet system make up the intricate web of Russian administration. In Chapter VI a brief attempt is made to explain how priorities of tasks are decided upon, obligations determined and performance of them secured.

CHAPTER I

What Russian Politics are About

Politics, in the Soviet Union as in any other country, are the complex of activities by which the circumstances of a country—its inheritance both of material conditions and of traditionally accepted attitudes—are shaped into a tolerable life for its people—tolerable in the sense that they will in fact tolerate it.

Material Inheritance

The territory of the U.S.S.R. in itself has sufficed to make the political experience of its people very different from that of western Europe. The area of the country is 8,512,000 square miles. No part of this vast area extends into latitudes farther south than those of the continent of Europe, and part of the mainland extends some eight hundred miles north of the Arctic circle. Moscow has four or five months of frost in the year, and even the northern parts of the Crimea have three or four. In some 47 per cent of the territory the soil below the surface to varying depths remains permanently frozen. Distance from the sea produces an extreme range of temperature, extending in part of eastern Siberia from a monthly mean of $-60°F.$ in January to $60°F.$ in July, and in exceptional seasons more than half as much again in either direction. Over large parts of the territory summer is extremely short and winter conditions such as to prevent agricultural work. Only parts of the Crimean and Baltic coasts enjoy a temperate climate. The soil includes, in the black-earth belt, extending from the Ukraine south-eastward, some of the best grain-growing land in the world, and some well-watered valleys in the Caucasus and central Asia are fertile, but in general the country is poorly endowed for agriculture. Much of the Asian south is desert, and more than half the country to the north has poor soil added to an unfavourable climate. In most parts the rainfall is poor or unreliable. The mineral resources, rich in the country as a whole, are scarce in European Russia. Mountains defend most of the southern frontier but present little obstacle to internal movement, though forest, frost and flood make for poor overland communication across the Siberian plain. Rivers provide better natural

21

routes, but few in any part of the country are naturally navigable by vessels of economic size or provide an outlet to an ice-free sea. In the south the east-west communications by land are good. To the north-west the land frontier in its natural state was blocked by forest and marsh, and the extent of northern coastal waters navigable for any considerable part of the year was, until recently, narrowly limited. The best communications with Europe lay down the rivers running south to the Black Sea.

The first Russian state, centred on Kiev, on this southern river system, derived its Christianity, in the Greek form, and its considerable early civilisation from the Eastern Roman Empire of Constantinople, thus adding cultural to physical isolation from western Europe. The open plains to the south-east brought invasion by the Tatars, which in 1240 put an end to Kiev as the Russian capital, and for some five centuries cut Russia off from the Black Sea as well. It was left to the principalities of the northern forests, among which Moscow took the lead, to reassemble, resettle and expand the country. In 1547 the Prince of Moscow was crowned Tsar (Caesar), and in 1589 the Metropolitan of the Russian Church, who had settled there in 1326, was at the Tsar's instance raised to the status of Patriarch, the two titles implying a claim to the succession to the Roman-Byzantine inheritance, vacant since the fall of Constantinople to the Turks in 1485. At the accession of Peter the Great (1682 as joint Tsar under a regency and 1689 as effective ruler) Russia was still without an outlet by sea to Europe either to the north—otherwise than round the North Cape—or to the south. During his reign, however, both routes were opened, and the former was safeguarded by the foundation of St. Petersburg, to which the capital was transferred; the route to the south was again lost. The move to the east into northern Siberia, which may be dated from 1578, met with very little resistance from the scattered tribes, and by the middle of the seventeenth century it brough the Russians to the Pacific. The land acquired, however, was not inviting to the voluntary settler, and the expansion was a venture of the Tsars for the sake of the tribute in furs paid by the native tribes. Another motive was early found in the utilisation of the territory as a penal colony, and this continued, with subsequent differentiation between convicts and exiles—the latter usually quite leniently treated—almost without interruption up to the revolution. Free settlement was early encouraged but not very successfully, and reliance was put mainly upon plantation of crown serfs and cossacks. In the south, where resistance was stronger, systematic garrisoning and settlement led the way and slowly gained ground against Tatar resistance. The progress culminated in 1783 in the conquest of the Khanate of the Crimea. There followed a rapid expansion into the Caucasus at the expense of the Turks and into central Asia; the latter ended in 1884 with the capture of Merv on the Afghan frontier, and British dissuasion from further advance.

The restrictions on development set by distance and natural obstacles were overcome only with the spread of railways in the second half of the nineteenth century, centrally organised, like much in Russia, as a military operation. The trans-Siberian railway, which after long delays set out from the Urals in 1891 and by 1904 formed, by way of the Chinese Eastern Railway, a continuous route to the Pacific, first made the exploitation of the resources of southern Siberia a practical proposition. Even in their earlier stages the railways began to open up some of the best agricultural land in both European and Asiatic Russia and to make possible the full utilisation of Russia's scattered mineral resources. An expansion of the economy resulted, which, though belated, was rapid, even if by the time of the revolution it had not yet attained the rate of growth of western Europe. Such forces of growth were reflected in a marked acceleration of the increase of population which allowed of a rise in Siberia alone from 1,540,000 European inhabitants to 9,500,000 within a century (1816–1914), while the population of old European Russia, supported by industrialisation and the influx of food from the new lands, was itself trebled. The population of the whole empire in 1913 stood at about 165,700,000; the population of the U.S.S.R., after the recovery in the Second World War of an area more or less equivalent to the losses of territory suffered in the First and in the upheaval of the revolution, had by the census of 15th January 1959 risen to some 208,827,000. Of these some 114,508,000 were Great Russians, now widely dispersed throughout all republics of the Union. There were some 36,981,000 Ukrainians and 7,829,000 Belorussians. Of the non-Slavonic peoples the largest group were those of Turkic speech, who numbered almost 23,000,000, including 3,581,000 Kazahs, 4,969,000 Tatars and 2,929,000 Azerbaidjanis.

Administrative Tradition

Isolation from Europe gave Russia a distinctive administrative tradition. Preoccupation with defence, national consolidation and colonisation of territories, of which the vastness threatened further disintegration, made it markedly military in character. The Tsar was, as his full title proclaimed him, an autocrat. Such possible germs of representative institutions as there were in Russian tradition vanished in the seventeenth century. The Tsars' original body of advisers, the *Duma* of boyars, was soon turned by the expansion of the state into a turbulent assembly of formerly independent nobles imperfectly reconciled to their subjection to Moscow. Its power for evil or for good was, however, weakened by the increasing dilution of the traditional nobility with administrative and other servants of the Tsar, and Ivan IV instituted in opposition to it a wider assembly, the *Zemski Sobor* (Assembly of the Land), which included not only the members of the *Duma* and the ecclesiastical synod but also representatives of the Tsar's administration and of the merchants who were his fiscal agents. The 'time of troubles', the period of disputed successions, violence and foreign intervention which followed upon his death, and the insecurity of the first Tsar of the house of Romanov which emerged from it, gave to the *Zemski Sobor* temporary importance and something of the character of a parliament in which for a time even the peasantry was represented. The mere size of the country, however, was inimical to such a development; to some meetings of the *Sobor* the provincial merchants were not invited at all. Moreover, the rapid advance of serfdom in the first half of the seventeenth century cut at the roots of popular representative institutions against the authority of the throne allowed of the decline of the assembly as soon as there was again a Tsar sufficiently firmly established to exercise that authority. From the time of Alexei (1645–76), the second Tsar of the house of Romanov, its meetings became rare; for the last twenty-two years of his reign and the six years of his successor it did not meet at all, and it was last convoked by Peter the Great in 1698 to pass judgment on his sister, the former regent Sophia, for plotting rebellion against him. The reforms of Peter put an end both to the *Zemski Sobor* and to the *Duma*, which had throughout continued to lead a more or less real existence apart from the larger body. His Westernising tendencies looked not to the parliamentarianism of the European maritime fringe of his day but to the relative administrative efficiency of central Europe.

The central machinery of government as it reached the nineteenth century contained organs with names suggesting representation, but the terms were misleading. Peter's Governing Senate was an appointed tribunal which by that time had become merely a supreme appeal court. The Council of State, instituted in 1810, was a form of nominated legislative council. Its membership (which included all the ministers) was entirely under the Tsar's command, but even this form of legislative procedure was found inconvenient by the autocracy. It relied rather on a smaller body, the Committee of Ministers, which was set up in 1802, but by reason of the responsibility of each of the ministers directly and severally to the Tsar was never allowed to grow into a cabinet. A measure passed by this body was not in name a law (*zakon*) but had equally binding force, as did any measure issued in the name of the Tsar. Both bodies showed a tendency to inflation of membership. In 1861 there was instituted a Council of Ministers, as distinct from the Committee, but this was from the first rendered inoperative by the requirement that it should consider only business proposed to it by the Tsar. It remained open to him to consult informally with such ministers as he wished or, if he preferred, to ignore them all. Among them was the Procurator-General, reputedly described by Peter as 'the all-seeing eye of the Tsar'[1] and combining the normal duties of a Minister of Justice with a general supervision over the whole administration. The administrative work of the ministries might be duplicated at will by the Tsar's private secretariat, and for the greater part of the nineteenth century the police work was so duplicated.

Local administration until the late nineteenth century was under firm central control. The country was divided by Peter the Great into areas under appointed governors (*gubernator*). The number of these governorships (*gubernija*) had risen to seventy-seven by the beginning of the twentieth century, in addition to a number of unincorporated areas known as regions (*oblastj*). The governor was assisted by an advisory council of departmental heads, including the agent of the Procurator-General, but whatever their influence at the centre their advice locally was not binding on him. The strength of the governors made it difficult to induce the nobility to participate in local administration. One of the principal reforms of Peter the Great was to build up a new nobility obliged to life-long state service, military or civil, and open to all attaining an appropriate rank in such service, the higher ranks—down to major and its civil equivalent—conferring hereditary nobility, the lower a personal status of noble. In recompense for their obligations, and as a further manifestation of the same rigid national discipline, the institution of serfdom, which during the preceding century of insecurity had been increasingly imposed upon the peasantry, was systematised by the registration of serfs, and in the course of the eighteenth century it was even intensified and further extended. Under Peter's successors the nobility was able to obtain a relaxation of the conditions applying to it, and in 1762 it secured from Peter III its release from all obligations to state service. The peasantry, being less well placed to press for favours, had to wait another century to get rid of its share of the burden. Meanwhile the authority of the lord over his serfs extended to transportation to Siberia and to sale, including sale

---

[1] Quoted by M. Kovalevsky, *Russian Political Institutions* (1902), p. 128.

apart from the land until the practice was forbidden in 1798. Catherine II in 1785 acceded to the demand of the nobility for greater exclusiveness by raising the ranks in state service which should confer hereditary or personal noble status. She also sought to utilise the nobility in local administration by the creation of assemblies of nobles for the several districts and for the governorships within which they were grouped. Their powers extended beyond the regulation of the affairs of their own order, and the appointment of their own marshals of the nobility, to matters of general concern, including the nomination of judicial and police officials in their areas. In general, however, the nobles declined to be interested in affairs outside their own estates. The institutions of urban administration established at the same time were similarly unsuccessful, although more broadly based.

The reorganisation of the system of local government in the reign of Alexander II was dependent upon the reform for which he was best remembered: the emancipation of the serfs in February 1861. This provided for the privately owned estate serfs to be given their freedom without, in principle, any compensation to the lords, although the owners of the poorer lands who had taken to utilising the labour of their serfs in non-agricultural pursuits, including new industrial departures, were in fact recompensed for the loss of value by the substantial over-valuation of their land at the peasants' expense. Of the cultivable land the landlords were to retain between a third and a half according to the quality of the soil, while for the rest they were to be compensated by an advance from the state, of which the emancipated peasants were to pay off the greater part by redemption dues over a period of some fifty years. Emancipation without dues but with only a quarter of the normal allocation of land was offered and about 6 per cent accepted. For the payment of their redemption dues and taxes the peasants were made collectively responsible through the already existing general village assembly of householders, or *mir*. This assembly elected its own elder, and in addition to its fiscal responsibilities was given general authority to regulate village affairs, including the periodic repartition of the land where this traditional form of tenure was retained. Increasingly, as government support was withdrawn from it, such tenure gave way to individual ownership, though not necessarily to consolidation of individual holdings, and the *mir* lost this function. There remained at village level, and at the higher level of the *volostj* (the traditional groupings of villages which had remained among state serfs and which were now reintroduced to the former privately owned villages), a curious form of local government based on inverted class discrimination. Only the members, the emancipated serfs, participated, but the powers of general regulation extended to all persons in the area other than the landed gentry. Opinion soon developed in favour of the replacement of this by an all-class institution, but this was only achieved at the level of the *volostj* in 1917, when it was too late.

At the level of the governorship and district (*uezd*) there was a system of local government providing representation for all owners of real property, not equally but on a scale heavily weighted in favour of wealth. To the land assemblies, or *zemstvos*, instituted in 1864 for thirty-four governorships, three categories of electors—individual owners of land or factories of a certain value, individual urban house and property owners, and peasant communes—elected their representatives for a term of three years by means of three separate electoral colleges. This was probably as liberal as the system could be made, while the conversion from serfdom was still incomplete. The *zemstvos* were not given freedom to select their own chairman; the marshal of the nobility for the area was to act as such *ex officio*. The length of their session was limited to twenty days at the higher level and ten at the lower. Between sessions their functions were entrusted to an 'administration' (*zemskaja uprava*), elected by them subject to the governor's veto and paid, as the members of the *zemstvos* themselves were not. After the general fashion of continental Europe, these inner bodies were obliged to act as agencies of the central authorities and under their supervision, as well as on behalf of their own *zemstvos*. In 1890, however, in the reign of Alexander III, this relative liberalism was modified. Representation was put on a class instead of a property basis. The nobility became an electoral category on their own, other private landowners, such as the new capitalist, who was buying up the estates, joined the townsmen in a single category, and the weighting in the nobles' favour was increased. The peasant class lost its direct representation altogether; the *volostj* meeting was now to put up two candidates of whom the governor should select one. The elective principle was from the first qualified by the representation granted to the agents of the central ministries and to the church. Yet something was achieved; from 1873 the *zemstvos* began to acquire the power to make by-laws for the regulation of local affairs, and rendered useful service despite their lack of financial resources and the veto left to higher authorities. In the field of education especially they made good progress, and in the more fortunately placed parts of the country gave promise of the early extinction of illiteracy. Much is said to have been done for the improvement of local statistical services and for hospitals and other health services. A means was at last found of engaging the services of at least the minor nobility in work for the public good, and employment increasingly became available in the new administrations for the intelligentsia.

In the towns there were comparable developments. A municipal law of 1870 provided that the town *dumas* should be elected by property owners and taxpayers with weighting, after the Prussian or Austrian fashion, in favour of the richer among them and the further election of the *uprava* by these bodies. In 1892 the weighting for wealth was dropped in favour of election by wards, but the taxpayers were excluded and the qualifying holding of property was raised, particularly for the larger towns, so that less than 1 per cent of the urban population then had the vote. Half of the *uprava* remained in office from one four-year term of the *Duma* to the next, so that the incoming *Duma* elected only half the membership of the effective governing body. Powers were similar to those of a *zemstvo*, though with greater freedom from the governor's veto, and the *uprava* was, like those of the *zemstvos*, utilised by the central authorities as part of the bureaucratic hierarchy of administration.

The judicial system also underwent in 1864 a drastic reformation, making it one of the most liberal in continental Europe, with a jury system, an independent judiciary and an unpaid magistracy after the British fashion. This system, however, was soon eroded; various classes of cases were withdrawn from trial by jury, and the local procurator was in 1884 given the power of veto over the appointment of jurors. In more than half the governorships, it seems the new system of courts never came into being. The Justices of the Peace were abolished outside the towns and replaced by a new official combining the functions of a magistrate with administrative supervision over the peasant local government of the *volostj*. Above all, nothing was ever done to reform the police, which remained inefficient, multiple in structure and virtually unchecked in the exercise of its powers. In an article published in 1883 denouncing the country's prison system Prince Kropotkin asserted 'not that the principles of Russian penal institutions are worse than those applied to the same institutions in western Europe. I am rather inclined to hold the contrary.... In Russia, however, principles are always ruined in application.'[1] The opinion could be given a wider extension.

The late development and industrialisation of Russia was reflected in the lack of towns. The medieval growth of urban life, like so much else in Russia, was stunted by the country's preoccupation with military security. In the middle of the nineteenth century there were only thirty-two towns of over 20,000 people, but by 1900 there were sixty-five, and of these nine had over 150,000, a standard which

[1] Prince Kropotkin, 'Russia's Prisons', *The Nineteenth Century*, January, 1833, pp. 27–8.

at the earlier date was reached by only the two capitals. Even so, many of them differed little from villages in the density or form of construction of their buildings, in their possession of the amenities of urban life, or in the occupations and outlooks of their inhabitants. Even in the early years of the twentieth century probably a majority of urban workers—of whom these were in all under 3,000,000 in 1917—still held some land, and in other ways maintained their connection with the villages. As there was hardly any proletariat, so also there was hardly any bourgeoisie. The merchants and craftsmen of the country towns, such as there were of them, lacked the cohesion and self-assurance of that class in western Europe. The new industrialisation was slow to produce a conscious group of Russian businessmen. Development was largely by foreign capital and partly by foreign skill, and at the cost of the accumulation of a heavy burden of foreign debt, and of the export of the country's increasing but still scanty supplies of wheat, which the peasant could himself rarely afford to eat.

Russian agriculture, on which the whole edifice rested, remained highly inefficient, with far lower yields than in Western countries, and this was true of the holdings of the gentry as well as of their former serfs. To the traditional incompetence of Russian landowners at estate management the emancipation added a serious shortage of labour, as the peasant, though barely able to wrest a living from his own land, refused to work that of his former master. Despite the provision of credit on favourable terms to the nobles, they found it increasingly difficult to make farming pay. Already by the late 'eighties it was reported that a quarter of the noble estates left by the emancipation had been mortgaged to the land bank and another quarter sold. Sometimes the purchasers were foreigners; often they were the more enterprising of the peasants. In the opening years of the twentieth century the substantial yeoman with a holding of several times the size of those of his neighbours and with the resources to employ the labour of others became a new feature of Russian rural society. But if some succeeded, many failed, sliding hopelessly into debt.

Attitudes

Despite their increasing acquisitions from the nobles and the possibility of expansion into the new areas of the empire, the demand of the peasants for more land remained the principal disruptive force in Russia throughout the period from emancipation to the revolution of 1917. The emancipation settlement had assigned to the landlords land which the peasants felt to be their own, and the fact that they could have made more efficient use of what land they had did not diminish the sense of grievance. There remained also the question of status. The emancipation of 1861 had left the peasants—the great majority of the population—still less than full citizens. They were bound to their villages no less than before, not to their lords by obligations of service but to the *mir* by the collective obligation for payment to the state. They remained subject to a separate system of courts applying a separate rural customary law. Collective responsibility for obligations was gradually eroded and in most places abolished in 1903, and in the following year official concern at the rising waves of rural unrest and violence brought the cancellation of much of the burden of debt for redemption dues as well as other relaxations. It left little time to build the peasants into the social structure before Russia had to face a world war. Discontent was increasingly manifest also among the urban workers. It was, in fact, the same discontent, for the workers were peasants and their grievances went with them into the towns. Industrial strikes had already started in the 'seventies, and became increasingly frequent. The opinion of their employers, too, as it developed, came to distrust and resent a system of government which, while it offered protection against foreign competition, had little regard for the opinion of those engaged in practical business. The nobility itself was by no means to be relied upon as a pillar of the existing order. The reluctance of the autocracy to entrust it with any effective responsibility for public affairs, the exclusiveness which it had itself sought and the gulf set between it and the people by recent serfdom and illiteracy, had left it with very little belief in its own powers of leadership. In so far as this generally serious and well-intentioned aristocracy looked abroad for the intellectual stimulus which it could not find in Russia, it met with thought which condemned its social position. But the element in Russian society most fitted to detonate the explosive situation created by Russia's many discontents was the intelligentsia, the products of its institutions of higher education. The intelligentsia was a mixture of all classes, including in large numbers the nobility, but by its education it was set apart from all classes of the archaic Russian social system, and unfitted for any employment which Russia's undeveloped economic life and its unintellectual administration had to offer, at least until the end of the nineteenth century. For want of more constructive outlets it was driven to conspiracy as an habitual exercise. Uninstructed and unrestrained by responsibility and the test of practice, it ceaselessly pursued mainly foreign ideas to their logical but often unreasonable ends.

The bias imparted to the dispositions of the generality of persons comprised within a nation by the forces operating at any given time upon them, from the facts of geography to the balance of personalities, may be called the national character. It is a pattern which remains in the formed character of the individual, in institutions and conventional behaviour, in literature, the form of the language, and habits of thought, and in other facts, though it has no permanence or life of its own. The features of the Russian national character at the time of the revolution which struck observers as characteristic arose very obviously out of the country's circumstances. Among 'the people' (*narod*), which in pre-revolutionary usage invariably meant the peasants, there prevailed a rustic torpor; an unreliability and unpunctuality, reflecting the seasonal cycle of long idleness and short intense effort which the climate dictates; a susceptibility to religious enthusiasm, often of a destructive kind; a tolerant but profound distrust of the stranger, the townsman, the educated. Among the last there was a dark awareness of indebtedness to the people, a pride in Russia's peasant power of endurance, often expressed in religious terms as holiness proved through suffering. There was a sense of not belonging to Europe, a consciousness of being materially backward yet of having superior qualities, a desire to emulate the achievements of the foreigner, combined with resentment and distaste for the inhumanity of his ways. Through the society as a whole there prevailed a sense of solidarity, and an acceptance of the necessity of leadership was combined with a critical attitude to particular leaders which, observers thought as early as the Crimean War, might bring down the Tsar himself in the event of a national defeat. And long before the revolution there was a foreboding of change, pronounced even among the nobility.

In August 1905 Russia was obliged to accept defeat at the hands of Japan after an eighteen-month succession of military disasters. It was a shock for the world, the first obvious defeat by an Asiatic power of a power accounted European. For Russia it resulted in a revolutionary fracture of the old regime which, though it left the Tsar on the throne, left him less than an autocrat. This was a complex affair. Mounting agrarian discontent broke in renewed violence in February 1905, its urban and industrial reflection was disastrously handled by the authorities, and general discontent with incompetence and oppression had already led to the assassination of the Minister of the Interior in the middle of the previous year. To these forces there was added an unwonted stirring of political organisation, from the Marxist Social Democrats to the liberal gentlemen of the *zemstvos*.

The disturbances of 1905 culminated in the last few months of the year in a wave of industrial unrest which in St. Petersburg assumed the proportions of a general strike, loosely co-ordinated by the Soviet (or Council) of Workers Deputies, and in similar manifestations in Moscow. The conflict led to Russia's first acceptance of liberal democracy as known in western Europe, expressed in the creation of the State *Duma* and the reconstitution of the Council of Ministers into something like a cabinet with a chairman of its own, comparable in position and function to a prime minister. From this opening of the prospect of political life there resulted the appearance for the first time in Russia of political parties which were something other than conspiratorial groups with disruptive aims. A *Duma* directly elected, though on a restricted franchise, was promised by the Tsar as early as February 1905, and as danger advanced the concession was extended to include universal suffrage. In his October manifesto of the same year the Tsar undertook to make no law without its consent, though he retained to himself the power of a veto. A Council of State, reformed to provide for the election of half the members on a restricted franchise, remained as a strong and conservative second chamber. Increasingly as order was restored the Tsar showed reluctance to accept the limitations on his power. Four *Dumas* were called; for two months in 1906, for a little over four in 1907, from 1907 to 1912, and finally from 1912 to the fall of the regime in 1917. Their markedly critical attitude to the administration was indicated in the short lives of the first two and in the changing composition of all four. The attitude of the authorities undermined the majority of the new liberal (Constitutional Democrat) party in the first *Duma* to the advantage of both right and extreme left in the second, and a change in the electoral law diminished the left as well in the third and fourth. The ministers were independent of the *Duma* and responsible only to the Tsar, who could and did maintain ministers not enjoying the confidence of the *Duma*, and even ignored those ministers for unofficial advisers of his own disastrous choosing. Nevertheless, even the last of the *Dumas* remained highly critical of maladministration during the war of 1914–18, and was able upon occasion to force a ministerial resignation. Political life had begun in Russia. But it was late. It needed peace and a wise Tsar; it was given neither. The war which broke out in 1914 brought early losses to Russia more crushing than any other state had to endure. The tender growth of industry and the transport system broke down from neglect, overloading and lack of hands, and famine threatened St. Petersburg itself. The military successes of 1916 were a last effort; thereafter Russia was sustained by the will of her allies rather than her own.

Doctrinal Equipment

The theories of society propounded by Karl Marx early found favour with Russians, and the first translation of his principal work, *Das Kapital*, was into Russian. However, Marx distrusted his Russian disciples and specifically declared his doctrine inapplicable to Russian circumstances. Marx was a Rhineland German and the basis of his thought was German philosophy and a practical interest in German politics. To these elements he added an acquaintance with French socialism and British economics, and observation of social conditions in both countries. His appeal to his age lay in the fact that he professed to see as inevitable, and laboriously assembled arguments to prove imminent, what many people felt to be morally right: the emancipation of the new factory workers for whom the traditional social structure seemed unable to provide any tolerable place. This he achieved by his adaptation of the dialectic of Hegel —the process by which an original state generates its own opposite and ultimately clashes with it to produce a synthesis which is neither, yet contains and transcends both. Marx removed it from the realm of ideas, where its conservative inventor had placed it, to that of material—by which he meant economic—facts. He held that the tools or processes used by men at each of the predetermined stages of development—what he called the forces of production—in some way enabled the owners of them to make themselves the ruling class, having control of the state, which, as Marx used the term, meant only the coercive machinery of society, by which to hold down the opposing classes. As such it would wish to hold its advantage as long as it could, but progress could not be arrested. As the economic process outgrew the social structure, so a revolutionary situation would come to fruition to bring in the new ruling class. Factory production, he held, depended upon, and so designated as the appropriate ruling class, the proletariat, which his compatriot, patron and colleague, Friedrich Engels, defined as the class 'whose means of livelihood depend entirely upon the sale of its labour'. This, he held, was the last of all possible classes. With its arrival in power the process would be at an end, and, with no other classes to hold down, the state as he defined it would wither away. This 'dialectical materialism' offered no reason why it would be the last of the classes, why, for instance, the peasantry should not be yet another; it merely assumed it.

This in itself ruled out Russia, with no ruling bourgeoisie to be overthrown, no proletariat to overthrow it and peasants everywhere. Marx, having a practical eye for a revolutionary situation, found Russia interesting and expressed the intention of revising his work to show where that country fitted in, but in fact he did not do so. With the flexibility which was characteristic of his theories he chose to consider that Russia might escape the capitalist stage of development, progressing from feudalism to an agrarian socialism and being carried on from there by the revolution made by the proletariat in the more advanced countries of the West. Accordingly he gave his support against the Russian Marxists to the advocates of a revolution based upon the traditional Russian *mir*. These, the populists (*narodnik*), the principal category of active Russian political opinion in the 'sixties and 'seventies, were not a party so much as a trend, the adherents of which agreed only on the necessity of going to 'the people' to teach them their destiny and, as some held, to learn from them their supposed peculiar rustic virtues. But in 1881 one of the two factions into which the populist movement had lately split effectively put it out of action for the rest of the century by assassinating the Tsar, Alexander II, to whom the peasants, expecting further benefits from their liberator, were still strongly attached. The vacuum which they left gave the Marxists their chance, even without the blessing of Marx. To organise, however, was not easy.

In 1898 there was founded the Russian Social Democrat Party, the name then traditionally adopted by Marxist parties. The founding congress hardly had time to produce a manifesto lamenting the difficulty of its task before the participants were arrested. In 1903, what for continuity's sake was called the Second Congress had to start all over again, meeting abroad. It promptly split into two opposing factions, which, despite attempts to achieve unity in 1905, in order to exploit the advantageous situation of that year, never came together again. By this time populism was back in the field in the form of the Social Revolutionary Party, which was founded in 1902, and by reason of its advocacy of aims and methods comprehensible to the peasants, the seizing of the land for those who tilled it and the use of violence, was now making good progress in the rural parts, where trust in the autocracy had faded. Things were more difficult for the Marxists. Their doctrine had no place for the peasant and his land-hungry small-scale farming, which they considered reactionary, while violence, they thought, could effect little in the working out of the laws of history. Nor in the absence of capitalism and bourgeois domination in Russia could they offer any very inspiring prospect of rapid results. Their first leaders drifted into the school of thought known as Legal Marxism, which advocated the establishment of capitalism, often in terms hardly distinguishable from those used by the liberals, in confidence that having been got into this situation the proletariat would be able to get itself out again. Another wing (which became known as the Economists) favoured a policy of trade-unionist industrial action for immediate benefits without too much regard for the larger issue of the transformation of society. Marxism, like most Western theories, did not get very far in Russia until it had been worked over into a peculiarly Russian form.

This transformation was effected by V. I. Uljanov, who for conspiratorial purposes took the name of Lenin, one of the second generation of Russian Marxists, an intellectual born in 1870 of upper-class parentage, like most of the leaders of the movement at the time. He rapidly made himself the leader of one of the factions into which the Social Democrat Party split on its second foundation in 1903, originally the smaller faction, though happy for accidental reasons in possession of the name of Bolshevik (of the majority), which by his skill in organisation it soon proceeded to justify. Lenin quietly admitted into the doctrine the possibility, which no previous Marxist would have accepted, that one class might make two revolutions, and he subsequently went on to suggest that it might make them without any very considerable interval in between. Moreover, he found a justification for alliance with the peasants, which is best expressed in his pamphlet *Two Tactics of Social Democracy*, written in August 1905, to provide the party with a line for the revolutionary situation developing in that year: 'The proletariat must carry through to completion the democratic revolution by uniting to itself the mass of the peasantry in order to crush by force the opposition of the autocracy, and to paralyse the instability of the bourgeoisie. The proletariat must complete the socialist revolution by uniting to itself the mass of semi-proletarian elements in the population; in order to break by force the opposition of the bourgeoisie and to paralyse the instability of the peasantry and of the petty-bourgeoisie.' The word 'democratic', despite its place in the party's own name, was not at this time used by Marxists in any approving sense. By 'democratic revolution' Lenin meant the revolution believed to be imminent which would 'for the first time make it possible for the bourgeoisie to rule as a class'. However, even with the most elaborate plans for taking the bourgeois horse to the water, there was no certainty that it would drink. It was still not clear how, if the bourgeoisie could not or would not rule, the proletariat was to overthrow it. In 1905 this problem did not have to be faced. The revolution of that year was not from the Bolshevik point of view effective.

The first effective shift in the location of power was that of March 1917, known by reason of the different Russian calendar of that time as the February Revolution. In this the Tsar abdicated, and his designated successor, his brother, refused to take the throne until called to it by a representative constituent assembly. Until this could be arranged effective control of affairs passed to a provisional government under Prince Lvov, the leader of the Union of Zemstvos, and with representation of the Social Revolutionaries in the person of Kerenski, who, on the reconstruction of the government in July, took over the chairmanship. From May onward the Menshevik faction of the Social Democrat Party was also represented in the government, together with minor socialist groupings, but without the Bolsheviks. Marxists agreed that this was the democratic revolution. The question was thus posed of how long they had to wait before its successor. Lenin solved this immediately on his arrival in the capital in April by declaring it already in progress.

Yet if in shaping the course of events Lenin's organising skill counted for more than Marx's analysis, it was not without consequence that the makers of the second revolution of 1917 were trained in Marxist teaching and believed it relevant to their country's situation, or that their successors in power apparently still do. Their beliefs affect their interpretation of events in terms of causes and motives and their estimation of the probable consequences of their own actions, even though for lack of practical guidance in Marx those actions are often applications to their new ends of methods traditional in Russia. The Soviet state is not simply old Russia, and the accepted beliefs are an important part of the reason why it is not. Merely to discern historical inevitability and to know oneself on its side is gratifying, and the knowledge may have added materially to the self-assurance of the Russian leaders. Dialectical materialism, though unhelpful as an explanation of revolutions or a guide to the making of them, remains an influential part of the inheritance, though perhaps for its Hegelian rather than its Marxian elements. The idea of sudden qualitative change was in itself immediately attractive to those discontented with things as they were, which in Russia was an almost universal condition. The idea of contradiction, which is yet no absurdity but part of the order of things, has remained no less attractive to the new regime, which has, by reason of the rawness of its theories and the original nature of the state which it set up, frequently needed to justify changes of front. Stalin's statement of the revised attitude to the withering away of the state is the classical example. 'We are,' he said, 'in favour of the state dying out, and at the same time we stand for the strengthening of the dictatorship of the proletariat, which represents the most powerful and mighty authority of all forms of state which have existed up to the present day. The highest possible development of the power of the state, with the object of preparing the conditions for the dying out of the state—that is the Marxist formula. Is it "contradictory"? Yes, it is "contradictory", but this contradiction is a living thing and completely reflects Marxist doctrine.'[1] The coexistence of opposites as part of the process of change—though with the end probably envisaged in the terms of the dialectic of Marx in which there is no true synthesis but a simple supersession of one opposite by the other rather than that of Hegel—may be seen in the current doctrine of the relations between socialist and capitalist states. To see contradictions as the way of history's unfolding was to be predisposed to the creation of contradictions wherever these might loosen an undesired stability, whether to refine the party before the revolution, to subjugate the peasantry in the early years of the new regime, or to undermine the potentially hostile alliance of foreign powers. In general, a disposition to see things in terms of conflict does not make for conciliatory or trusting policies, even where these are objectively possible. To see history in terms of self-initiating stages of social development to a pattern and towards an end prescribed in the nature of things is not conducive to belief in the historical significance of the individual.

If Marx's emphasis on the economic causation of history was an embarrassment to his Russian disciples, while they were seeking in his name to overthrow the Tsarist state, it was a source of strength to them when they found themselves in power with an accomplished revolution behind them and a new state to build. Industrialisation was the prime need of Russia if it was ever to play a leading role in the world in competition with the powers of the West. They were not the first to see this. A systematic policy of industrialisation might have been pursued had there been no revolution. It is less likely that it would have been given prominence had the revolution been made under the leadership of the Social Revolutionaries or others committed to the interests of the peasant. But there was none so disposed to give attention to this necessity and to the economic factors generally as those who were accustomed to speak in terms of factories and the social product, and of whom self-respect demanded that they provide with all due speed the causes for what had already happened. This was not the Marxism of Marx, which in fact it stood back on its Hegelian head, making the material, in Marx's economic sense, dependent on the human will, but it was an almost inescapable result of the application of Marxism to Russian circumstances. In its immediate effects the revolution retarded development, hindered the recovery of industry from the disruption of war by impractical ideas of workers' control and extinguished the more economic units of agricultural exploitation by the encouragement given

[1] Report of Central Committee to Sixteenth Party Congress, published in *Leninism* (English translation of *Voprosy Leninizma*) (10th edn. 1934) II. 342.

to the peasant allies to seize what they could. But it was from the first unlikely that the followers of Marx would be content so to leave things. Their realisation of the importance of doing something about the economy did not mean that they had at the outset any clear vision of what they ought to do in any given situation, or of the magnitude of the task of management to which they were committing their new state. Lenin completely underestimated the skills required for running the economy once capitalism had laid the foundations and provided the means of communication. For the most part, he held, they amounted only to the 'simple operations of registration, recording and checking ... quite within the reach of all literate persons'.[1] But Lenin himself was no man to be deterred by the possibility of the unseen obstacle. Looking back in 1923, he quoted with approval the dictum of Napoleon, 'On s'engage, et puis on voit', and instanced the New Economic Policy as one of the successful pieces of improvisation produced in the course of the engagement joined in November 1917.[2]

Engels declared that 'So long as the proletariat uses the state it does not use it in the interests of freedom, but in order to hold down its adversaries, and as soon as it becomes possible to speak of freedom, the state as such ceases to exist.' This last dimly envisaged event was remote from the practical considerations of the more effectual of the Russian revolutionaries long before Stalin provided his ingenious dialectical explanation of the neglect of it. More originally, Stalin added that the state would be needed even when the ultimate classless society called communism should have been reached, so long as there were still capitalist powers around to threaten it. There remained of Engels' declaration only the justification for strong government. The purpose of the communist cannot be to put checks on the power of the state, as seemed to the American Founding Fathers and the nineteenth-century liberals to be the wisdom of the constitution-maker, but to see that the right class wields it. Marxist belief thus made for a continuation of authoritarian rule no less than did Russian lack of experience of anything else.

How far the makers of the revolution were also committed by their Marxist faith to a dictatorship of the party over and through the proletariat was not at this time clear beyond dispute to the Marxists themselves. Marx was not very helpful. He asserted that in preparing the revolution the communist element in working-class politics, being the most advanced and resolute and having the

[1] V. I. Lenin, *The State and Revolution* (1917), in his works (Russian edn.), Vol. 25 (1949), p. 392.

[2] Lenin, *Our Revolution*, Works, Vol. 33 (1950), p. 439.

advantage of knowing where it was going, 'pushes forward all others', but about the post-revolutionary phase he had nothing to say. It was all rather remote, and he was a practical man. Even Lenin, whose contribution to the elaboration of Marxism consisted largely in the development of the theory and practice of the party, had little to say about this later phase. But in practice the Russian Marxists, drawing upon the conspiratorial party tradition of the days of autocracy and not the parliamentary experience which became available only in the time of the *Duma*, fell naturally into the assumption that they must continue to 'press forward' by their party's own direct action and not merely through participation in the working of constituted machinery. After the revolution Lenin resisted the wish of Trotski and others to make a specific declaration in favour of party dictatorship, but in practice it was assumed that, like the state itself, this other regrettable necessity must continue for so long as there was still opposition to be beaten down.

For anything as specific as the organisation of the party it was useless to look to Marx. Already by the time of the revolution, however, the matter had been actively debated among the Marxists for some time, and the dominant Bolshevik faction was equipped with a firm tradition mainly of Lenin's making. His trust was in the disciplined striking force. It must, he said, contain 'chiefly people whose occupation is revolutionary activity', and, in direct contrast to the more familiar trade-union type of workers' organisation, it must be 'not very broad and as secret as possible'. It must have its members in the factory but, in virtue of their profession of revolutionaries, under orders of the party committee, not in virtue of their employment as industrial workers. For 'broad democracy' within the party he had little use, and he specifically rejected an 'immoderate use of the elective principle'. These means were related to the pre-revolutionary situation; the secretiveness was justified by Lenin on the ground of the necessity to exclude the prying eye of the police, but it was possible to argue that in the period of continuing insecurity much of the same sort of care was still needed. By the time of the revolution this attitude had become the distinguishing mark of the Bolshevik against other factions.

This does not mean that Russian communism was narrowly lost for democracy. Lenin was more thorough, more ruthless and more far-seeing than his Menshevik adversaries, but they hardly differed from him on specific issues. At the time when they were still in the ascendant they were even more strongly convinced than he of the inadmissibility of the expression by members of dissenting opinions, and Trotski, who to his own undoing combined the hardness of the Bolsheviks with the doctrinal inflexibility and personal attachments

of the Mensheviks, seems to have been earlier than Lenin in making
his claim for 'the leadership's organised distrust of the members, a
distrust manifesting itself in vigilant control from above over the
party'.

A name for the principle on which the party was organised was
found in a resolution of the Bolshevik conference of December 1905
held at Tammerfors in Finland, which declared 'democratic centralism' to be 'the indisputable basis of party organisation', though
without explaining what it was. In the following year Lenin provided the definition: 'The principle of democratic centralism and of
autonomy of the local units means full and reciprocal freedom of
criticism so long as unity in a specific action is not destroyed thereby, and the inadmissibility of any criticism whatever which undermines or makes difficult unity on any action decided upon by the
party.'[1] In practice, difficulty was found in agreeing whether at any
given moment the party had made up its mind or not. Lenin at the
time of providing this definition was seeking to reverse a decision
which the Mensheviks, who in principle accepted his formulation,
wished to preserve. He was able to raise the issue not because the
decision was in some way provisional, but because he was Lenin.

Marxist discourse contrasts such 'democratic centralism' with
'bureaucratic centralism', in which orders are passed down from the
centre without preliminary sounding of opinion below. It was the
principal of criticism of the Titoists against the school of Stalin that,
though bureaucratic centralism was a necessary element in a
socialist state—in the army, in the security services and in a situation such as that of the early days of the Soviet regime when there
were large areas of the country without proletariat or communist
sympathisers—it was the duty of the communist regime to build
up democratic centralism against it. In Russia, they claimed, on
the contrary bureaucratic centralism had itself been made into a
system.

An important feature of the background of the party which
seized power at the revolution, though much the same would have
been true of any other of the Russian conspiratorial parties, was the
importance which it attached to theory. Right conduct, it held, stems
from right belief, and a heterodox explanation of a social situation
was presumptive evidence of a disposition to improper courses of
action. To express views which could be paralleled in the writings
of the discredited, in Bakunin or in Blanqui, was to be discredited
oneself; and, conversely, to fall from favour with the majority or
controlling group in the party was to stand convicted of heterodox

[1] Lenin, *Freedom of Criticism and Unity of Action*, Works, Vol. 10 (1947),
p. 409.

views. This was the pure spirit of the Russian intelligentsia, as of any school of thought which, deprived of the possibility of direct observation of action, is obliged to infer it from principles. Again, the attitude survived into the post-revolutionary situation in which the circumstances which produced it no longer obtained. It has, however, elements of practical utility. The myth of orthodoxy in application of the teachings of Marx and Engels and their legitimate successors to situations which they could not foresee has been one of the principal props of the new regime. To oblige their opponents to argue their cases in an idiom of which those established in control of the apostolic party are themselves the acknowledged masters has throughout been a source of great advantage to the latter and a valuable means of discipline. In 1955 Stalin's views on the stage reached by the revolution, his clarification of a distinction, of dubious Marxian authority, between communism and a state of socialism prior to it, could be brought into action to remind Mr. Molotov that he was not invulnerable, and of recent years the authority of Lenin could be called to the aid of the party in dissociating itself from the more malodorous aspects of Stalinism.

The Manner of Seizing Power

In contrast to the largely spontaneous outbursts of 1905 and March (or February) 1917, exploited by the extremist parties but not of their own creation, that of November (or October) 1917 was deliberately engineered by Lenin and made possible by years of careful preparation of the party. Lenin was himself on the spot, as he had not been at the start of either of the previous developments, having been enabled by the Germans to reach Petrograd at the beginning of April. By exploiting the fluid situation of a country which had undergone a change of regime and committed itself to the reformation of its administrative system in the middle of a disastrous war, by building up the power of the soviets and the congresses of soviets against the provisional government, and raising all the disruptive issues which the latter wished for the time being to keep quiet, he created a situation where power could be seized without the need to fight for it. The peasants were doing his work. The troops at the strategic points were on his side. There was little resistance in Petrograd, some in Moscow and a few of the garrison towns, none anywhere else. There was also not much seizure of power anywhere else, but the capitals once conquered in centralised Russia, the rest could be expected to follow. Many issues still remained to be sorted out. Stalin, who surveyed these events from the editorial office of the party newspaper, later named 'peace, the agrarian revolution and freedom for the nationalities' as the three principal factors out of which the Bolsheviks built up their support.[1] In fact, peace was not to be obtained except on the most humiliating terms, the surrender at Brest-Litovsk on the 3rd March the following year of all the western borderlands, conquered since the time of Peter the Great, except the northern outlet to the sea. Even from that it was felt advisable to withdraw, and the capital returned to its ancient seat at Moscow, where it has ever since remained. Even Brest-Litovsk did not guarantee peace, for its effect was to trigger off among the Tsarist generals, the Czechoslovak former prisoners of war and Russia's late allies an armed resistance which might have otherwise been postponed. The new regime had to continue the fight up to the latter part of 1920. The agrarian revolution was achieved on terms which Marxists could not possibly allow to become permanent, and freedom for the nationalities was also to prove at variance with their principles. Nevertheless, as an example of technique, the seizure of power taught lessons to those who were able to learn. It was an example of what might be achieved by temporary alliances based upon the moods of the moment, and it showed that the advantage in such manoeuvres lay with the party least involved in loyalties to temporary allies. It was an example of the advantage of organisation, of self-confidence, of knowing what you want when others do not. It was a lesson to the ambitious within the party, and it was Stalin, the Georgian whom Lenin had recruited as his expert on nationality problems and agent in the underground who, comparatively small though his part in the event itself had been, showed the subtlety of mind to follow it most consistently.

The Issues

The Russian revolution, like any revolutionary movement, left no clear heir to the power which it overthrew, and in the politics of Russia since the revolution the motive of retaining power, enlisting support and eliminating rivals, has always been predominant. The Marxists, as specialists in revolution, had studied the precedents and in particular the lessons of the French revolution. They knew that the first organisers of change might themselves be overthrown by others more extreme if they were not vigilant to frustrate and outbid them. In particular they were aware of the danger of a Bonaparte, and the necessity to keep the military power amenable to orders though strong enough for action. Russian political life

[1] J. Stalin, 'The October Revolution and the National Policy of the Russian Communists', Works (Russian edn.), V, p. 113.

from the bottom to the top has been penetrated by realisation of the danger of the unguarded moment.

Next to this motive has been that of economic priorities. The economic bias of Marxism has made the Soviet Union into a single vast firm with the consequent problems: finding and organising an effective force of managers, keeping them loyal and skilled and interested, rationalising departmental organisation, budgeting and allocating resources. This last has been far from simple. The revolution was made at a moment of opportunity but not of plenty. It was not possible to amass and apply the immense capital required for the development of the resources lately revealed into a solid foundation of basic industry without denial of the desire for a better standard of living which was already emerging and was bound to develop with the further urbanisation which industrial growth implied. Yet there could be no other stimulus to effort except the traditional and tempting Russian method of coercion. The food supply in Russia had always been unreliable for both climatic and organisational reasons, and had been apt to break down in famine, particularly in times of war and disturbance. The new regime had to provide a basic security of food supply while diverting more to its developing towns. It could not do this with such a diminution in the efficiency of agriculture as was implied in its own encouragement of peasant seizure of lands. Its traditional advocacy of retention of the large estates by entrusting them to some form of co-operative management by the peasants was bound to seem a more tempting solution. And yet the difficulties which existed without the ill-will of the cultivators could only be increased by incurring it. These have throughout been the topics of a constant debate within the Soviet political system, and most of them are not settled yet.

The traditional concerns about the frontier and security have retained their old urgency. Apart from foreign intervention Brest-Litovsk had stimulated new nationalisms in the territories now cut off from Russia. Moscow was presented with Moscow's old problem of winning them back, and in particular of again forcing back the frontiers of the west. From the timing of the revolution in the middle of a world war there resulted a mutual resentment between the Soviet and the non-Soviet world, intensified by the decision almost inevitable for a revolutionary government to disown Russia's immense foreign debt. The need to prevent encirclement, real or supposed, and to ward off intervention, which at least from the direction of Japan still continued to threaten in the 'thirties, have been prime motives of Soviet Russia throughout its history. Here lay yet another incentive to industrialisation and also to the relocation of industry away from the frontiers. An obvious response to the pre-occupation with foreign danger has been, in view of the official doctrine's internationalist associations, the direct appeal to peoples over the heads of their governments. The demands thus made upon foreign communists and their obvious relation to exclusively Russian interests, however, have operated to keep the number of Russia's committed supporters small and to alienate much sympathy which might have been gained among the uncommitted.

Another force with which the regime has throughout had to reckon has been the desire to protect local interests and peculiarities. Before the revolution there had been little divergence on national grounds within the territories to which the Bolsheviks found themselves heirs. Even in the newer territories of central Asia government, though severe, had not been discriminatory, but already with the influx of Russian colonists material interests were beginning to diverge. In particular, the native races were becoming concerned about the shortage of land. Thus when the tight hold of the centre over them was removed by the disorders of 1917 there were many who were willing to seize the opportunity for establishing their independence. This soon came into opposition with the internationalism of the Marxists, which once the state was found to be necessary, had little to distinguish it from old-fashioned imperialism. Nor was it enough that the former empire should remain united; it must also be uniform. Already before the revolution even the Great Russians, who had previously been remarkably uniform in character and way of life in spite of their wide territorial dispersion, were beginning to develop local differences, and in the *zemstvo* governorships these extended to differences of political practice. But the new society was to be a socialist one, and the binding interpretation of what was implied in socialism was that of Moscow. Its determination of economic priorities necessarily came into conflict with local concern for the balance of the local economy, as well as with conservatism and caution, and its unwillingness to compromise has left it with a permanent burden of discontent and unreliability.

For such and other reasons, notably the professional interests of officials, there has been a tendency to the formation of a variety of local alliances for protection against the centre. Clearly these still persist generally throughout the country, and particularly where circumstances favour them, as in remote areas, areas with a common minority culture and a local language which compels the centre to some reliance on local assistance, or where they are supported by personal relationship. All this is comprised within the sin of 'familyness', which is constantly being denounced in official pronouncements and publications. The term covers much more than nepotism, though that is part of the problem. The leaders themselves for their own purposes have been obliged to create very powerful particular interests, of a different but no less dangerous type. The various corps of officials, who, for lack of popular competence and enthusiasm, and by reason of the very nature of the work, have had to be established, continued or revived to run the machine, are disposed to such offences as 'preserving the honour of the uniform'—covering up the faults of other persons in the same service. The authorities have felt obliged to devote much thought to (again in their own idiom) keeping the line open for 'signals' from below. Often this has meant laying more lines, complicating the administrative structure at a heavy cost in manpower and in convenience of working.

The Periods

The circumstances and issues of politics have changed greatly in relative importance with the passage of time since the revolution. Soviet writers, as Marxists, mark off periods in economic terms, and in general this coincides conveniently with the changing balance of political themes. We need not accept also the myth of consistency which they simultaneously maintain and in which they are often supported by opponents apt to see their worst excesses implicit in their earliest acts. Our distinction of periods, like any other, is artificial.

The first period of the regime, extending to the spring of 1921, is economically described as that of 'war communism', and may politically be called that of the anti-Bolshevik menace. The dominant themes were peace—its conclusion on tolerable terms and its preservation—defence against foreign intervention and the civil war against the few remaining supporters of the imperial family and the more numerous upholders of military ideas of sound government, the maintenance of the food supply and the reversal of the flight from the famine and disorders of the towns, and the working out of the implications of the decree of general nationalisation issued on the 28th June 1918. Lenin and his supporters were possibly led by circumstances to carry their communist principles into effect faster than they had intended. For the successful conclusion of the complex of wars in which they were involved they needed urgently to restore the country's economic life, and their nationalisation may also have been intended to forestall German or other claims to foreign assets. Moreover, they needed to keep ahead of the extremism which in a revolutionary situation can easily mobilise support against moderation. Enthusiasm was high, and ideas such as direct management of all economic enterprises from the centre, or workers' control, or both at once, communal living and the moneyless economy based upon allocation of goods in kind—or the similar idea of the lawless state based on public interest and economic planning—seemed feasible, and died out only over the years. The myth of the coming revolution in western Europe, which would solve most of Russia's difficulties, lived on to the end of the period.

In politics the main concern of the Bolsheviks was to get rid of the Constituent Assembly. Before their seizure of power they had been its strongest advocates in order to embarrass the provisional government. They could not now repudiate it, yet they could not hope to control it. The elections produced only 175 Bolshevik members out of a total of 707, which included 414 of the Social Revolutionary Party. Lenin took precautions against the Assembly's going the wrong way; he exploited a split among the Social Revolutionaries, and used it to question the validity of their majority; he arranged a meeting of the Congress of Soviets, over which he had already begun to exercise influence, for three days after the Assembly was due to meet. When it met in January 1918, and still proved refractory, he dissolved it by force of arms and prevented it from meeting again. The Congress of Soviets, thus presented with a *fait accompli*, duly declared itself the permanent, instead of, as previously, the provisional, government of Russia. The popular demand for a constitution was satisfied by one of the Bolsheviks' own making approved by another Congress of Soviets in July 1918.

In the internal affairs of the party the Leninist standards of discipline, which in the period of revolution and war the Bolsheviks had had to relax, were increasingly asserted. This culminated in the denunciation by the Tenth Congress of the party, meeting in March 1921, of 'deviation' and 'fractionalism'—holding any discussion by groups within the party of views not approved by the leadership—as impermissible, and the prescription of a periodic 'cleansing' (*chistka*)—or 'purge', as it has generally been translated—as the remedy. This measure was at the time conceived in terms of public examination of records leading to reprimand or expulsion of offenders, without its later more sinister connotations. The same congress opened the way to a new period by acceptance of the New Economic Policy (N.E.P.).

The occasion of the N.E.P. was the mounting discontent in the country, caused mainly by realisation that internal peace was not to be achieved as easily as had once been hoped, by continued food shortages and by peasant unrest resulting from the violent methods adopted to remedy these at the expense of the food-producers. They came to a head in February–March 1921 in the expression of specifically anti-Bolshevik—though not anti-soviet or counter-revolutionary—demands by the men of the naval base, and former Bolshevik stronghold, of Kronstadt, which the Bolsheviks felt obliged to beat down by military action, during the meeting of the Tenth Congress. The new policy represented an attempt at conciliation; the peasants were to be permitted to sell their produce in the open market after settlement of fixed obligations to the state instead of being subject to arbitrary requisition. In the main this settled their active discontent and enabled many of them to achieve comparative prosperity, but it did not remove their heightened distrust of the towns and their consequent reluctance to supply them with food or to show such agricultural efficiency as might attract a new expropriation, and it did not make the minute holdings resulting from the land redistribution any more economic as units of cultivation. Limited yet substantial revival of private enterprise was permitted in commerce and the greater part of industry, the state restricting its field of monopoly to what, in the military terminology favoured by the Marxists, it called the 'commanding heights' of heavy industry. Foreign capital was again allowed access to Russia under government-granted concessions. Lenin admitted that it was a partial return to capitalism and expressed the hope that state enterprise would prove itself more efficient in free competition. At least it brought some return to law and judicial procedure—though the *Che-ka* (the revolution's secret police) continued active—and to traditional ideas of orderly administration, to increased readiness to make use of officials who had served under the Tsar, and to the abandonment of the Marxist idea of limiting officials to 'workmen's wages'. Willingness to compromise with non-Marxist views, at least in inessentials, was shown also in the admission of federal institutions to the system of government. There was much in all this which many sincere Bolsheviks could hardly have accepted from anyone but Lenin—especially since over much of the field it was not brilliantly successful, for capital was understandably timid—and when the N.E.P. was little over a year old his influence—not moderate but always prudent—was virtually removed. Already at the end of May 1922 a stroke seriously reduced his physical powers, and two more strokes, in the latter part of the year and the beginning of the next, left him paralysed until his death in January 1924. Out of the public eye, the struggle for the succession was already well advanced. Trotski was, after Lenin, unquestionably the most brilliant figure of the revolution, and for his achievements as its military leader the most popular, though not the most judicious. Yet Stalin, obscure, in intellect and in fame, had secured a unique central position, with command of two key departments of the state administration and at the same time of the yet unrealised power of the party's administrative machinery, formally confirmed by his election as its General Secretary just two months before Lenin's first stroke. Lenin distrusted Trotski's judgment, but in his last months he came increasingly to fear Stalin's ambition and dishonesty, and, given time and strength, would probably have sought to break his former protégé. His judgments on both men were proved correct. Stalin triumphed by the means of which Lenin had himself advertised the efficacy, by organisation—though through the office, the personal file and the manipulation of postings rather than through the public meeting and the pamphlet—and by adroit changes of policy. In the wide spread of party opinions he took the safe dead centre. Against Trotski's bold and arduous course of immediate and rapid industrialisation and a firm hand with the trade unions and peasants, for which the country then had little heart, he advocated the more cautious policies of the party's principal propagandist Buharin. He opposed Trotski's argument for more democracy within the party—not even Trotski suggested the possibility of its extension outside the party—which alarmed many with less personal interest in the consolidation of bureaucracy than Stalin had. He enlisted to his cause the general desire for a *détente* in international relations by casting doubt on the safety of his rival's revolutionary zeal. Trotski was manoeuvred into isolation, largely by exploitation of his own strong sense of Bolshevik discipline, and expelled from the party in November 1927, and from Russia in January 1929.

The period extending from the Fifteenth Party Congress of December 1927, which passed the directives for the preparation of the first Five Year Plan, to the Eighteenth, of March 1939, which approved the third Five Year Plan—some fourteen months after it had come into operation—has a political unity as the period of determination of the content of Stalinism when the location of power was no longer contestable by political action, and only the use which Stalin was to make of it was in doubt. Within it, however, there is a significant change of subject in the year 1934, which began with the election of Andrei Zhdanov as one of the secretaries of the party Central Committee and closed with the murder of Sergei Kirov. In the earlier part the economic theme was clearly dominant. Without any special experience or original ideas in this field, and without any guidance in the writings and practices of Lenin, Stalin found himself obliged to produce some solution for the pressing problems of economic power more positive and more gratifying to communist prejudices than the discredited N.E.P. Having eliminated Trotski, Stalin was driven to adopt the essentials of Trotski's policies, and in many respects to exceed them in boldness of conception and ruthlessness of application. The first Five Year Plan, which came into operation in October 1928 and was accepted by a party conference in the following April, inaugurated a rapid return to the stringencies of war communism without its wilder idealistic enthusiasms. Though the official claim of its completion in four years was clearly not literally true, its success in its own material terms of increased industrial production far exceeded all reasonable expectation, and, it seems, helped to build up Stalin's own faith in the efficacy of organisational methods to solve all problems and so in his own omnicompetence. Intensive collectivisation of agriculture, for which the Fifteenth Congress had given authority, entered on its full compulsive phase in 1929, and had virtually achieved the complete extinction of the private farmer before, at the end of 1930, Stalin halted it as a product of official excess of zeal. This in part it probably was, but Stalin's magnanimity did not extend to the reversal of its achievements. From 3.8 per cent of the total crop area in 1928 the share of socialised agriculture apparently rose to 98.4 per cent in 1936. Here results in terms of production were less favourable: peasant embitterment and resistance and government reprisals kept output down and cost the country some half of its livestock, but the land was for the first time made substantially amenable to the will of Moscow, and Stalin could hope to make good by mechanisation what had been lost.

In the second part of the period, in the middle 'thirties, the issues of Soviet politics again became more complex, as Stalin sought to impose on others the legend of his own infallibility, of which he had convinced himself, and the personal control of all aspects of the country's life which it justified. In Zhdanov he found the intellectual powers which he himself lacked and which he needed for the manipulation of his subjects' minds. A rigid orthodoxy based upon minute oversight of all aspects of cultural life, isolation from all unauthorised contact with the outside world, suppression and rewriting of inconvenient internal sources of information and the conscious revival of Russian tradition favourable to autocracy, were the main elements of the new policy. The motives for the murder of Kirov, one of the more moderate of the Stalinists, may have been personal and, if political, were certainly muddled, but the motives of Stalin in utilising it as the occasion for a new phase of the process of purges in party and state are fairly clearly related to this development. The process began with a general examination of the records of party members which reduced the total membership between 1933 and the beginning of 1937 almost by half, and from 1936 to 1939 it passed to a wider field in the form of the mass arrests, summary trials, transportations and shootings associated with the name of Yezhov, the People's Commissar for Internal Affairs of the time.

In each phase persons who might in some way have stood in the way of the new legend were conspicuously numerous among the victims. These included almost all close associates of Lenin except those notoriously clients of Stalin himself, a very high proportion of other members of long standing or exalted position in the party, the leaders of the Communist Parties of the minority nationalities, foreigners, including foreign communists, and real or supposed friends of foreigners. Zinoviev and Kamenev, Stalin's first allies against Trotski, whose deposition from influence in the party had been contemporary with that of Trotski himself, were brought back under the lights for trial and execution, and their fellows and successors were similarly played off one against the other and in turn overthrown. More tangible considerations perhaps dictated the mass elimination of the loyal but untrained communists in the technical and administrative posts of industry who were obstructing the rise of the new managerial class which Stalin had created, and of the possibly unreliable senior officers of the army, at whose mercy he probably foresaw that he might in the near future be placed by war, for this was the period of the rise to power of Hitler, partly through the misjudgments of the Russians themselves. The party was changed from an arena where a struggle for power was fought out with ideological weapons to a highly specialised instrument of administration. The period concluded with the triumphant Stalin's revision of Leninism at the Eighteenth Congress to provide for the continuance of the state for an indefinite period even after the happy attainment of communism.

The period from 1939 until Stalin's death in 1953 is not marked off by any changes of economic structure such as distinguished those before it. Nevertheless Soviet official opinion seems now to recognise its distinctiveness as the period when Stalin finally got out of hand, when, in Mr. Khrushchov's words, he 'thought that now he could decide all things alone, and that all he needed' (as advisers) 'were statisticians; he treated all others in such a way that they could only listen and praise him',[1] though, on Mr. Khrushchov's own showing, his regard for the opinions of others had been minimal before. Political issues, in the sense of matters for negotiation, hardly existed at the highest level. In another sense, too, the range of politics was narrowed. Throughout the period the scene was dominated by external relations, the opportunities and perils presented by a world at war. Territorial expansion added five new republics to the Union and enlarged three others, and invasion brought a serious danger of the regime's total collapse. During the

[1] N. S. Khrushchov, speech in closed session at the Twentieth Congress of the party, 1956.

war of 1941–5 military problems were solved by substantially conventional military machinery and, as in other countries, left little room for the more varied concerns of peace. 'Soviet patriotism', devised in the immediate pre-war years to replace the party's original internationalism, was necessarily given increased prominence in official propaganda, and its already marked traditional Great-Russian content, the promotion of Great-Russian historical legend, literature, way of life and political influence to the detriment of what remained of the independence of the nationalities, was perhaps intensified by suspicion of the reliability of the latter aroused in Stalin's mind by the defection of some of them in the days of their first contact with the German invaders. This trend was not reversed on the coming of peace, but there disappeared other trends of the war period, concessions to Western opinion and to necessity, particularly a greater tolerance of breaches of collectivisation in agriculture. The official answer to the immense material and moral problems of the post-war period proved immediately to be a return to rigid planning, collectivisation and control, to extreme measures to stop the gaps in the isolation of the Soviet people from the outside world, and (for some of the nationalities at least) to purges. In general, however, though the regime's repression of opponents remained severe, the purge in the manner of the 'thirties was after 1939 a thing of the past, replaced by an elaborate and constant system of supervision. The end of the war left Russia secure and influential in the world as never before since the revolution, but not apparently more trusting. The Stalin myth was greatly enhanced probably in his own mind as well as in those of others. It seems unlikely that his participation in military affairs was quite as inept as Khrushchov suggested, and it is now again officially in order to praise it; but we can patiently await more evidence. For whatever reason, the courses of action on which he insisted, such as the defence of Stalingrad, were pursued through to success, much as in the economic battles of previous years. In the post-war years he showed a self-assurance greater than ever before, and amid clamorous adulation laid down the law in a succession of fields in which he had no specialised knowledge whatever. Under his authority Zhdanov's regimentation of Russian thought became absolute. The party had greatly expanded and had a force of new men at its disposal with reputations gained in the activities of wartime, and in particular in the army. Stalin's policy seems to have been to ignore those at the top, who might be dangerous, particularly the generals, whose independent reputations might challenge his own, and to make full use of those lower down who had shown the capacity to be serviceable. Now again the succession was becoming a matter of obvious concern in the top ranks of the party. New rivalries appeared which seemed to centre particularly about the opposition between Zhdanov and Malenkov, Stalin's protégé and deputy in the control of the party machine. With the death of Zhdanov in August 1948 the field seemed open to Malenkov, and his dead rival's retainers were hastily removed from all posts of influence.

Power next to the throne, however, depended on continued occupancy of the throne, and the death of Stalin in March 1953 left a gap of too distinctive a shape to be filled by a designated heir even had Stalin so far forgotten his skills in the balancing of men's ambitions as to provide one. Beria, who with the private army and influence network of the security services seemed nearest to supreme personal power, was early eliminated, and Malenkov was, by weakness or miscalculation, induced to renounce the highest party office for the leadership of the formal government, which previous experience indicated, and subsequent practice seems to confirm, to be of no comparable potency as a source of power. Painfully acquired awareness of the perils of not being first in a monarchical order brought back into usage the arts of politics—bidding by aspirants to management of the country's potentialities for the acquiescence of those who have power to give them trouble. The ouster, in 1958, of Molotov and the other strangely diverse opponents of Khrushchov on whom the latter was able to pin the label of the 'anti-party group' shows a revival of realisation that the party monolith has parts which can be manoeuvred one against the other, and, almost certainly, a rare, and probably unrepeatable, instance of readiness to bring the power of the army into play. The immediate curbing of that power, in the person of Zhukov, and the fall of Khrushchov himself in October 1964, discreetly and decorously contrived in response, it seems, to revulsion among his immediate associates at his flamboyant style and propensity to ill-considered and potentially disruptive reform, left an oligarchy seemly, conservative, conciliatory to the more easily appeased pressures, such as those of consumers and peasants, but as suspicious as any of its predecessors of intellectuals and their unhealthy interest in the world beyond the frontiers. This order looks both more complex and more tolerable to those who must live under it than its predecessor, but it seems as likely to prove cyclical as linearly progressive towards liberalisation. The Khrushchov experience suggests both that the Soviet pattern of government still tends to autocracy and that successive autocrats may find themselves less able to count on security of tenure.

The Participants

As in any other country, the relative importance of the various issues of politics has been different not only at different times but also for different men. The ordinary Soviet 'citizen', so designated for lack of a claim to the party style of 'comrade', rarely appears in the press, and then usually in a discreditable light. He is found feathering his own nest at the public cost—usually through the inattention of some official 'comrade', who shares in the blame—neglecting his work or otherwise failing in social discipline. Here, as generally, the bias of the Soviet press towards the pathological distorts the picture. We have, however, from other sources enough evidence to form some model of the citizen's world. For him the revolution is a fact, beneficial on the whole; the rightness of his country and the obtuseness of authority are as axiomatic as for his counterpart in any other society; the making or unmaking of ministers and of laws are activities as remote as they were to his grandfather, and verbal conformity and the recognition of influence are senses highly developed as necessary to existence. His concern appears to be to make life as predictable as possible, to live his own life, to avoid officials and to keep out of trouble. In the early days of the new order there were hopes of a dramatic liberation—particularly, among the minor nationalities, hopes of national liberation—but there can be little of this now. Among a section of the youth enthusiasm may still be high, but it soon fades. The same desire for predictability and a little peace is probably the motive of the small official. His 'bureaucracy', which the official organs constantly denounce, is a desire for orderly procedure in which not every case is an exception and the line from higher authority is sometimes silent.

Soviet terminology suggests benevolence but little respect for this class. The 'masses' are always an object, though an important one, rather than a subject—material to be manipulated, to be persuaded and conciliated rather than coerced, but of themselves inert. The 'population' (naselenie) which faces the Soviet official is not quite the 'public' of his Western counterpart; usage suggests something more submissive, more in need of protection, less spontaneously disciplined.

A much larger proportion of the population, however, than in most societies—those with ambition enough to interest themselves in the wide prospects which the Soviet system offers, as army officers, managers, leading officials and specialists, 'activists' (regular workers in the party and active supporters of it)—needs to play politics in the sense of basing action on some conscious assessment of the views and motives of government and its agents. They must submit to a much closer supervision than the less ambitious, and the best way to counter it is probably to seek the favour of the well placed. They must advertise themselves, and this generally means undertaking a variety of voluntary tasks, in the permitted social organisations, in the recurrent government drives and campaigns and, above all, in the party, to which closed circle the ambitious man must sooner or later secure admittance. They do not usually, unless they hold or aspire to party office, need to know all the tangled ropes of Marxist philosophy, though, like everybody else, they must accept it, and, unlike the more lowly, may need to make occasional unexceptionable utterances. But especially they must give results in their own fields of employment, perform, secure the performance, or conceal the non-performance of assignments which are habitually a little too big. For people in this position technical incompetence is probably now the only completely irredeemable flaw. Understandably for the generality of them the world revolves around a particular department in the government service; there is little time to look beyond it and its immediate neighbours to see the system as a whole.

For those within the managerial élite who are regularly in interaction with the sovereign policy-makers the position is different. The circle can hardly be considered to extend beyond the twenty members and secretaries of the central directing body of the party, a fair proportion of the sixty or so secretaries of the republican parties and perhaps a few of their associates, ministers of the union government and a few from the government of each union republic, a party secretary or two and perhaps a state official from each of some two hundred non-federal units, together with a few private secretaries and heads of the more frequently consulted specialist agencies—perhaps some seven or eight hundred persons in all. These, though widely scattered, form something like a true political society, with power to advise, and perhaps even to promote policies of their own liking. They need the skill of the politician to sense changes of wind in the upper air and to turn with them in good time, to understand the moods and motives of those below and to secure co-operation from them without committing themselves. They also, like their subordinates, are judged by results, and failure means a rapid return from real influence and prosperity to obscurity. These are the men who must always bear in mind the contingency of a coming purge and how best to avoid it. They cannot allow themselves the safety of silence, but must have the alertness and subtlety to detect what is happening and demonstrate in orthodox terms and with references to texts its rightness and inevitability. Among them are most of the men with a close knowledge of the outside world, and they are kept reasonably well informed of both central decisions and external events. That they are not, in consequence—as probably they are not—a cancer of cynicism at the heart of the Soviet system is probably due to the rigorous process of selection by which they have reached the top, with its implicit emphasis on right ideas as ancillary, but necessary, to material achievement, and to the general human proneness to suppose that what is good for oneself is self-evidently right.

The size of the sovereign decision-taking body—that which needs to consider no limitation on its range of action other than that of physical possibility—has clearly varied from time to time. It is reasonable to say that in the time of Stalin it consisted of one man, with the rest able to do little more than guess, at their own considerable risk, what was going on in his mind. Now there are probably more active participants; and though there have been, and will be, other aspirants to the sole lead, it will probably require a subtlety more than Stalinian to possess it in tranquillity. Such things are more easily done a first time.

We probably have not to suppose that even at this level the practitioners see the system whole, though Stalin may at times have stood back from his work to wonder at his own artistry, and perhaps even Molotov may have reflected with modest pride on the skill which kept him in the safe, if less satisfying, role of the reliable second from prerevolutionary days until his decline and downfall in the ascendancy of Khrushchov. At this level the concern must be to keep the balance of power, to prevent its accumulation in other hands, to appreciate how much is possible with the given material and how that material may be maximised. This obviously requires an intimate knowledge of personality and great skill and tact in manipulation. Such a man must know, as Trotski suggests Stalin did, how so to involve his colleagues in his schemes as to make them feel committed to courses which they would otherwise find distasteful, and yet contrive to look beyond the new ally to his riddance should he seek to become the master.

CHAPTER II

Soviets, Union and Constitutional State

The Invention of the Soviets

On the form of the socialist state after the revolution Marx was of little assistance. His principal venture into the practical was in 1871, when, for his own short-term advantage in the political manoeuvres of the first International, he constituted himself the champion of the Paris Commune, which enjoyed a brief two months of independence upon the close of the Franco-Prussian War. In an address preserved in his writings as *The Civil War in France* he described this creation as according to its constitution it should have been: the representative assembly elected for a short term, the revocability of all deputies, the absence of any separation of powers, the control by local bodies over the police and officials, the restriction of all state servants to workmen's wages, the elective, responsible and revocable judges and magistrates, and the district and national assemblies elected up from the local bodies. He approved the dominance of the towns over the countryside, which, he suggested, secured to the peasants their natural leaders in the urban working men, and he proclaimed the whole a chance-discovered form for the dictatorship of the proletariat. In fact, it was manifestly nothing of the sort, and the declaration of support for violence served only to alarm and estrange the British trade unions and others whose support Marx was seeking. Consequently the attempt was soon forgotten by him and by others, and the work which it produced, though reprinted and from time to time commented upon, was not taken very seriously.

As we have seen, soviets of workers' deputies first appeared in Russia—in St. Petersburg and Moscow, and subsequently in a few other towns—in the course of the troubles of 1905, as co-ordinating bodies among the mass of strike committees. The word 'soviet' in itself is politically neutral, meaning merely 'council', as in the title of the old Council of State. The thing in itself was in 1905 of no one pronounced political complexion. Most of the existing political parties were represented in the St. Petersburg soviet, including both wings of the Social Democrats; and the dominant figure in it, who exploited most effectively its possibilities for theatrical demonstra-

56

tion, was Trotski, who stood between the two. Even the newly
formed liberal grouping, though it did not join, sent a message expressing its solidarity. This soviet was a body of somewhat fluid
membership with, at its largest, some 560 members and an executive committee composed principally of Social Revolutionaries and
Social Democrats of the two schools. Lenin, who arrived in St.
Petersburg during the period of its activity, expressed interest in it
and appreciation of Trotski's work, but himself took no part and
apparently saw in it no principle capable of further application. Its
dramatic appearance on the scene, however, gave prestige to the
form, and when subsequently troubles again developed it was
imitated. In 1917 soviets began to form, not only among the workers
but also in the army and navy and among the peasantry. Their
political allegiance was still not certain, though those in peasant
areas were dominated almost exclusively by the Social Revolutionaries.

At the beginning of the 1917 Lenin apparently began to see new
possibilities in the soviets. In an address delivered in Switzerland in
January of that year he recalled that in certain towns in Russia
they had 'really functioned in the capacity of a new state power'.[1]
In March of the same year, by which time they had already reappeared in Russia, he proclaimed the soviets to be a 'new, unofficial, still comparatively weak, workers' government'.[2] A few
days after this appeared in print he was on his way home, and on
the day of his arrival he first brandished overtly the stick he had
devised to beat the provisional government with. In the 'April
theses', ostensibly points for discussion in the formulation of party
policy, he declared: 'not a parliamentary republic—a return to that
from the soviet of workers' deputies would be a step backward—but a
republic of soviets of workers' agricultural labourers' and peasants'
deputies throughout the country, from the bottom to the top'.[3] His
addition to their description accorded with his discovery of the
utility of the peasants. In an article in the recently revived party
newspaper *Pravda*, in defence of the theses, he proclaimed the
authority of the soviets to be of 'exactly the same type as the Paris
Commune of 1871',[4] thus placing them in the direct line of Marxist
succession. They were to be based not on any parliamentary discussion but on direct mass action and on 'outright seizure', words
which, though unspecific, were in themselves attractive to the
peasants. The police and army were to be replaced by the arming

[1] Lenin, *Report on the Revolution of* 1905, Works, Vol. 23 (1949), pp. 240–1.
[2] Lenin, *Letters from Afar*, Letter I, Works, Vol. 23 (1949), p. 298.
[3] Works, Vol. 24 (1949), p. 5.
[4] *On the Diarchy*, Works, Vol. 24 (1949), pp. 19–20.

of the whole people, who were themselves to maintain order; and officials, in so far as they were retained at all, were to be reduced to the status of simple agents of the people, subject, as in Marx's vision of the Paris Commune, to summary dismissal.

Though Lenin never withdrew his hastily granted recognition of the state of soviets as the form appropriate to the period of the dictatorship of the proletariat, his attachment to the soviets as in fact they existed was intermittent in the succeeding months. The party's April Conference, to which the theses were presented, duly adopted his slogan 'All Power to the Soviets' as a direct challenge to the authority of the provisional government, but in a pamphlet written in preparation for the Sixth Party Congress in the following July he himself urged its withdrawal.[1] The provisional government had for the first time brought itself to take a firm hand with Lenin, driving him into hiding over the Finnish frontier and imprisoning some of his supporters, including Trotski, while the majority in the principal soviets, though ready enough to accept Bolshevik slogans, remained unamenable to Bolshevik control to a degree which threatened the delicate strategy of the minority with disaster. In September he revived the slogan,[2] with equally good cause. At the beginning of that month there had been the first movement of army officers against the provisional government, representing military exasperation with the lack of effective guidance from the capital. The threat was the salvation of the Bolsheviks, the section of the revolutionaries who best knew what they wanted and were prepared to provide firm leadership towards getting it and to throw upon their less resolute rivals the suspicion of complicity with the supposed counter-revolutionary elements. Shortly afterwards they gained for the first time a majority in the Petrograd soviet, where Trotski, now their ally, returned to the chair, and in the soviets of Moscow and other towns. The return at the same time of the peasant soldiers deserting at Bolshevik instigation from the front, and finding in their villages that the Social Revolutionaries had achieved little for them in concrete terms of land, gave them their first control of some even of the rural soviets. The soviets had suddenly become a useful instrument, though not one in the possession of which Lenin could feel entirely secure, even when power was seized in its name in November.

The soviets had already ceased to be purely local. The first All-

---

[1] *On the Slogans*, Works, Vol. 25 (1949), pp. 164–70. In an article published in *Pravda* in the middle of the previous month he was still strongly advocating the slogan (Works, Vol. 25, pp. 134–5).

[2] 'One of the Root Questions of the Revolution', published in *Rabochi Putj*, 27th (14th) September 1917, Works, Vol. 25 (1949), pp. 340–7.

Russian Congress of Soviets had met in the middle of June. It was not a success from the Bolsheviks' point of view; the 882 delegates included only 105 Bolsheviks as against 285 Social Revolutionaries and 248 Mensheviks, and a Bolshevik motion for the assumption of power from the provisional government was defeated. Like the earliest soviets, the congress resolved to establish an inner executive and administrative body to manage business until the next congress. Even this proved to be as big as 250, of whom in the first instance only thirty-five were Bolsheviks. The Second and Third Congresses of Soviets, though neither provided the Bolsheviks with a majority, were rather better managed by them. The *coup d'état* of November, and the dispersal of the Constituent Assembly of the following January, were staged a few days in advance of the congress meeting, so that the congresses had merely to take delivery of, in the first case, provisional, and in the second, permanent authority as the parliament of Russia, and in this they concurred. In practice it was not the congress but the All-Russian Central Executive Committee, its inner body, which exercised the parliamentary function, in so far as it was exercised at all, and which continued so to do until 1936. But the transfer of power to executive committees was not confined to the congresses, where it could hardly have been avoided, but was found also in the local soviets. The Petrograd (St. Petersburg) soviet of 1917 was from the first managed, and virtually replaced, by its executive committee. Already at the Eighth Congress of the party (to be distinguished from the Congresses of Soviets), held in March 1919, we find a delegate complaining publicly that 'in fact there is a tendency to liquidate the soviets and to convert Russia into a country of executive committees'. Soon there even appeared inner bodies within these inner bodies; and as the functions of the Soviet state became increasingly managerial, this tendency, directed towards the production of agencies of a size and type of membership suitable to such functions, became increasingly pronounced in party, in state, and throughout the system.

In September 1917 Lenin protested against the common interpretation of the slogan 'All Power to the Soviets' as meaning 'a ministry from the parties of the soviet majority', which, he held, would mean leaving in being the whole old official machinery. Instead the people must be involved directly in the whole process of government, including administration. However, Lenin soon brought himself to accept, as from practical considerations it was inevitable that he should, a ministry, though without a majority in the soviets, of which he was himself the chairman. The Second Congress of Soviets, which accepted the revolution of November, resolved 'to form for the administration of the country for the time until the convocation of the Constituent Assembly'—which in the event meant permanently—'a provisional workers' and peasants' government to be known as the Council of People's Commissars'. The choice of title was apparently largely accidental; the Bolsheviks desired to avoid the associations of the word 'minister' and apparently added the word 'people's' (*narodni*) to the word 'commissars', to differentiate them from other commissars already thrown up by the revolution and so named in imitation of the French revolution. The departments entrusted to these officials mostly bore designations familiar in conventional political systems, including, with some peculiarities of terminology, that of Russia—internal affairs, foreign affairs, finance, justice, posts and telegraphs, agriculture, labour, commerce and industry, the army and navy—at first organised as a committee but soon thereafter reorganised into two commissariats —and so on. Thus the ministries were never really in abeyance. The new men took over existing machines, and in the succeeding months the traditional manners of operation of the latter soon reasserted themselves. One of the motives directing events was the desire of the administrators to recover control of their former local branches. In the early days the soviets had been encouraged to seize control of the local offices as one means of disorganisation. With the Bolshevik conquest of power, however, there was a change of emphasis. In December 1917 we find the People's Commissariat for Internal Affairs, while continuing to invite the soviets to seize all government offices, directing them at the same time to co-ordinate their activities with the general decrees of the central authority. It reported that it was itself responsible for unifying their actions and accordingly invited them to submit reports.[1] Soon after the revolution we get complaints of the loss of independence by the soviets and their departments in consequence of the action of officials sent out from the centre.

An ingenious justification was found for this state of affairs in the evolution of the doctrine of dual subordination. By this, departments of lower soviets were to be responsible both to the executive committee, and so the soviet, at the level of which they worked, and also to the corresponding department in their own line of business at the next higher level up to the ministry. The same principle of dual subordination applied to the executive committees themselves, making them, in the terms of Article 101 of the current constitution of the U.S.S.R., 'accountable both to the soviets of toilers' deputies which elected them, and to the executive organ of the superior soviet of toilers' deputies'. In practice the vertical line, as Soviet

---

[1] S. Dobrin, 'Soviet Federalism and the Principle of Dual Subordination', *Transactions of the Grotius Society*, Vol. XXX (1944), p. 269.

administrative theory styles it, leading up towards the centre, has
proved more effective than the horizontal line of control by the local
soviets. The device facilitated a return to the administrative state
while preserving for the new regime the moral advantage of the new
myth of mass political action.

By-passing the soviets, however, was not enough. The centre still
needed their services, and for this it had to reorganise them, especially the rural soviets, where, despite the steady drift away from the
Social Revolutionary allegiance to the advantage of the Bolsheviks,
a conflict of wills still remained. The alliance of the peasantry and
the proletariat was one of convenience and not of conviction.
Marxists, with their attachment to industrial forms of organisation,
were, from the first, disposed to believe in the superiority of collective over individual peasant agriculture, and to favour the retention
of the larger estates for use as collective farms. They took over the
populist slogans of seizures and redistribution only as a tactical
move, necessary for the seizure of power. The necessities of the
retention of power, when once they had the towns to feed, drove
them no less firmly back to their principles. From the earliest days
military revolutionary committees had been posted in the villages
to force upon the peasants the surrender of an adequate proportion
of their crops. For a more permanent solution they looked to the
resentments for which the increasing differentiation, in respect of
wealth, of a peasant society offered foundations. To describe and
damn the larger peasant, defined as from time to time suited them,
they made use of the term 'kulak', which in its pre-revolutionary
usage vaguely suggested sharp practice—from the merchant's giving
of short weight to the usurer's expropriation of the impoverished
peasant who had increasingly been falling into his clutches. Against
him they brought into action the committees of the poor. 'Their
main task was to split the village....,' Zinoviev explained at the
Sixth Congress of Soviets in November 1918, when that task had
been completed. 'They are not really elective bodies. They were
appointed by visiting representatives of the executive committees or
of party organs.... There are committees of the poor consisting of
a few people—the best people in the village. They hold it under
their control although sometimes they are not its elected representatives, and side by side with them there still exist some remnants of
the old soviet, a couple of people.... We rejected ... the suggestion
that these soviet remnants should be allowed to continue their existence side by side with the committees of the poor as food sections.'
The old soviet had been smashed by emissaries from outside the
village—in fact from the town. It remained to put something in
its place. 'On the transition from the neutralisation of the middle

peasant (at the end of 1918) to a policy of establishing a firm alliance with him', the same Congress of Soviets 'passed a decree upon the re-election of soviets with the aim of improving their composition. The immediate conduct of the re-election the congress left to the committees of the poor. On the completion of the re-election at the beginning of 1919 the committees of the poor were liquidated and their function transferred to the newly elected soviets.'[1] The story was repeated in the mass collectivisation phase of 1929–30. Again groups of poor peasants were organised, but this time the village soviets themselves were required to organise them. When many of them failed to do so, and some themselves opposed collectivisation, the authorities satisfied themselves of 'the necessity of re-election, review, examination of personal composition of the backward village soviets which do not manage the new tasks',[2] and acted accordingly.

Already by this stage the soviets, as a distinctive institution underlying and determining the character of the state, were dead. They had never been the motive force, though perhaps the fact that they were there had affected the way in which more positive forces operated. As a tool the village soviet remained of some importance while the collectivisation of agriculture continued; a legal instrument of 1930 laid upon them the duty of speeding its progress, and to that end relieved them of the more general competence, prescribed by an instrument of 1924, to provide for all local needs. They were given the power to enquire into the internal management of the private farms and to confiscate the land of people not fulfilling their production plan or their obligation to the state. This task done, they were left, as the town soviets were already, as merely part of the local administrative structure and, very largely, an otiose part.

An order on district and higher congresses of soviets was issued in 1928 giving them power of supervision over the village soviets. The shift of the operative function away from the village was completed in 1936 when the new constitution provided, for the first time,

---

[1] A. A. Askerov, et al. in *Sovetskoe Gosudarstvennoe Pravo* (1948), p. 124. Of the result of the process Lenin admitted at the Eighth Congress of the party (March 1919) that 'The low cultural level brings it about that the soviets—although by their programme they should be the organ of administration by the working people, are now, in fact, the organ of administration for the working people, by the most progressive stratum of the proletariat' (i.e. the party) 'but not by the working masses. Here there is before us a task which we cannot solve otherwise than by protracted education.' His successors were not so much troubled by the fact that the task remained unsolved.

[2] Ja. Berman in *Sovetskoe Gosudarstvo i Revoljutsija Prava*, No. 2 of 1930, pp. 21–2 (periodical quoted in further references as *S.G. i R.P.*).

for directly elected local 'soviets of working people's deputies' (no longer of 'workers' in the narrower class sense) at all levels of the administrative system—village, settlement or town, district, area, region or territory, and in autonomous regions and national areas, apart from the new directly elected Supreme Soviets in republics.

The Union

The losses of territory of the early days presented the Bolsheviks with a major problem of policy. Some Marxist national groupings, confident of early international triumph, professed indifference to vulgar nationalistic desires for self-determination; the Poles, being the most subject to temptation, were particularly austere in their resistance to it. Similar considerations disposed the Russians to be generous. But as experience of independence produced in the former Russian territories a variety of governments, more or less socialist, but mostly such as the Bolsheviks regarded as bourgeois, they could not but desire to see their own form of state prevail. Stalin specifically called self-determination a right of the working masses only and declared that it should be 'a means for the struggle for socialism and subordinate to the principles of socialism'.[1] Lenin was, as ever, more circumspect, but his actions agreed. From the first, aid and pressure were applied from Moscow to that end. In Poland and Finland there was, by reason of the strength of the nationalist sentiments, little that they could do. In the Baltic provinces the same forces, though weaker, were effectively backed by foreign armed assistance. In the Ukraine and Belorussia the situation was very different; there was a general realisation that their interest lay in association with Russia, though, in the fashion of the time, this early took the form of a demand for federation. The first governments set up were not acceptable to the Bolsheviks, and they fell in the latter part of 1918 with the Germans, with whom they had been obliged to ally themselves. Governments of Soviet form and largely made in Moscow took their place and, though not proceeding at once to formal federation, entered into treaty relations with Russia, which involved extensive adoption of Russian legislation and close administrative integration. The recession of resistance and intervention in the Caucasus had similar consequences. Farther east it led rather to direct incorporation in the new Russia.

As Marxists, the new rulers of Russia were against all forms of

[1] Report on the national question to the Third All-Russian Congress of Soviets of Workers', Soldiers' and Peasants' Deputies, 15th January 1918—Stalin, Works, IV, p. 32.

federalism. Engels's dictum that 'the proletariat can use only the form of the one and indivisible state' followed obviously from their principles. The proletarians of all lands were, as the Communist Manifesto demands, to unite. Since the state was merely an instrument of a class it was reasonable that this united class should have a united state, and the larger the better. It could work across frontiers drawn against it, but for it to draw frontiers across its own territory would merely play into the hands of the bougeoisie. 'Federation', Lenin wrote in a curious definition of his attitude in December 1913, 'means a union of equals depending upon common consent. . . . We reject federation on principle; it weakens economic links; it is an unfit form for our state. . . . We are for autonomy for all parts. We are for the right of secession (but not for secession itself for all). Autonomy is our plan for the building of a democratic state. Secession is not at all our plan. . . . In general we are against secession. . . . The right to secession is an exception from our general proposition of centralism. This exception is essential in view of Russian Black-Hundred nationalism.'[1] The objection to a union of equals was understandable in one committed to believing that some were right while others were wrong. The objection to any actual secession from a communist state, while recognising the right, followed equally from communist reasoning. The people should readily accept communism when once it was shown to them; from a wish to secede bourgois motives were to be inferred. Also of interest was Lenin's approval of autonomy, by which, subsequent practice and terminology has shown, he understood freedom from such control of day-to-day operations as is exercised by a head office over a branch.[2] It did not exclude the possibility of such occasional forms of influence as legislation. Subsequently Lenin brought himself to accept the term 'federation', and so made its popular appeal available to his cause, by identifying it with autonomy in his sense. This identification was expressed in the Russian Soviet Federated Socialist Republic (R.S.F.S.R.) established by the 1918 constitution. Despite the name of the new state, the constitution made no provision for federal institutions, but only for certain units designated as autonomous (originally eight autonomous republics and thirteen autonomous regions, to which were later added national areas). Stalin even went so far as to extend the term 'autonomy' to cover

[1] Letter to S. G. Shaumjan, 6th December 1913 (new style)—in Lenin's Works, Vol. 19 (1948), pp. 453–4. The black hundreds referred to were the strong-arm bands frequently involved, often with official connivance, in violence against Jews, minority nationalities and intellectuals in the closing years of the empire.
[2] S. Dobrin, op. cit., p. 281.

the relations with Russia of former possessions, such as Azerbaidjan, then ostensibly still independent though in treaty relations
with it. The criterion of fitness for the establishment of an autonomous unit within the Soviet state is nationality, which, as it has in
practice been defined, means language. The readiness of the authorities in Moscow to recognise the existence of such distinct language
groups and to give form to their previously unwritten languages
seems to have even exceeded the demand, and the grant of autonomous status which followed has survived even the decline of the
people concerned, in consequence of population movements and
other forces, into a minority within the area to which it gives its
name. The political substance of the award of such status, however,
has progressively declined. Thus in the early years of the new state
the autonomous republics had within their governments, apart from
ministries directly subordinate to those of the R.S.F.S.R., others not
directly under any ministry at the higher level, though subject to
the All-Russian Central Executive Committee; that is to say, to the
central parliament. The latter variety of ministry was designated
'autonomous', thus giving substance to the same word in its Leninist sense in the title of the republics. By the constitution of 1924,
however, they lost this distinction, and all ministries of autonomous
republics became directly subordinate to some ministry at the next
higher level. They differ from the autonomous regions and national
areas only in having the titular forms of republics—constitutions,
Supreme Soviets (since 1936), ministers, and Supreme Courts.
Autonomous regions and national areas differ from purely administrative regions and areas only in the use for official business of their
national languages.

The first Council of People's Commissars of 1917, although conventional in pattern, contained already one significant innovation—
the People's Commissariat for Nationalities, of which the commissar was Stalin. It was a ragged affair, composed of sections set up
as the occasion demanded for the various nationalities in which the
Soviet government happened at any given moment to be interested,
mainly those of the old Russian Empire, but extending so far as at
one time to include a Yugoslav section. The functions of these were
wide, extending from cultural affairs to contact behind enemy lines
in the period of civil war and intervention. By 1922 the commissariat had become a small government on its own, duplicating, in
respect of the territories with which it was concerned, the functions
of the other commissariats, particularly those of an economic character, which brought it into conflict with some of the latter. It was
consequently abolished in 1923 with the entry into force of the
new constitution. But it left behind it the centralising tradition

established by its formidable commissar, and also a new representative institution. The Soviet of Nationalities was established in May 1920 as a consultative body, meeting under the chairmanship of the Commissar for Nationalities and including representatives of the several peoples for which he was responsible. With the abolition of the commissariat it was taken within the Central Executive Committee as an equal second chamber.

In December 1922 the R.S.F.S.R., the Ukraine, Belorussia and the Transcaucasian S.F.S.R., newly formed under Russian pressure by the three republics of Georgia, Armenia and Azerbaidjan, agreed to unite into a new federation to be called the Union of Soviet Socialist Republics. The federal constitution was adopted on the 6th July 1923 by the Central Executive Committee of the R.S.F.S.R. in which the other federating units were already represented, and confirmed by the All-Russian Congress of Soviets on the 31st January 1924. The former body now became the Soviet of the Union, forming together with the Soviet of Nationalities the All-Union Central Executive Committee, or effective parliament of the new federation. The All-Union Congress of Soviets, as the nominal parliament became, remained unicameral. As the constitution also recognised for the first time a further inner body within the Central Executive Committee, the Praesidium, which had, in fact, been in existence for some time, the curious structure was presented of three rings, each elected by that outside it of which only the second was split into two chambers.

In the manner of the distinction between the two elements of the Central Executive Committee, the American analogy seemed to have counted for something. The Soviet of the Union was to be constituted on the basis of population, after a fashion comparable with the House of Representatives, while the Soviet of Nationalities was to represent the equality of the federated units after the fashion of the American Senate. The product, however, was something very different from the American model. One of its peculiarities was that it provided equal representation, five members each, for all republics—both the four federating 'Union Republics' and the autonomous republics included within the R.S.F.S.R., which were presumably in some sense less than federal. The autonomous regions were to have one deputy each. By the constitution of 1936 this was modified and a distinction was made between Union republics and autonomous republics. The former were to be represented by twenty-five deputies, the latter by eleven, while autonomous regions received five, and the new category of national areas one each. For the 1966 election the union republic representation was increased to thirty-two each.

But in the Soviet Union the representative machinery is always
less important than the administration. The 1924 constitution distinguished three categories of people's commissariats, 'all-union',
'unified' and 'republican'. The first, existing only at federal level,
provided for the traditionally centralised functions of any federal
state: foreign affairs, military and naval affairs, foreign trade—
though in this field the republics retained until 1931 certain powers
—communications, water transport and post and telegraphs. The
second category, renamed in the 1936 constitution 'union republican', contained the majority of the people's commissariats at both
levels as well as the Supreme Council of the Economy, the agency
supervising the management of state economic activities. The third
category, existing only at the republican level, contained the commissariats for internal affairs, justice, education, health and social
welfare. Here, in contrast to the arrangement of the representative
organs, a distinction was, as we have seen, drawn in the 1924 constitution between the union republics and the autonomous republics.
The autonomous republics had ceased to be autonomous and autonomy had become the mark of the union republic.

The result is not a federal system in the terminology of the non-
Soviet world. To say so is not to condemn it. Federalism is a con-
cept evolved mainly for the practical purpose of describing the sort
of relations which the central authorities of the U.S.A. maintain
with the several component states, and most of the countries to
which we are accustomed to apply it owe something to the American example. If we declare that the Soviet Union contains in its
constitution a number of obviously unfederal provisions, we imply
by this merely distinction from this familiar tradition. Soviet
autonomy-federalism recognises no indefeasible rights in the federated units, and prescribes no field of regulation as belonging exclusively to them. Apart from its principal peculiarity, the unified or
union-republican commissariats or, as they have been styled since
1946, ministries, it leaves to the central authorities 'the determination of the basic principles' in a number of fields for which they
are not departmentally responsible. The number of such fields has
decreased, but only with the extension of the responsibility of
federal departments, and there would seem now to be no field in
which, even on the face of the constitution, such a power is required.

The most important of all the federal powers is that to make the
national economic plans for the whole of the U.S.S.R., and the consolidated state budget, which includes and provides the means for
the budgets of the union republics and the local soviets within
them. In addition, the constitution provides that 'in the event
of divergence between the laws of the union republics and a law of

the Union, the union law prevails', and decisions and orders of the federal Council of Ministers are similarly binding throughout the Union (Article 67). No restriction is made in the provisions with regard to the subject of legislation. The Praesidium of the Supreme Soviet of the Union (Praesidium of the Central Executive Committee in 1924) has power to annul the degrees or orders of the Council of Ministers (people's commissars) of a union republic for illegality. Until 1936 it had the same power over acts of the less productive legislative bodies, the republican Central Executive Committees, and, subject to later endorsement by its own Central Executive Committee), the republican Congresses of Soviets. The list of ministries and their allocation as between the various categories have been left readily variable, and have been frequently varied by administrative decisions at the federal level. Neither constitution of the Soviet Union has provided protection by provisions specially difficult of amendment and subject to interpretation by a body independent of the federal administration. The federal Supreme Court was empowered in 1924 to render decisions concerning the constitutionality of decrees of the union republics upon demand of the federal authorities, but no provision was made for passing judgment on the constitutionality of federal measures, and the power was not included at all in the 1936 constitution.

Non-Leninist federalism implies limitation, acceptance of local and sectional interests. Its presence in a Marxist society would be surprising in view of Marxist ideas of history and state power. Any divergence of the Russian giant-firm state from the implications of the doctrine has not been in such a direction as to make it more probable. It is a unitary structure in which the several elements—administrative units, economic enterprises, etc.—participate not with different rights and interest but with varying 'subordination' (*podchinenie*)—that is, place of attachment to the common frame. Even the national forms of culture accepted in principle have, like all forms, always been held subject to change to accord with changing economic substance. As the directors of all change, economic and otherwise, are Russian by residence and predominantly by origin, there has been a marked tendency to extend the language, literature and mythology of the Russians to the other Soviet peoples. Russian is the general second language in education and administration, and even the minority languages have of latter years been given a Russian aspect by the introduction of the practice of writing most of them in the cyrillic alphabet, even where, as in the Moldavian (Rumanian) language, a latin alphabet was established, or, as in some of the previously unwritten minority tongues, had already been introduced by Soviet scholars. The spread throughout the

Soviet Union of a new uniform pattern of life is tending to break up such material conditions for federalism as exist. The primary concern for economic efficiency demands that the boundaries of federal units be habitually disregarded in making appointments to posts, including those conventionally considered political. There seems to be evidence that some regard is paid to the convenience of having a post staffed by a native of the territory concerned but that this motive is of low priority. A variety of organisations and societies, including the party itself, are organised on a basis which factually disregards the existence of the federation.

Soviet autonomy-federalism, however, is not without its utility. It has served, as have federal forms in other countries, to induce divergent communities to associate and to remain together pending the emergence, by whatever means, of a closer union. The early autonomy of the insubstantial nationalities within the restricted area of Russia served for advertisement and persuasion to the larger communities on its frontiers, which were subsequently gathered into the Soviet Union. Even from the point of view of the people themselves, this was at least a process more conducive to happiness than annexation by mere force, though Bolshevik impatience and intolerance led to the frequent use of force as well. The forms of autonomy, and the greater dignity of having it called federation, have probably gratified local pride to some extent. There is advantage in terms of public relations, though there is also administrative inconvenience, in having the local language recognised for official business—and the Soviet Union is not exempt from the rule that good relations make for efficiency. The possession of autonomous status probably confers also some practical advantage on the inhabitants of the minority areas. The qualifying population for establishment of, for example, an autonomous region seems to be lower than that required for a purely administrative region, and the institutions are similar. In a hierarchically administered state this is important. It means that appeals from district decision may be heard not only in the local language and possibly by local men but also probably at a more accessible spot than would otherwise be the case. It does not, however, exclude the possibility of an unlimited amount of interference from higher levels.

From the original four, the union republics have now increased to fifteen. The Transcaucasian S.F.S.R. was in 1936 dissolved into its three component parts and each was admitted as a union republic. In 1925 the Turkmen and Uzbek union republics were created as part of the partition and pacification of Turkestan, formerly an autonomous republic; in 1929 the Tadjik, and in 1936 the Kirgiz, union republics were set up in the same region, and also in 1936 the

Kazakh republic was advanced in status. During the Second World War the three formerly Russian Baltic republics of Lithuania, Latvia and Esthonia were reannexed, purged and constituted union republics, and the territories annexed from Rumania and Finland, together with autonomous republics formerly within the R.S.F.S.R., were constituted into the Moldavian and Karelo-Finnish republics respectively, of which the latter was dissolved and absorbed into the R.S.F.S.R. in 1956. Stalin in his introduction to the 1936 constitution expressed three criteria of suitability for the promotion of lower autonomous units to union republican status. They must lie on the frontiers of the Soviet Union, because otherwise it would not be possible for them to exercise the right granted by the federal constitution (Article 17 of the 1936 constitution) freely to secede from the U.S.S.R.; they must have populations of at least one million, and the nationality which gave them their name must be in a majority. It does not seem that all this was seriously meant. The right of secession was declaredly not intended to be exercised, and could not be exercised by some of the present union republics without cutting off others, and even a region of the R.S.F.S.R., from contact with Moscow. Again, it is not clear why it is essential that the name-nationality must be in a majority in a union republic, when this is no longer so of some of the autonomous republics and regions or national areas, and it does not seem that the Karelo-Finnish republic ever possessed this qualification for union status. It seems probable that Stalin was merely seeking to discourage inconvenient demands for promotion, and in his position he did not have to be too particular about the weight of the arguments which he used.

Most of the autonomous republics and autonomous regions and all the national areas are within the R.S.F.S.R. *Autonomous republics* there are the Bashkir, Dagestan, Kabarda-Balkar, Kalmyk, Mari, Mordovian, North Ossetian, Tatar, Udmurt, Chechen-Ingush and Chuvash on the southern and eastern fringes of European Russia; the Karelian (formerly the Karelo-Finnish union republic) on the Finnish frontier; Komi in the north; the Yakut republic covering a vast area of northern central Siberia; and the Burjat (formerly Burjat-Mongol) and Tuva on the southern frontier. In Azerbaidjan there is the Nahichevan autonomous republic, in Georgia the Abhazian and the Adjarian, in Uzbekistan the Kara-Kalpak. Tuva, semi-independent before the war, was first annexed as an autonomous region and advanced in October 1961. *Autonomous* regions in the R.S.F.S.R. are the Adygei and Karachai-Cherkess in the Northern Caucasus; Gorny Altai and Hakass in south central Siberia; and the Jewish in the Far East. The last was a half-hearted Russian alternative to Zionism and is exceptional in that the name-nationality apparently never was, and still is not, strongly represented among its population. Nagorny Karabah autonomous region is in Azerbaidjan, the South Ossetian in Georgia, and the Gorny Badahshan in Tadjikistan. There are ten *national areas*, all in the R.S.F.S.R. Two, for sections of the Burjats detached from the main mass, lie in southern Siberia and four lie along the arctic coast and together extend for some two-thirds of the whole union's length from west to east. One, as vast, is farther south in central and one in western Siberia. One is in north Kamchatka, and one at the extreme eastern edge of European Russia. No autonomous or national unit is contained within another. All are subordinate directly to a union republic or to one of the purely administrative subdivisions, though this was not always so.

The federal constitution provides (Article 18 of 1936) that the territory of a union republic may not be altered without its consent. There is no similar guarantee for autonomous republics or for lesser autonomous units either in the federal constitution or in the constitutions of the republics, and in fact five such units were dissolved during the Second World War: the Crimean, Volga German, Chechen-Ingush and Kalmyk republics and the Karachai region. In January 1957 the last three regained autonomy (the Kalmyks as a region until July 1958). Their peoples, and the Balkars, were to be repatriated in two to four years. Union republics have lost territory, by consent or otherwise. Part of the Karelo-Finnish republic was transferred to the R.S.F.S.R. in 1945, and in 1956 the rest of the republic acceded to the R.S.F.S.R., ostensibly of its own free will, thus extinguishing its union-republican status. In 1955 the R.S.F.S.R. itself ceded the Crimea to the Ukraine, in 1956 and 1963 the Kazakh republic ceded territory to the Uzbek, and in 1957 Georgia ceded to the R.S.F.S.R. its part of Chechen-Ingush territory. Minor frontier adjustments have been fairly frequent.

The insubstantial nature of the autonomy of Union republics was emphasised at the end of 1962 by the establishment of a single economic district as the unit of management for the economies of Uzbekistan, Kirgizia, Tadjikistan, Turkmenistan and the cotton-growing part of Kazahstan. While the financial budgeting of the republics remained in principle free it was thus left without much room for manoeuvre. Joint organs for specialised functions of economic management—building, cotton growing and irrigation and the management of state farms—were set up. At the same time a special bureau of the party central committee was instituted to supervise the affairs of the same republics as, in the following year, was one for the three Transcaucasian republics of Georgia, Armenia and Azerbaidjan;

this was a less conspicuous affront to national sentiment only in that the party, in its internal arrangements, had never held itself bound to show much respect for the forms of autonomy. Like others of the less popular reforms of Mr. Khrushchov the economic district had a short life after his fall; its abolition was announced at the end of December 1964.

Administrative Areas

Where there are no claims of nationality administrative areas are based upon considerations of management of the economy and in particular of agriculture, since the greater part of industry has been centrally controlled. The structure therefore is extremely fluid and constantly changes with changing ideas of convenience, unimpeded by the civic particularism which makes alteration difficult in a liberal state. Thus one region in the R.S.F.S.R. which elected its regional soviet with the rest on 3rd March 1957 was abolished on 23rd April.

Immediately after the revolution soviets were set up in the town and village areas of the pre-revolutionary administrative structure, with congresses of soviets at the levels of the *volostj*, the *uezd* and the governorship (*gubernija*), still retaining its old name although now without a governor. It was accepted from the first, however, that more suitable units must be found, and local experiments were early made in the grouping of governorships. The outlines of a new system were accepted by the Central Executive Committee in March 1921, but in April 1923 the Twelfth Congress of the party demanded that development be restricted for the time being to two selected representative regions. By the beginning of the following year, however, change was well under way and continued gradually, though until well into the 'thirties the old and the new units were simultaneously in existence in different parts of the country. The new policy was for larger units than previously; in place of the *volostj* the *raion* (generally translated as 'district'); in place of the *uezd* the *okrug* (usually translated as 'area', though 'circuit' might be a more accurate rendering); and in place of the governorship the *oblastj* (region), supposed to be a unit of distinctive economic character containing both manufacturing industry and agriculture. Certain units of regional status were given the designation of *krai* (territory) by reason of the inclusion within them of units themselves designated as regions. The latter were the autonomous regions included within the R.S.F.S.R. before the war, of which five still remain, and also two purely administrative regions in Khabarovsk territory in the Russian Far East. This local variant was removed in February

1956 by the separation of one of the regions, that of Kamchatka, from the territory, and the abolition of the other. In the course of the forced economic development of Kazahstan under Khrushchov, however, four more territories containing administrative regions were set up there: one, for the virgin lands, survived his downfall by a year. The Primorski (Litoral) territory—between the north–south stretch of the Manchurian frontier and the Pacific—has never contained any units of regional status, and probably owes its designation to the fact that it was formed in 1938 by the division of the former Far Eastern territory, the rest of which became a 'territory' of more normal type. The small 'rural locality'—as the official translation of the constitution renders the Russian term *selo*, the 'village' in the more usual but misleading translation—remained. It was convenient for purposes of control, so long as there were private peasants and a consequent need for the local officials to know them and their resources in detail. In 1924 there was some consolidation, but it was claimed in 1929 that this had been a mistake, unfitting the 'Village' soviets for their task, and had been reversed.[1] At about the same time the idea of abolishing the village soviets as superfluous, and giving their functions to the new collective farms gained some currency. The authorities, however, soon decided against it, and it was denounced as Social-Revolutionary in origin—and also anarcho-syndicalist.[2] The towns remained separate from the surrounding rural areas, with subordination to district or to region (or to republic where there are no regions, and, for the few largest cities, even where there are) according to their size and economic significance, and the largest were themselves divided into districts (*raion*) with their own soviets.

At first only the R.S.F.S.R. was divided into regions and areas, so that elsewhere districts and large town were of republican subordination. In 1930 the decision was taken to abolish the *okrug* as an unnecessary link in the chain of control. Rather, it was suggested, the *oblastj* should direct groups of districts according to their economic characteristics, without regard for territorial contiguity. Thus Moscow region was reported in 1931 to have divided its districts into five and subsequently six, groups according to their predominant economic activities: heavy industry, light industry, grain-growing, market-gardening with dairying and animal husbandry, technical crops and crafts.[3] Again, however, the change took some time to carry out, and areas were still in existence in the late 1930s. At the same time there were repeated complaints that regions and

[1] A. Luzhin, *Ot volosti—k raionu* (1929), p. 123.
[2] Ja. Berman in *S.G. i R.P.*, No. 2 of 1920, p. 21.
[3] M. Jurgin in *S.G. i R.P.*, No. 2 of 1931, pp. 89–90.

republics were finding difficulty in controlling the large number of districts directly subject to them, which in 1930 averaged 129 and reached 585 in the Ukraine and some 230 in the Siberian territory. In the period preceding and immediately following the Second World War there was a tendency to steady increase in the number of units at all levels above the village, to provide for the constant settlement and development of new areas and also to allow of more detailed management. Already by the outbreak of war the number of regions had exceeded the number of the old governorships, and by the beginning of 1953 there were, apart from the autonomous and national units, 6 territories, all in the R.S.F.S.R., and 144 regions—R.S.F.S.R. 55 (including three in Tatar and two in Bashkir autonomous republics and two in Khabarovsk territory). Ukraine 25, Uzbek 9, Tadjik 3, Kazah 16, Belorussia 12, Turkmen 4, Kirgiz 6, Lithuania 4, Latvia 3, Estonia 3, Azerbaidjan 2, Georgia 2. By then 26 administrative areas (*okrug*) had reappeared —in the Moldavian, Armenian and Karelo-Finnish republics and in some of the Russian autonomous republics—and there were 4,418 districts, 1,498 towns of varying status, 511 districts within the towns and some 76,000 'villages', of varying local designations, and settlements (*posjolok*) having their own soviets—apparently something under 2,400 of these last being 'workers' settlements' or 'settlements of urban type'; with a status somewhat superior to that of an ordinary village.[1] The new administrative *okrugs* and the regional division of Azerbaidjan and Georgia, completed in 1952, were the product of a new acute phase of the persistent concern over effective supervision of districts by higher authorities. In the Baltic republics the administrative structure was not changed from the pre-war pattern to the Russian three-tier system until collectivisation of agriculture had been completed in about 1950, and in Latvia and Esthonia this process of administrative reorganisation continued into 1952. Shortly after the death of Stalin, though it was perhaps due to the organisational fluidity characteristic of the Soviet Union rather than to that event, the *okrugs* began to be abolished again, and none of them is now in existence. Similarly the regions in the Tatar and Bashkir autonomous republics, and in Lithuania, Latvia, Esthonia, Azerbaidjan and Georgia, were all abolished during 1953. In 1955 the Tadjik union republic also abolished two of its administrative regions, leaving only the one geographically most remote from the centre.

Throughout the period of these two trends there was a more

---

[1] *Izvestia*, 11th January, 1953: figure for settlements calculated back from figure for the beginning of 1955, *Narodnoe Hozjajstvo SSSR* (Central Statistical Administration), 1956, p. 26.

consistent process of reduction of numbers of district and village-soviet areas. The consolidation, in the interests of tighter control as much as of agricultural technology, of collective farms—with, in some cases, their conversion into state farms—from some 254,000 units in the early part of 1950 to 87,500 by the end of 1955 and under 40,000 by the end of 1962 made nonsense of the very small village. Cases were reported in 1953 where a single collective farm covered the area of four or more village soviets. Though themselves consolidated over the previous two years 49 per cent of all village soviets in the R.S.F.S.R. still had under a thousand inhabitants and some only 200–300. By October 1964 their numbers were stated to have been further halved since 1953, to a total, for the whole U.S.S.R., of 39,898, giving them an average of some one farm apiece. The actual distribution did not appear to meet even this dubious standard of rationality. Of 342 village soviets in Tula region over 150 each served two or three fragments of various state farms; only 104 were concerned with a single collective farm and 48 with a single state farm. Village soviets, it was recognised, had by then largely ceased to be concerned with agricultural matters; they were urged to give more attention to matters of social welfare.[1]

The district soviets were similarly relieved of their previously predominant agricultural concerns—though in principle only of the administrative means of doing anything practical about them—only in the succeeding phase of Mr. Khrushchov's inventions for agricultural management. In March 1962 the party Central Committee decreed the establishment, for areas larger than those of districts, of 'collective-state' (or 'state-collective' where state farms predominated) 'farm production administrations', and in the following November it was ruled that the party's committees in agricultural areas should be based on the new units. In the tradition of Soviet administration the district soviets, though deprived of their agricultural administrations in favour of the new bodies, were forced into the same organisational mould as the party. As reported at the beginning of 1964 districts in the R.S.F.S.R. had been reduced in the process from 1,946 to 1,049 (1,845 in the whole U.S.S.R.), of which 938 (U.S.S.R. 1,723) answered to the then separate rural regional organs in party and soviet structures. All but 143 in particularly difficult locations (the far North, the mountainous areas, etc.) coincided with the production administrations. The other 111 districts (U.S.S.R. 122), answering to the industrial network of higher authorities, were mostly deviant from tradition in that their territory was not continuous; typically it consisted of a number of minor towns and workers' settlements, though a few village soviets

[1] M. A. Shafir in *S.G. i P.*, No. 10 of 1964.

were included within such units. Reunification of the local administrative system in party and state, immediately after Khrushchov's fall, was almost a total reversion. The districts not only recovered their industrial parts but, somewhat surprisingly, resumed substantially their old dimensions, allegedly because they had in the interim become unmanageably large. The agricultural administrations, however, though now again under party district committee supervision, were not re-subordinated to the district soviets (or their executive committees).

With even less obvious justification the amalgamation of village soviets seems to have been not only halted but, if only temporarily and locally, reversed, though long-heralded federal and republican legislation of early 1968 on them and on settlement soviets has not obviously found them much new to do or any substantial means of doing it. There were in April 1967, 40,178 'villages', 3,452 'settlements of urban type', 1,884 towns (822 of them subordinate to higher levels than district), 413 districts within towns, 2,959 other districts, 105 regions and again 6 territories.[1]

The 'economic-administrative districts' set up from May 1957 (and merged in November 1962 into larger 'economic districts') as units of Khrushchov's industrial management reforms left no trace on the administrative map on their abolition in October 1965, since they had consisted of groupings of the existing regions.

One persistent trend of change over recent years owes little to individual ingenuity. The progressive urbanisation of the country is strikingly expressed in the advancements, announced at a rate of two or three a week, of villages or previously dependent rural settlements and inhabited points to the status of 'workers' settlements' or 'settlements of urban type'—where they acquire their own soviets— and thence through the two main grades of town (subordinate to district—or to another town; subordinate to a region, territory or republic not divided into regions), if not extinguished by amalgamation. The districts within the towns have been declining in numbers, either by merger or by abolition.

Population is probably a minor consideration in the formation of administrative areas in this management-oriented system; it cannot be decisive in any system. In January 1959 territories varied in population between 1,142,000 (Khabarovsk) and 3,762,000 (Krasnodar), and regions in the R.S.F.S.R. between 221,000 (Kamchatka) or 236,000 (Magadan—in area the second largest in the R.S.F.S.R.) and 2,993,000 (Perm) or 4,044,000 (Sverdlovsk), apart from the special cases of Moscow (some 11 million, with over 5 million in

[1] *Verhovny sovet SSSR* (Moscow 1967), pp. 274–5. The corresponding R.S.F.S.R. figures were 22,287; 3,452; 949 (505); 251, 1,720; 49; 6.

the town and immediate environs) and Leningrad ($4\frac{1}{2}$ million and something under $3\frac{1}{2}$ million respectively). The autonomous regions of the R.S.F.S.R. varied between 157,000 (Gorny Altai) and 411,000 (Hakass); in other republics they were smaller. For districts we have only an average: in the R.S.F.S.R. in 1967 something under 42,000. The town category overlaps widely in this respect with that of workers' settlements. Of the 1,679 towns in January 1959, 489 had less than 10,000 inhabitants, while 30 of the 2,940 workers' settlements had over 20,000. Predominantly, however, the settlements are at the lower end of the scale. Towns with over 50,000 inhabitants numbered 304, and of these 25 had over 500,000.[1]

Collective Administration

The revolutionary regime, we have seen, early abandoned its objections to a government of the traditional type, and the people's commissars and their officials soon settled into the ministerial tradition as it was known in Russia. In the first days there was a tendency for local soviets also to develop their own councils of people's commissars, but this was early discouraged. The place for the ministry was its traditional one—at the top. Even the emphasis on collective administration, or 'collegiality' (*kolegialjnostj*) with which this acceptance of the traditional pattern was hedged has been constantly challenged by reality in the form of a demand for results from unpopular and onerous policies and the need to fix individual responsibility for performance.

Where the task is purely formal principle can largely be allowed to prevail. The Praesidium of the Central Executive Committee—an inner group not constitutionally recognised until 1923, but certainly in being before then—seems to have been intended to keep a watch over the inherited administrative structure in the intervals between the sessions of the Central Executive Committee, though it early lost the power to exercise any effective influence over it. But it was also entrusted with the powers traditionally belonging to a head of state—dissolving and calling the legislature, instituting and conferring honours and awards, sending and receiving diplomatic missions, etc. Soviet sources commonly refer to its successor, the Praesidium of the Supreme Soviet, as the 'collective president' of the U.S.S.R. The new state of soviets was the negation of an autocracy and demonstrated this in not giving itself an individual head. But there are certain of the conventional functions of the head of state which cannot conveniently be regularly performed by more than one man—such as the receiving of foreign diplomatic representa-

[1] *Naradnoe Hozjajstvo SSSR* 1959, p. 34.

tives, the signing of legislation, and the presenting of decorations. Such functions were entrusted to the chairman of the Praesidium. It has been an office of little power, held by the worthy rather than the influential (see pp. 112–13).

A similar principle of collective headship was from the early days applied in the people's commissariats themselves. The commissar was not to be left with unchecked authority. Instead he was to be assisted and limited by a ministry 'collegium' composed of his deputy commissars and other principal officials appointed by the Council of People's Commissars. These might appeal against his decisions to the latter body, or, as was originally provided, to the Praesidium of the Central Executive Committee. As in most other matters, there has been some fluctuation of policy on this point. In March 1934, by resolution of the Seventeenth Party Congress, the collegium, in the commissariat or elsewhere, was abolished 'for the purpose of strengthening personal responsibility'. The commissar was to have not more than two deputies, and was to be assisted by an advisory council of forty to seventy members, half of them or more representatives of organisations and enterprises under the commissariat. In March 1936 the collegium was revived as indispensable, though without a constitutional right of appeal against ministerial decisions and without abolishing the councils. As yet their articulation into the administrative system as in practice it is required to work is imperfect. A plenary session of the party Central Committee in July 1955 demanded improvement in the work of the ministry collegia, though it stressed that responsibility was to remain personal. This same duality between personal responsibility and the necessity for collective discussion applies, in Soviet writings, throughout the system of government, down to the local soviet.

In the economic sphere the symbolic defence of collegiality was longer maintained. Though commissariats existed from the first for such functions of economic significance as transport, food, labour and posts and telegraphs, the management of manufacturing industry was from 1920 to January 1932 entrusted to a Supreme Council of the Economy. With its dissolution into commissariats for the several industries only planning remained nominally collective. Even there, the chairman, as with heads of administrative boards in other political systems, assumed, by reason of his personal standing and his duty to speak for his office, in the government and elsewhere, the character of a minister—usually a very senior one. The collective body receded into the role of a collegium.

The Khrushchov reforms, from the institution of local councils of the economy (sovnarhoz) in 1957, through the re-centralisation by the planning bodies and an intricate structure of State Committees, to the restoration of the name of the Supreme Council itself in March 1963, relied heavily on collective forms. The chairmen, however, remained ministers, at republican or central level, either *ex officio* or by personal designation.

The early bolshevik factory was managed by a board formed as to two-thirds of representatives of workers, and as to one-third of representatives of the technical staff approved by the workers' trade union. Lenin soon saw the need to make one person responsible, and 'one-man headship (*edinonachalie*) was permanently established as the official principle, with 'collegiality' retained as a reminder that workers should be carried along with official policy rather than overridden. So long as competent managers, like competent military commanders, were suspect to the regime their personal responsibility was checked by placing almost equal responsibility upon the secretary of the factory party committee and the head of the trade-union branch. In the autumn of 1929, however, this 'triangle' system was also condemned by the party. The manager was fully in command; the relations of the party committee to him have never since been precisely defined, though it remains a power; the trade unions, hammered by Stalin, counted for little until his death. Since then consultation in the factory has again been urged and a somewhat larger place has been found for the unions.

In agriculture, general participation in management has retained a larger formal role. In the collective farm (*kolhoz*) the cultivators are in form co-operative owners, not employed persons, and control the farm through their general assembly and a management board elected by it. But the difference is more apparent than real; the collective farm has long been managed by its appointed chairman. In the Khrushchov period there was a marked swing to the form of the state farm (*sovhoz*)— run as an industrial enterprise; together with the amalgamation of the collective farms into larger units and the centralisation of control over both types of farm through the production administrations this further reduced the scope for management by assembly. In view of the pressure on agriculture for ever-elusive results this is unlikely to be revised in fact.

The Function of Soviet Constitutionalism

A constitution is a body of conventional relations and practices, departure from which in political action is apt to cause offence and friction. In this sense every political association has a constitution; there are some limits beyond which the organisers of the association's affairs would be ill-advised to go, though the limits may be very wide and it may be difficult to say in advance of the event where they lie. A written constitution is an attempt to formulate a significant part of this working constitution for the guidance of the participants in political action, usually upon association into a new state or as a condition of the continuance of obedience to an established ruler or system of rule which the subjects find it in their power to challenge. The idea of limitation is always present, and to be a useful guide to those whose conduct it purports to regulate the written constitution must indicate with reasonable clarity where the limitations lie, what sorts of action will be held to constitute a breach of it, and how wrong action will be proceeded against. A constitution which gives no such guidance, or which suggests that action will be taken which, in fact, nobody is in a position to take, is a bad constitution, such as littered the ground of Europe in the 1850s, or that of South America to the present day. For a genuine federation, as we have described it—that is to say, a federation in the American tradition—a written constitution is almost indispensable. The associating parties must know what they are surrendering, and will wish to indicate clearly the point up to which co-operation can be counted upon and beyond which there will be trouble. A written constitution may have other functions, and in course of time any satisfactory constitution acquires them. In particular it becomes a symbol of the state itself, venerated, even if unread. But this is no role for a new constitution.

The Soviet Union does not have the most obvious motives for adopting a written constitution. It is not a true federation, and by its official creed it can accept no limitation upon the will of those conventionally accepted as standing for the working people. It is true—as we have suggested that it is true for any state—that in practice some limitation must be accepted, if only at the point where further action in a given direction would provoke physical resistance on a large scale. This means that the leaders or those working under their orders must not offend too many influential people at the same time. But these are limitations such as cannot be conveniently defined in documentary form for permanent application; they are matters for tact.

Three constitutions have been made in Moscow for the whole of its dominions since the revolution: that of 1918, setting up the R.S.F.S.R.; that of 1923–4, recognising the establishment of the U.S.S.R.; and that of the 3rd December 1936, formerly known as the Stalin constitution, which is still in force. Under the last two of these the union republics and the autonomous republics have each made their own constitutions. The occasions of the two earlier constitutions are readily apparent. In 1918 there was the wish to fill the gap left by the dissolution of the Constituent Assembly and formally to declare the outcome of the revolution settled. In 1923–4 the formation of the federation itself is an adequate explanation. In 1936 the motivation was less obvious. Stalin himself provided an explanation at the extraordinary Eighth Congress of Soviets to which it was introduced on the 26th November 1936. He contended that the basic condition of the state had changed, and as a Marxist he stated this in economic terms. The New Economic Policy, which had been at its height in 1924, had left few traces by 1936. The *kulak* problem had been solved. The basis of society had been changed with the extinction of hostile class interest and its replacement by a friendly association of transformed classes. The working class could no longer be called a proletariat, and its dictatorship had entered into a second stage, which Stalin confusingly described also as the first stage of communism. This intermediate period he designated socialism, and for this the new constitution was to provide. It was an order in which 'all citizens have equal rights' and yet not equal positions, since 'personal labour . . . determines the position of every citizen in society'. The discrimination of the earlier stage was no longer needed, but essentials were unchanged. Stalin declared that 'the draft of the new constitution preserves the regime of the dictatorship of the working class, just as it also preserves unchanged the present leading position of the Communist Party of the U.S.S.R.'. For the reason why a change of incidentals needed to be made with such ceremony we must look outside Stalin's speech to the circumstances of the time. The rise of Hitler to power in Germany, and the explosive international situation of which the dangers were belatedly beginning to dawn on Stalin and his associates, gave them cause to seek to give assurances of reliability to potential allies abroad. A period of extensive purges in the party in the interest of the Stalin connection, with the wider and more violent action of the succeeding years in the making, called for similar assurances at home. Probably most Russian Marxists envisage, and many hope to see, a day when each man's duty, the nature of which is not for them in question, will be clear to him and he will perform it without the supervision and coercion needed while ends are still in dispute. They knew in 1936 that this stage had not yet come, but they needed the good opinion which it alone could bring them. They had to realise at once on their prospective inheritance.

The manner of the making of the 1936 constitution suggests this intent. On the 1st February 1935 the plenary session of the Central Committee of the party instructed Molotov to lay proposals before the Seventh Congress of Soviets, then already meeting, and gave him specific directions on the content of these. The Congress of

Soviets unanimously approved the proposals, and its Central Executive Committee designated a drafting commission under Stalin to prepare the text. This was again submitted to the party Central Committee on the 1st June 1936 and approved. After that, by an entirely new departure, it was released for general public discussion in which, it was alleged, some 36,500,000 people participated. But though, it is said, 154,000 amendments were suggested by the public, only forty-three were accepted, and only one of these, the substitution of direct for indirect election to the Soviet of Nationalities, was of more than verbal significance. It may be inferred that the leaders desired the appearance, and probably the reality, of wide public support, but not if it would prevent them from getting their own way in all material respects. Formal enactment followed at the last of the Congresses of Soviets.

The Supreme Soviet of 1962, at its first sitting, in March of that year, set up a commission under Mr. Khrushchov to prepare a new constitution, and after his fall its mandate was renewed, with his successor in the party's chief secretarial post (i.e. leadership) as chairman. Neither the impulsive and individual innovativeness of the former regime nor the stolid conservatism of the latter has given much promise that a significantly more liberal political style might result. As in 1936, desire for favourable publicity seems the most likely aim. Progress, if any, remains undeclared.

Contents of the Constitution

The 1936 constitution consists of thirteen chapters, designated respectively as: The Social Structure (Chapter I), The State Structure (Chapter II), The Higher Organs of State Authority in the U.S.S.R. (Chapter III), The Higher Organs of State Authority in the Union Republics (Chapter IV), The Organs of State Administration of the U.S.S.R. (Chapter V), The Organs of State Administration of Union Republics (Chapter VI), The Higher Organs of State Authority in the Autonomous Soviet Socialist Republics (Chapter VII), The Local Organs of State Authority (Chapter VIII), The Courts and the Procurator Service (Chapter IX), Fundamental Rights and Duties of Citizens (Chapter X), The Electoral System (Chapter XI), Arms, Flag and Capital City (Chapter XII), Procedure for Constitutional Amendment (Chapter XIII). The distinction between state authority and state administration is that between organs constituted in principle by elections and those constituted by appointment, the former including both the soviets and Supreme Soviets and their Praesidia and Executive Committees, the latter including the ministers and the Council of Ministers as a whole. This distinction is indicative of a way of looking at politics quite distinct from the early Marxists ideas, according to which the people would be actively involved in administration. It seems also to be at variance with the system as in fact it operates, but in a different sense, in that the principle of appointment extends to offices nominally in the elective line. The term 'local' as contained in the designation of Chapter VIII covers all levels of the system from the region down to the village—that is to say, all levels at which the soviet is not designated 'supreme'.

Chapters I and X are both declarations of faith rather than statement of verifiable facts or prescriptions which can be enforced against any person or public body by a court of law. There is no provision for, or evidence of, their ever being so pleaded. The rights stated are sometimes meaningless. Thus Article 7 (in Chapter I) states that 'every household in a collective farm . . . has for its personal use a small plot of household land as its personal property . . . a dwelling-house, livestock, poultry and minor agricultural implements . . .', and Article 125 (in Chapter X), guaranteeing the citizen's basic freedoms, states that 'these civil rights are ensured by placing at the disposal of the toilers and their organisations printing presses, stocks of paper, public buildings and streets, means of communication and other material conditions for the exercise of these rights'. Yet neither poultry nor printing paper is provided free; the state's role is the purely negative one of seeing that the peasant does not have enough of the former to be independent of the collective farm and rationing the latter to the very limited number of organisations permitted to engage in printing on a scale just sufficient for the circulation which it is thought that they should have. Other rights, though of ascertainable meaning, are in no way secured against circumvention. Thus Article 127 provides that 'citizen of the U.S.S.R. are guaranteed inviolability of the person. No person may be placed under arrest except by decision of a court or with the sanction of a procurator'. Yet there is evidence of arrests being made on the basis of blank warrants provided in advance by the procurators, or even without them, and there seems to be nothing to prevent this. We now appear to have the highest authority for believing that Stalin personally issued orders for the arrest of individuals.[1] It is probable that his subordinates did the like. It is questionable whether constitution-makers in the Soviet Union or elsewhere are wise to guarantee rights of which they lack either the means or the will to ensure the protection. The solemn affirmation of rights may help to build up respect for them, but repeated violation is apt to destroy respect for the law itself. One article in

[1] Khrushchov, closed-session speech Twentieth Congress.

Chapter X, however, is important. Article 126, which guarantees the rights of Soviet citizens to unite in trade unions, co-operative societies, sports clubs, and so on, adds that 'the most active and politically conscious citizens in the ranks of the working class, working peasants and working intelligentsia voluntarily unite in the Communist Party of the Soviet Union, which is the vanguard of the toilers in their struggle to build communist society and is the guiding nucleus of all organisations of the toilers both social and state'. This is the first mention of the party in a Russian constitution. It appears in humble company, but it is unique of its kind, and, unlike the other forms of organisation mentioned in the same article, it is not declared to be open to all Soviet citizens. The constitution does not say who is to distinguish the degree of activity and political consciousness of aspirants.

Chapter II states at some length the rights of the federated units: to have their own constitutions, which take 'account of the specific features of the republic', and are 'drawn up in full conformity with the constitution of the U.S.S.R.' (Article 16); to secede from the U.S.S.R. (17); not to have their territory altered without their consent (18); to maintain direct relations with foreign states even to the extent of concluding agreements and exchanging diplomatic and consular representatives (18a); to have their own military formations (18b); and to retain full sovereignty except as defined in the constitution (15). The federal powers, however, by which the republican powers are limited, are defined in Article 14 on very comprehensive terms, including, as we have seen, determination of basic principles in a number of spheres for which the federation is not departmentally responsible. It is hard to think of any power which is left exclusively to the federating units, but if there is one it could readily be removed if its existence were found inconvenient; the item which vests in the federal authorities the 'determination of the principles of legislation concerning marriage and the family' was added in 1947. Recent changes reverse the trend, replacing exclusive by shared jurisdiction. Some powers granted were never intended to be operative; Article 17 has been explicitly so declared, and Article 18 seems to present no difficulty in practice. Articles 18a and 18b have not been applied, for though the union republics maintain ministries of foreign affairs, offers from foreign powers to establish direct relations have been refused, and they do not maintain defence ministries or, apparently, forces at all. Ministries are moved at will from the all-union to the union-republican category when it is desired to establish a branch in one republic or more. The order of the Praesidium of the federal Supreme Soviet making the change usually also 'recognises the necessity' that a corresponding

ministry should be established at republican level. When it is no
longer desired to act through a branch at republican level the ministry is as lightly returned to all-union status.

On political structure and machinery the constitution is too detailed for convenience. The specification in Chapter II of the territorial division of the several union republics down to regional level,
deleted in February 1957 when these matters were transferred to the
republics' own competence, used to require amendment at almost
every session of the Supreme Soviet, and the articles in Chapter V
which set out the designations of the ministries and similar bodies
represented in the federal government still do. The increase in the
early 'fifties in the number of republics divided into regions required the insertion of additional articles at the end of Chapter II,
which were deleted on the abolition of those regions in 1953. Most
changes have consisted in deletions and insertions in the existing
articles. Shortly after the session—twenty days after that of May
1957—further changes of ministries or other institutions are made
by edict, and they continue to appear at similar intervals until the
next session comes along to confirm them, if by then they have not
already been reversed.

The machinery provided in Chapters III–VIII and XI of the
constitution forms the subject of our Chapter III, and Chapter IX
comes into our Chapter V.

Here we need only note that in the field of legislation there is
what appears to be a superfluity of means. Thus Article 32 states
that 'the legislative power of the U.S.S.R. is exercised exclusively by
the Supreme Soviet of the U.S.S.R.' But Article 49 states that the
Praesidium of the Supreme Soviet 'issues edicts' (*ukaz*), and it does
not say about what. Article 66 states that 'the Council of Ministers
of the U.S.S.R. issues decrees (*postanovlenie*) and dispositions (*rasporjazhenie*) on the basis and in pursuance of the laws in operation
and verifies their execution', and a similar power is given to ministers individually to make such orders in their own fields (Article 73).
Even so, the constitution does not indicate the full extent of the
duplication, since it makes no mention of the machinery of the
party or the measures which it enacts either alone or conjointly
with one or more of the organs of the state.

Thus Article 32 suggests that the previous rejection of the separation of powers has been abandoned. But in fact the 'legislative
power' (*zakonodateljnaja vlastj*) is only power to make the 'lex'
(*zakon*), formal law so designated. In fact comparatively few of the
rules which Soviet citizens have to obey are made in this form. As
under the Tsars, most of the rule-making is done by ministers,
either individually or collectively, in the Council of Ministers. The

other means are for the more solemn regulations. There is no distinct executive power, but only a 'highest executive and administrative organ of the state authority', the Council of Ministers (Article 64), which is 'responsible and accountable' (Article 65) to the Supreme Soviet as 'highest organ of state authority' (Article 30), or between its sessions to the Praesidium (Article 65). The acts by which the Supreme Soviet makes ministerial and other appointments are spoken of by Russian theorists as 'acts of supreme administrations'. For the other traditional division of state power, the judicial, there is the apparently more positive provision of Article 112, that 'judges are independent and subject only to the law', but this article has no ascertainable meaning; we will return to it in Chapter V.

Amendment of the constitution is in fact by the ordinary procedure for legislation—a vote in each house of the Supreme Soviet separately. Article 146 requires 'a majority of not less than two-thirds of the vote in each of its chambers', but as in practice no law (and no other proposal of however little importance) has ever failed to get a unanimous vote this provision is inoperative. Amendment after the event is a common practice. Thus, apart from the incessant changes of areas and ministries, school fees for higher education were imposed in 1940, contrary to Article 121, which as then worded guaranteed free education to all; foreign affairs and defence were added to the powers of union republics in February 1944; family legislation was added to the federal powers in July 1944; the age of eligibility to the Supreme Soviet was raised in October 1945 —and all these changes were reconciled with the constitution by its amendment only in February 1947. In normal times the delay is shorter. No provision is made for the interpretation of the constitution other than that of sub-paragraph c of Article 49, which lists the interpretation of laws of the U.S.S.R. in general as one of the functions of the Praesidium of the Supreme Soviet; that is to say, a body formally an offshoot of the legislature itself. No mention is made of the possibility of declaring any act unconstitutional. It is hard to see that with so little binding force over other legislation the constitution can properly be described, as it is in its title, as a 'fundamental law'.

As we have seen, the rights of the union republics as guaranteed in the federal constitution include a constitution of their own 'which takes account of the specific features of the republics'. In practice these specific features seem to be very few. The official Soviet law textbooks cite as examples of such differences the provision in some constitutions for the existence within them of autonomous republics and regions, and differences in the number of republican ministries.

In fact there is not very much else to point to, and these differences themselves are not very considerable; the republics are bound by federal recommendations as to the union-republican ministries to be set up, and republican ministries are very few. Otherwise the constitution follows the same model almost word for word. Such constitutions are made by the Supreme Soviet of the republic subject to confirmation by the Supreme Soviet of the U.S.S.R. The constitutions of autonomous republics within the R.S.F.S.R. are completely uniform. They are made by the Supreme Soviet of the autonomous republic, subject to confirmation by the Supreme Soviet of the R.S.F.S.R. The procedure in other union republics is presumably similar. The charters of autonomous regions, which correspond to constitutions and represent their principal distinction from ordinary regions administered under general legislation, are similarly confirmed by higher authority, and similarly seem to be uniform.

Utility of the Constitution

Stalin presented the constitution in 1936 as record rather than as precept. Thus he said to the Congress of Soviets: ' The draft of this new constitution is a summary of the path that has been traversed, a summary of the gains already achieved. In other words, it is a registration and legislative embodiment of what has already been achieved and won in actual fact.' The implication of this is that if the constitution and practice differ it may be the constitution which should be changed, in that it has ceased to be a registration and legislative embodiment of the latest achievement. In this lies the theoretical case for the *ex post facto* amendments. Such a record may be useful, nevertheless; but by reason of its inaccuracy, imprecision, incompleteness and impermanence it is unlikely that the Soviet constitution is much consulted by practical administrators, or by those who have to deal with them, for the purpose of finding out what the present organisation of the system of government is. Its false emphasis, as for example on the relations of elected bodies to their inner bodies, is likely to make it a poor guide for this purpose. The constitution has a large distribution within the Soviet Union, but it is likely that this is for educational rather than for practical purposes.

To obtain information on how the system works, one must look to the general legislation as well as to the constitution, and rather to the former than to the latter. This is thin and unhelpful if one considers only the published acts of the Supreme Soviet: voluminous but still often unhelpful if the published and reported acts of the

Council of Ministers, the ministries and the various economic bodies is added. Presumably the practising official, seeking to know what the law is at the moment, has the internal instructions of the public service to guide him—more probably more of them than in other countries of a confidential nature. Some officials may be supposed to have the party directives, open or restricted, on which these are based. But the difficulty of maintaining uniformity of practice in such circumstances is probably still such as to constitute a major force of friction within the Soviet system. It must be particularly hard for the public, which cannot know how it stands with regard to the authorities on many particular issues, and must therefore make a large number of unnecessary applications and enquiries, though private contacts may obviate the need always to put these through official channels. We who stand outside the system are similarly in the dark. We may supplement the information of the written constitution by the same published sources, by the party charter, and other party measures, but the real constitution is obviously unwritten and consists in understandings as between persons.

But constitutions can have other functions: they are also ideology. Only in so far as they are intended for propaganda abroad can the constitutional documents of the Soviet Union perhaps be discounted as political institutions; that is to say, as means to facilitate the attainment of agreement among individuals. Their internal propaganda value, if they have any, makes for good government; that is to say, for the acceptance of the restraints of government without a sense of frustration of will. It is probably that they have some such value; to Soviet citizens, repeatedly told that their constitution is the most enlightened in the world, it probably seems so. To the federated and autonomous units their own constitutions are probably of some value as symbols of statehood.

What Remains?

The soviets and the union being almost entirely historically based myths, and the constitution a vehicle for the propagation of mythology, we must seek elsewhere the functioning machinery of the state. Much of it is of a fairly conventional type, inherited from the pre-revolutionary regime or borrowed from abroad, though very heavily modified in operation to meet the requirements of totalitarianism. Underlying and interwoven with it, however, is the distinctive Russian communist invention, the disciplined managing corps called a party.

CHAPTER III

Conventional State Machinery

The Representative Bodies—What They Are

The Supreme Soviet of the U.S.S.R. consists of two houses: the Soviet of the Union, popularly elected on the basis of one deputy for every 300,000 of the population (Article 34 of the 1936 constitution); and the Soviet of Nationalities, similarly elected on the basis of thirty-two (before the 1966 election, twenty-five) for each union republic, eleven for an autonomous republic, five for an autonomous region, and one for a national area. The relation of deputies to population in the former house cannot be precise, since to form constituencies the regions, though usually subdivided, are never grouped together. Any region of less than 600,000 population, therefore, presumably has one deputy, and above that a rise of less than 300,000 brings no increase. In the elections to the Soviet of Nationalities the inhabitants of autonomous or national units have votes for the representatives of the union republics to which the units belong, as well as those of the units themselves. In addition to the members thus elected to the two houses, there were before 1966 varying numbers of members (fourteen in 1962) elected for special constituencies for the armed forces stationed abroad; half sat in each house. Thereafter military polling stations were annexed, apparently arbitrarily, to constituencies at home. At the 1954, 1958, 1962 and 1966 elections the Soviet of the Union had 708, 738, 791 and 767 members, the Soviet of Nationalities 639, 640, 652 and 750. Presumably the intent of the latest reforms is to get back to something like the near equality of the houses elected in 1937, the only pre-World War election under the present constitution—569 and 574 members respectively. Growth of population, on the one hand, and territorial acquisition and changes of status, upward or downward, of the units represented in the Soviet of Nationalities, on the other are apt to disrupt this balance. For much of their business the two houses meet in joint session of all 1,517 deputies.

The two houses are elected at the same time for a four-year term. The first post-war election was held in February, the next four in March, the 1966 election in June. Casual vacancies are filled by by-elections as they occur.

The fifteen union republics have each a Supreme Soviet of some 400–500 members, which is unicameral even in those republics which contain autonomous republics. The autonomous republics have somewhat smaller unicameral Supreme Soviets. In both classes representation is related to population. In the R.S.F.S.R. there is one deputy to 150,000 inhabitants; in the Ukraine one to 100,000; in Belorussia and Kazahstan one to 20,000; in Uzbekistan, Georgia and Lithuania one to 15,000; in Azerbaidjan, Moldavia, Latvia and Esthonia one to 10,000; in Kirgizia, Tadjikistan, Armenia and Turkmenia one to 5,000. In the Tatar and Bashkir autonomous republics there is one to 15,000; in the Mordovian and Chuvash one to 12,000; in Udmurt one to 7,500; in the Dagestan, Burjat-Mongol and Mari republics one to 6,000; in Karelia one to 5,000; in Komi and the North Ossetian republic one to 4,000; in Kabarda one to 3,500; in the Yakut republic one to 3,000;[1] others are unknown. They also are elected for periods of four years, but not simultaneously with the Union Supreme Soviet. The first republican Supreme Soviet elections under the current constitution were held in 1938, and since the war they have been held in the years following the election to the Union Supreme Soviet—1947, 1951, 1955, 1959 and 1963 and 1967, in each case in February.

The various levels of the administrative structure—territories and regions, areas, districts, 'villages', towns and settlements—have their own soviets. In the latter part of the Khrushchov period a variation was introduced by the division of the party structures for the control of industry and of agriculture. Following the accepted principle that party and soviet structures should correspond two separate soviets were set up in each region of mixed economy (e.g. in five of the six territories and 37 of the 49 regions of the R.S.F.S.R.); a similar duplication in the districts was avoided by dividing the districts themselves into industrial and agricultural and attaching isolated industrial sites to reasonably convenient towns. Before the end of 1964, the year of Khrushchov's fall, this complex arrangement had yielded to the old simplicity.

At the 1967 elections there were 49,015 Soviets including autonomous regions and national areas, with a total membership of 2,045,419 (with some people serving on soviets at more than one level). The number of soviets was some 1,250 up on 1955, but about 3,250 short of the 1963 figure; the number of members, however, had increased fairly steadily, by some 32,000 and 35,000 over the

---

[1] Figures for union republics from constitutions as published in 1956. Figures for Karelia from constitution of Karelo-Finnish union republic as published in 1951. Figures for the other autonomous republics in R.S.F.S.R. from constitutions as published in 1955.

two successive intervals; the overall trend reflects policies of fewer, and more substantial units, particularly in the lower levels of the system, and wider popular participation. The size of the soviets is fixed by republican legislation within limits set by the republican constitution, except in the Baltic republics and Moldavia, for each class of territorial unit on a basis of population. The scales vary widely with density of settlement but, except among the towns, the resultant bodies are of very similar size—upward of sixty for a region—to as many as 200—some 35–60 for a national area or a district and 25–35 for a village.[1] Town soviets may run up from about district size to several hundreds.

The largest cities are necessarily somewhat exceptional in this respect. The size of their soviets is usually specifically provided for in the republican constitutions; contrary to the general trend it has often diminished as the population represented has increased. The Moscow City Soviet elected in 1955 had 813 members, as against 1,500 in 1953 and over 2,100 before the 1939 election, but by 1965 was back to 1,104. Leningrad in 1965 elected 605 members. Districts within towns commonly have soviets of district or small-town size, but in Moscow they run to some 250 members.

Local soviets are unicameral, elected for two-year terms (Article 95 of federal constitution)—in 1939, December 1947—January 1948, December 1950—January 1951, February 1953, and March of 1955, 1957, 1959, 1961, 1963, 1965 and 1967.

With the adoption of direct elections to the central legislatures the local soviets have ceased to be in any material sense 'the political foundation of the U.S.S.R.' (Article 2 of the federal constitution). In so far as they genuinely function they are 'local authorities', though involved in the general business of the state in a manner characteristic of the local-government bodies of continental Europe rather than of Britain. The Supreme Soviets, similarly, are now 'parliaments', despite the objections of Lenin, theoretically continued by his successors, to parliamentarianism. They may differ from the similar institutions of other countries in the quality of their performance but not in the nature of the task purported to be assigned to them. The state of soviets, if it was ever to be found in the Soviet Union, is there no longer.

The councils of the economy of Mr. Khrushchov's economic districts were not elected bodies. They were appointed formally by the Councils of Ministers of the Republics and answerable only to them, though in a republic which formed a single economic

---

[1] Of the 342 village soviets elected in 1963 in Tula region 249 had 25 deputies each, 42 had from 25 to 30, and 50 had over 30.—M. A. Shafir in *S.G. i P.*, No. 10 of 1964, p. 26.

district, or part of one, the appointed body overshadowed the appointing.

How They are Formed

Before 1936 only the village and town soviets were directly elected, the higher levels having congresses of soviets elected up by the soviets or congresses of soviets at the level below, right up to federal level. The franchise for the popular election at the lowest levels was not an equal one. Lenin and his successors habitually emphasised the distinction between their form of state, or 'proletarian democracy', and 'bourgeois democracy' in that the former frankly recognised its class basis, whereas the latter sought to conceal it. Certain classes of people were therefore excluded from the franchise: persons engaging in commerce or employing hired labour for profit, persons living on unearned income, priests and monks, members of the Imperial Family and holders of certain pre-revolutionary offices, such as the procurators and police officers. Aliens resident in the Soviet Union, however, enjoyed the franchise on equal terms with Soviet citizens and any discrimination on a basis of race, religion or sex was forbidden. Above the level of elections, in the congresses of soviets, advantage was given to the urban proletariat by providing a higher proportion of representation for the town than for the village soviets. Thus in the district congresses of soviets in the R.S.F.S.R. and the Ukraine there was one deputy for each 300 inhabitants in the villages and one for every sixty voters in the towns, or in plants or factories outside them. At the federal level these figures were 125,000 inhabitants and 25,000 voters respectively. The method of voting was open, and much was made of the fact that the election took place not in territorial units but in the factories wherever possible.

By the constitution of 1936 all this was changed. Enfranchised aliens and excluded classes both disappeared. The vote was given to 'all citizens of the U.S.S.R. who have reached the age of eighteen, irrespective of race or nationality, sex, religion, education, domicile, social origin, property status or past activities.' (Article 135.) The insane and persons expressly sentenced to loss of voting rights were alone excluded (though an extension of disqualification to all persons in custody was apparently still in practice in the post-war period[1]). Disqualification by the courts was abolished in 1958; the insane remain excluded.

The qualifying age for candidates was in 1936 similarly placed at eighteen, but by an edict of the Praesidium of the Supreme Soviet of

[1] Askerov, et al., op. cit., p. 332.

the 10th October 1945 this was raised to twenty-three for election to the federal Supreme Soviet, and by a similar edict of a year later it was made twenty-one for election to the Supreme Soviets of the union republics. The age of voting remains unchanged. Election to soviets and Supreme Soviets at all levels became direct, and the method prescribed was the secret ballot. In contrast to the system provided in Great Britain, however, the voter is required not to mark the name of the candidate for whom he wishes to vote but to cross out the name of the candidate for whom he does not wish to vote. Though still in the electoral regulations, this requirement ceased to be printed on the ballot paper in 1946 as a belated recognition of the fact that there had never been more than one candidate for any place at issue in any election, central or local.

All elections are held in single-member constituencies, so that for the bicameral federal Supreme Soviet the voter casts his vote in two constituencies of different sizes at the same time, or, if he lives in an autonomous or national unit, in three. The same polling stations are used and the votes are distinguished by the use of ballot papers of different colours. Elections of any one category—federal, republican or local—in any one republic are held on the same day—always a Sunday—though in republican or local elections different groups of republics may poll on different days, a week or sometimes more apart. Voters absent from their places of residence on polling day may obtain certificates entitling them to vote in the places where they happen to be for the candidates there standing, even, it seems, in local elections.

The conduct of the elections to a Supreme Soviet is entrusted to a Central Electoral Commission appointed by order of the Praesidium of that Supreme Soviet. Election commissions for elections to the Soviet of Nationalities are appointed by the Praesidia of Supreme Soviets and executive committees of soviets of the several autonomous and national units. Those for constituencies are appointed by the similar organs at regional level, or republic where there is no region, and those for polling stations by the executive committees of district or town soviets. The members are to be appointed from among members of the party, trade unions, youth organisations and various cultural societies, and upon their suggestion. Their political reliability is consequently unimpeachable.

The onus of registration lies not upon the voter but upon the lowest organs in the soviet system—the executive committees of village soviets, or of soviets of settlements, districts within towns where the towns are so divided, and the towns themselves where they are not. The issue of certificates to their registered voters who will be absent on polling day rests with the same authorities. Appeals against non-inclusion or other faults in the electoral lists lie to the district people's court, the lowest unit of the soviet judicial system, and its decision is final. To secure election the candidate is required to obtain an absolute majority of the vote cast provided that not less than half of those entitled to vote have in fact done so.

Article 141 of the constitution secures the rights to nominate candidates to public organisations and societies of the working people, Communist Party organisations, trade unions and co-operatives, youth organisations and cultural societies. Electoral regulations extend the exercise of the right also to assemblies of workers and other employees at their places of work, collective-farm members on their farms, and members of the armed forces in their units—and it is in fact by such bodies that the nominations are ostensibly at least always made. A Russian university textbook explains that 'in the U.S.S.R. it would be inappropriate to give the right of proposing candidates directly to individual persons. Firstly, citizens of the U.S.S.R. have every possibility of proposing this or that candidate at the general assemblies of collectives of toilers, or through the organs of social organisations. Secondly, the proposing of candidates by collectives and organisations of toilers corresponds to the high level of development or organised social consciousness in the Soviet state'.[1]

The nominations then made are finally sorted out and placed on the ballot paper by 'pre-election constituency conferences of representatives of the various collectives', which, it is agreed, always produce one single satisfactory candidature,[2] but there seems to be satisfactory evidence that the conference in fact has no sorting out to do. The lists put up by the nominating meetings may, in fact, contain several names, but that is because, particularly in the small constituencies used for local elections, any one factory may contain voters from several constituencies. When, in fact, the lists proposed by the various meetings are put side by side it is found always that they contain just sufficient real candidates to provide one for each constituency. There have generally been also some unreal candidates; it was the custom for Stalin himself and each of the leading figures of his entourage to have himself nominated in a number of constituencies, from all of which he would subsequently withdraw except in the one constituency where he was the only candidate. Khrushchov, though originally more discreet, was before his fall making similar use of this technique. Where such a bogus plurality of candidates was presented to the constituency conference, it did not attempt to cut it down but confirmed both

[1] Askerov, et al., op. cit., p. 324.
[2] Ibid., p. 325.

candidatures.[1] The candidate is registered with the constituency election commission. The ballot paper contains the candidate's name, the name of the organisation nominating him and the fact that he is a party member if he is. Party membership, however, plays no part in the campaign; all candidates are placed before the electorate as 'the bloc of communists and partyless people', and in the lists of candidates as published in the press party membership is not indicated.

The fact that the ballot paper is valid without marking has an important consequence for the conduct of the election, for the voter's only reason for using the screened voting booths for which all polling stations are required to be provided is to vote against the candidate. Official propaganda has done nothing to discourage open voting, but has rather favoured it as an act of civic courage. The press frequently publishes accounts of irregularities in the conduct of elections, such as the failure to provide voting booths or the failure (in the case of a by-election upon the amalgamation of two village soviets) to give any notice to the electors before polling day, but failure to insist on voters going through the forms of secret election is never mentioned, and there is no suggestion of improper influence on the selection of candidates. Where these things happen —and they evidently do—it is by design.

The absence of alternative candidates does not mean that the outcome is everywhere certain before polling takes place. At the local elections of 1939 and in all local elections since then a number of candidates have failed on the grounds that they had not secured the necessary absolute majority. Presumably this is due to the local occurrence of a very low poll, though some of the voters may have crossed the name out or else spoilt their ballot papers. In such a case the election is invalidated and has to be held again. But such cases are very few; there were only 125 in 1939 out of some 1,400,000 places at issue, and in 1967, 129 (119 of them in village soviets) out of 2,045,406. The same procedure is presumably followed for any subsequent election until a candidate does secure the necessary majority. In general, declared participation in elections is good beyond all belief. By 1937 it was already 96.8 per cent of the electorate, and since 1950 it has not fallen below 99.94. Local election polls have been equally good—99.96 per cent in 1967. Georgia repeatedly, and other republics at times, achieve polls of 99.99 per cent; Esthonia is content with a relaxed 99.46 (national 1966) or 99.64 (local 1967). The proportion of those voting in 1966 who voted for the candidate was 99.76 per cent for the Soviet of the

[1] T. H. R. Rigby in *Political Quarterly*, July–September 1953, p. 315 (central elections), and in *Australian Outlook*, March 1954, pp. 20–1 (local elections).

Union and 99.80 for that of Nationalities. In 1967 it varied between 99.37 and 99.99, in two autonomous republic supreme soviets (Chuvash and Nahichevan). It is therefore strange that any candidates at all fail to get the votes required. The cases may be arranged to simulate democracy, but they could be genuine; probably there is some local variation so that a degree of secretiveness which would be unsafe in one place may be indulged in in another.

Elections can have other purposes than the selection of representatives. Turnout can be used as an index of the regime's control over its subjects, as it was in the early days of some of the newer communist states. But with polls coming as near perfection as do those of the Soviet Union, even this function of elections is losing its point. The high proportion of voters participating is still regularly quoted but possibly mainly as a demonstration of solidarity aimed chiefly at the outside world. The provision of a special occasion for party workers and helpers to practise their skill as agitators is probably a more real consideration. In the 1950 local elections, 3,750,000 people were said to have been engaged in the work of the electoral commissions in the R.S.F.S.R. alone, and several million more as agitators and in similar capacities in the constituencies. It was claimed that in the 1955 local elections fourteen to fifteen million people were employed as agitators.

Elections are also demonstrations. Conducted as they are in a holiday atmosphere of music and flags and portraits of the leaders, they are a stimulating experience. This is comprehensible in the circumstances of the Soviet people, with their lack of any extensive previous experience of elections and their habituation over a long period to other purely symbolical demonstrations, such as May Day celebrations and meetings in support of the various campaigns of the authorities on issues of national or international affairs. Also the approach of election day is used, as are May Day and the anniversary of the revolution and formerly Stalin's birthday, as an occasion for a production drive and the demand of an extra display of energy to complete other tasks.

The analyses of membership presented to the opening sessions of the soviets by their mandates commissions are the principal official indications of the nature of the product of this process. Membership of one or other of the officially recognised social classes, party membership or candidate status, age, sex, education and possession of honours or decorations, are the categories employed. Thus in the Supreme Soviet elected in 1966 54 per cent of the members were shown as belonging to the intelligentsia, 26.6 per cent to the workers and 19.4 per cent to the collective farm members. Republican supreme soviets of 1967 had slightly more peasants and fewer of the intelligentsia, local soviets as a whole rather more so. Party members and candidate-members former 74.7 per cent (573 members) of the Soviet of the Union, and 75.7 per cent (568 members) of the Soviet of Nationalities—75.2 per cent of the whole. Intelligentsia and party members were both down in proportion, the former reversing a post-World War II trend, the latter continuing one. For the local soviet the proportion of party membership declines steeply as one goes down the scale from, the federation towards the village, and it also varies markedly from one republic to another. Thus in the 1947 election the proportion of party members in the local soviets in Armenia was stated to be 52.57 per cent, and in the newly acquired republics of Moldavia and Lithuania only 13.41 per cent and 11 per cent respectively.[1] In 1957, however, their proportions, while still among the lowest, had risen to 39.2 and 32.14 per cent respectively. Esthonia had 33.7. Armenia still had the highest proportion, with 59.6, followed by Kazahstan, with 49.99 per cent. The R.S.F.S.R. had 45.5.[2] By 1967 Moldavia, with 47.7 per cent, had moved up to second place, behind Azerbaidjan (50.48); Georgia was third (47.62), Armenia now fourth (47.50). The R.S.F.S.R. had 46.11. Esthonia at the bottom of the list, had 38.60; above it, with 42.3, was Lithuania. But these official statistics of composition are in some sense misleading. That by membership of the party is no doubt genuine, but not very important. By the rules of the party members are specifically charged to concert their actions on the basis of the party line, in soviets as in any other type of body. There is no body similarly able to act against them. The other members are non-party, not anti-party, and there is every reason to suppose that the party has had the decisive voice in their selection. The classification by social status is particularly unsatisfactory. Before the late 'thirties members of public bodies were apparently reluctant to classify themselves as belonging to the intelligentsia, and would if they could claim working class or peasant status, if only on the basis of a previous occupation which they had abandoned, or, it seems, often on the basis of family origin. Since the establishment of a new Soviet intelligentsia it has apparently been less usual to assume disguise in this respect, but there is still some evidence of a random element in the classification. Always a number of those classified as workers or peasants are found to be holding posts

[1] John Hazard, *Law and Social Change in the U.S.S.R.* (1953), pp. 75–6; and same author, 'Political, Administrative and Judicial Structure in the U.S.S.R. Since the War', *The Annals of the American Academy of Political and Social Science*, May 1949, p. 10.
[2] *Pravda*, 8th, 9th, 13th, 16th March 1957. *Verhovny Sovet SSSR*, 1967, *Vedomosti Verhovnogo Soveta SSSR*, No. 13 of 1967.

reckoned by Soviet standards as putting them in the intelligentsia. A figure of something over 80 per cent for that category has been calculated for earlier Supreme Soviets and seems to accord with Soviet accounts of the educational attainments of members of the 1966 houses: 50.2 per cent higher education, 21.2 per cent full secondary and 22.7 per cent part-secondary[1]—an ambiguous category but probably still productive of white collars.

Soviet sources have latterly offered contributions to, and largely confirmed, the more detailed analysis of membership previously conducted only outside the Soviet Union. A 1967 publication[2] shows 289 members of the 1966 houses as employed in full-time party office as secretaries or leading workers of party committees, or in similar positions in trade unions and the youth organisations—which form in fact a single service—and 229 in full-time state administration (supreme soviet praesidium chairmen, ministers, chairmen of soviet executive committees, etc.)—which in respect of career patterns is closely integrated with it. The armed forces had fifty-six, all of high officer rank. Managers of enterprises and comparable grades in industry numbered seventy; similar grades from the state farms were twenty-one and chairmen of collective farms ninety-nine. In various forms of intellectual work, including teachers, writers, composers, artists and doctors there were 154. There were 309 workers in industry (including foremen and brigade leaders) and ninety-five in state farms and 195 collective-farm members (other than chairmen). The picture which emerges is somewhat different from that maintained through several preceding elections; a trend to reduction of the party-state administration is continued, but an increase in the industrial group is markedly accelerated and one in the agricultural group even more so. The military and the intellectuals seem to have suffered reverses of previous trends in their favour.

About two-thirds (66.9 per cent) of those elected in 1966 had never served in the Supreme Soviet before;[3] this is standard for any two successive Supreme Soviets, and the repeated maintenance of consistency of composition against such rapid turnover suggests deliberate composition.

At the lower levels also there seems similarly to be a rapid turnover—of about two-thirds of supreme soviets of both union republics and autonomous republics in 1967 and half, or rather more, in local soviets.[4] In the past, and probably also in the present, more

[1] *Verhovny Sovet SSSR*, 1967, p. 278.
[2] Ibid., pp. 72–75.
[3] Ibid., pp. 276–7.
[4] Ibid.

CONVENTIONAL STATE MACHINERY

drastic cases can be found; only four of the members elected in 1948 to the Leningrad regional soviet were re-elected to it in 1950. Of the thirty-five members elected to the village soviet of Suharevo (Moscow region) in 1953, eighteen were new, and among the 1,500 elected to Moscow city soviet at the same elections there were 672 new members.

The Soviet constitution allows the electorate to recall its representatives in any directly elected body at any time. This right seems very rarely to have been exercised, but in late December 1956 one Latvian constituency was reported to have recalled its deputy to the republican Supreme Soviet for untrustworthiness and failure to carry out constituent's instructions. In October 1959 the federal Supreme Soviet passed a decree reasserting the power of recall, and in July 1963 a deputy was in fact recalled from the Soviet of Nationalities.

What They Do

Article 46 of the constitution states that the Supreme Soviet of the U.S.S.R. is convened by its Praesidium[1] twice a year, and that in addition the Praesidium may call an extraordinary session at its own discretion or on the demand of one of the union republics. According to Article 41 sessions of the two Houses begin and end simultaneously. Except in the war years, when only a few brief extraordinary sessions were held, the Supreme Soviet seems to have kept, on average, though not literally, to the legal requirements, but the meetings seldom last much more than a week in the year. The fifth Supreme Soviet, elected in 1958, sat from 27th to 31st March and 22nd to 25th December of that year, 27th to 31st October 1959, 14th and 15th January, 5th to 7th May and 20th to 23rd December 1960 and 6th to 8th December 1961—a total of twenty-six days. The sixth—of 1962—sat from 23rd to 25th April and 10th to 13th December 1962, 16th to 18th December 1963, 13th to 15th July and 9th to 11th December 1964, 1st to 2nd October and 7th to 9th December 1965—twenty-one days. The seventh—of 1966—held its first three sittings from 2nd to 3rd August and 15th to 19th December of that year and 10th to 12th October 1967. It is claimed as a prime virtue of the Supreme Soviet 'that it is a working institution, called not only to accept the laws but also to ensure their carrying into effect. This is the basis of the sessional order of its work. The Supreme Soviet of the U.S.S.R. does not, like bourgeois parliaments, sit almost without intermission, but is called for short sessions. Such a manner of operation permits the deputies, who after their election

[1] See p. 113.

remain workers in the economy, in science and culture, the state machinery and so on not to be cut off from their basic work and to keep check in real life on the carrying out of the laws and actively to promote their realisation'.[1]

The frequency of meetings of Supreme Soviets of union republics and autonomous republics is prescribed in their own constitutions, but all agree on the same minimum of two sessions a year. The frequency and duration of sessions of the R.S.F.S.R. Supreme Soviet and apparently those of other republics, correspond almost exactly to federal practice, thus perhaps remaining virtually constitutional by Soviet standards.

Sessions of local soviets are also covered by republican constitutions; that of the R.S.F.S.R. prescribes four meetings a year for soviets of regions, territories and towns divided into districts, and six for all others. Until March 1957 a monthly meeting was required of town and village soviets. Other republics agreed except Kazahstan which required only four meetings a year at district level and three at higher levels. A case for the reform in so far as it concerns the villages was made in 1954 in one of the more authoritative central organs: 'The necessity has developed to restrict the number of sessions held by village soviets in order to free the chairman for immediate organisational work in the villages. It is enough, in our opinion, if sessions of village soviets are held once in two months.'[2] In part it was perhaps a recognition of the futility of insistence on more meetings; compliance has throughout the system been chronically poor. In 1955 the soviets of two of the six territories and four of the fifty-four regions in the R.S.F.S.R. had held no sessions at all, while all the towns of republican subordination in the same republic, 66.6 per cent of area soviets, 40.3 per cent of settlement soviets and 36.5 per cent of those of villages had fallen short of the requirements of the law. The constant complaints on the subject in the press, even if now less fully quantified, do not suggest that new legislation for the local government system has produced any drastic advance in procedural decorum.

All soviets and the two Houses of the federal Supreme Soviet verify their own mandates, as is usual in the elected bodies of con-

[1] M. P. Kareva and G. I. Fedjkin, *Osnovy Sovetskogo Gosudarstva i Prava* (1953), p. 223.

[2] V. A. Nemtsev in *S.G. i P.*, No. 8 of 1954, p. 54. *S.G. i P.*, No. 3 of 1956, p. 8, agrees on the ground that only thus can village soviets reasonably give instructions to their executive committees—as to assert their authority over them they should—as to the subject on which they are to report at the next session, but, strangely, as late as 24th February 1957, and in *Pravda*, K. M. Ozolins, Chairman of the Praesidium of the Latvian Supreme Soviet, ridicules this argument.

tinental Europe—they would themselves hear disputes concerning the credentials of members if, as is not the case, there were any. The first business on the agenda of the two Houses of a newly elected Supreme Soviet meeting separately is to appoint their mandates commissions of thirty-one members each (since 1966, having risen gradually to that figure from the original eleven at 1937), which report back later. While they do their work the Supreme Soviet's other business is not suspended. Thus the Houses of the Supreme Soviet of 1962 appointed mandates commissions at their first sessions on 23rd April 1962 and heard their reports on the 24th, having in the meantime elected their other commissions and a new Council of Ministers, after making the usual changes to the constitution. The commission remains in being for the whole term of election of the House, and similarly reports on the credentials of any members elected in by-elections.

Each body of Supreme Soviet status has its own chairman and a number of deputy chairmen, who are elected by it at its first session before the adoption of agenda, and remain in office for its whole term of election unless released. Thus the federal Supreme Soviet has a chairman and four deputies for each House, the unicameral Supreme Soviet of the R.S.F.S.R. has a chairman and eight deputies, four republics prescribe four deputy chairmen, one three and the others two. When the two Houses of the federal Supreme Soviet meet in joint session, as they do for a large part of their business, the chairmen of the two Houses preside alternately. Between sessions the posts of the chairmen involve them in certain duties such as the signing of messages to foreign parliaments and perhaps some organisational work as well; they are not, however, traditionally full-time posts, though they may be becoming so. Mr. V. T. Lacis (to 1958) and Mr. Ja. V. Peive (1958–1966) of the Soviet of Nationalities combined the office with chairmanship of the Council of Ministers of Latvia. Mr. A. P. Volkov (to 1956) and Mr. P. P. Lobanov (1956–1962) of the Soviet of the Union held simultaneously the chairmanships of, respectively, the executive committee of Moscow regional soviet and the Academy of Agricultural Sciences. Mr. Volkov was released from his chairmanship on appointment to the federal Council of Ministers, but from May 1957 Mr. Lacis's and Peive's republican office carried *ex officio* membership of that body without requiring their resignation. Mr. I. V. Spiridonov of the Soviet of the Union since 1962, a career party official (secretary of the central committee, 1961–62), and Mr. Ju. I. Paleckis, of the Soviet of Nationalities since 1966, previously chairman of the Praesidium of the Supreme Soviet of Lithuania, do not appear to have simultaneously held any other office.

Local soviets elect a chairman from among their members for each meeting.

Also chosen by the Houses of a newly elected Supreme Soviet are the standing commissions. Until February 1957 these were three for each House: on legislative bills (since 1946, nineteen members), on budgets (twenty-seven, reduced in 1954 to twenty-six) and on foreign affairs (eleven). In the spirit of the 1957 emphasis on decentralisation of management and the rights of the nationalities the Soviet of Nationalities then formed an economic commission of thirty-one (a chairman plus two from each union republic). In 1966 this innovation was abolished, but each House now formed additionally commissions for: industry, transport and communications; construction and the building materials industry; agriculture; health and social security; popular instruction, science and culture; commerce and public amenity services. The budget commission now had fifty-one members, industry, etc. and agriculture forty-one, the rest thirty-one. Activities of commissions are now more publicised than formerly. Those on bills and the budget at least reportedly meet a few weeks before the Supreme Soviet—often jointly between the two Houses—and work largely in sub-committee having power to call officials. Findings seem to be concerted before the Houses meet. When the two Houses, after hearing the report of the Minister of Finance at a joint session, withdraw into separate session to hear the co-reports from the chairmen of their budget commissions they are invariably presented with identical recommendations for increases over the Minister's figure of expenditure and—always a larger increase—revenue. The assignments of the former to the several republics and of the latter to particular taxes is always identical, though the exposition may vary.

The standing commissions of local soviets have, at least in origin, rather different functions. They are the heirs to the 'sections' or groups of soviet deputies and 'activists'—interested citizens from outside the membership—formed by the lowest-level soviets for their several classes of business. The sections were one of the many attempts in the Soviet system to create a fluid outer layer of public support, and vigilance, around the organs of authority. By 1936 they had 3,639,061 members. They had their own inner bodies—or 'bureaux'—of three to five, including the head of the appropriate administrative department, but as the section itself had no executive powers the bureau's function was vague. In the reforms on the making of the new constitution the sections came to be replaced by the standing commissions, which differ from them principally in being established in local soviets of all levels, and not merely the lowest, in having no inner bureau, though they have a chairman and secretary, and if large enough a vice-chairman, and in that the activists now have no vote. It is not clear how the activists are disadvantaged thereby, since the votes can apparently only pass resolutions for the soviet's executive committee to endorse, or not. The largest soviets (regions and cities) are recorded as having up to fifteen of these bodies, and every village soviet should have three to five of them. The most common types are for the budget, for agriculture and for various social services, such as education and health; they are also formed for commerce, for local public works and building, for industry and communications, for 'socialist legality' (defence of the law against unauthorised infringements) *inter alia.* They may inspect, or depute members or activists to do so, though their power to inspect enterprises subordinate to higher authorities than their own soviets, or to pay expenses of inspection, has been questioned. They may attach a co-report to the departmental report to the soviet. The executive committee should invite them when measures or other matters concerning them are under consideration. It seems that in practice the executive committee often invites only their chairmen, or even fails to consult them at all, and ignores any co-reports submitted. If in their inspections the commissions detect criminal fault they are to report it direct to the procurator. It is evident that apart from this sending of 'signals' to higher authority they are valued for their utility in keeping the public aware of official aims and running campaigns, such as road repairs by voluntary communal labour. It is in this sense that *Izvestia* can report[1] that 'millions of working people are recruited for the commissions' work'. Reported numbers of activists engaged have risen by some half-million over a decade to 2,437,031 in 1964. All deputies, except members of executive committees, and in the largest towns certain other office holders, who are now exempt, are required to serve, though they are apparently not always eager. In 1964 1,502,766 of them were recorded in the 245,877 commissions. By April 1967 their numbers had risen to 1,666,513 and 301,760 respectively.

The Houses of the U.S.S.R. Supreme Soviet, at each meeting, assemble briefly in separate session to accept their agenda and deal with domestic business (by-election returns, etc.). Then, for the rest of the first morning they go into joint session for a theme address from the leadership on the main business of the sitting. Thereafter, at two sessions a day—morning and late afternoon—they consider their business, separately or jointly, and finally assemble for a concluding joint session—usually with a further major address. Since December 1958 they have two meeting places open to them: the Kremlin Great Hall—used also for meetings of the R.S.F.S.R.

[1] *Izvestia,* 3rd July 1953.

Supreme Soviet, party congresses and the larger conferences—and the new Kremlin theatre, and they alternate in use of them. Previously they had only the former, and scheduling was correspondingly more difficult.

They are required to vote in separate sessions upon all laws formally so designated, of which only those approving the annual plan and budget ordinarily take up much of their time—hence the predominance of December sittings. For other business largely appointments and resolutions of approval—they meet and vote together. Short sessions, usually to publicise a government move, are sometimes taken entirely in joint session. Interpellation of the government by groups of deputies at the February and May sittings of 1957—then unprecedented—and the December sitting of 1965 was taken jointly; it produced assurances of concern for cultural contacts abroad, and for an end to hydrogen bomb tests and observations on American activity in Vietnam. Voting, as in all soviets, is by show of hands.

The constitution (Article 38) gives the Houses equal initiative powers. Measures to confirm Praesidium edicts—numerous but all undebated—are introduced by the secretary of the Praesidium. Original legislation is usually introduced by a minister.

Participation in debate is relatively poor, and the speeches never give any indication of difference of opinion. A representative selection of members from different parts of the Union declares support for the measure, and in the debate on the budget suggest reasons why more provision should be made for particular purposes of interest to their own republics or regions, but never any manner in which this increase might be provided for to the detriment of other areas. In the local soviets the theme seems to be rather the claims of allegedly neglected services within the excessive range for which officials there, as elsewhere in the system, are held responsible, or cases of inefficiency or malpractice by individuals. It is evident that there also debate is lacking and speeches far from spontaneous. The practice of having all speeches prepared and approved by the chairman of the executive committee in advance has been officially condemned, though in consequence of the attitude of some chairmen members often seem still to find it safer. Advance notice to members to speak is approved.

Many important matters do not come before the Supreme Soviet for decision, notably the five-year (or, 1958–65, seven-year) plan, though measures to give effect to it do. The budget under the 1956 five-year plan was passed before acceptance of the plan by the party congress.

According to Soviet expositors there are three categories of

Supreme Soviet business: Laws (*zakon*), defined as 'Acts of Supreme Legislation'; Decrees (*postanovlenie*)—'Acts of Supreme Administration'; and a third category—'Acts of Supreme Supervision'.[1] The second category consists of acts making or confirming appointments; the third of resolutions—usually also called Decrees —approving reports from organisations subordinate to the Supreme Soviet. The distinction between the first two categories corresponds to the procedural distinction between business to be voted on in joint session and that which can only be voted in separate session. The two Houses individually may make 'decrees', but only for their internal matters such as appointment of commissions. The Supreme Soviet may also, and frequently does, pass resolutions expressing views on foreign relations, etc.

The 1962 Supreme Soviet passed at its first session seven laws, all confirming acts of the Praesidium, one of them (changing the State Committee structure in the Council of Ministers) consequentially amending the constitution (which the Praesidium cannot do); one confirmed the code of air law, one ended pre-call-up military training, one removed entertainment tax on sport, one strengthened the criminal penalty for bad upkeep of agricultural machinery and one for certain crimes of violence, one amended the code of principles of criminal legislation. Six decrees elected a new Praesidium, took note of the formal resignation of the old government and continued it in office *ad interim*, elected a new one, approved the report of the Minister of Foreign Affairs on disarmament talks in Geneva, elected a new supreme court and set up a commission to draft a new constitution. The Houses decreed the appointment of their standing commissions and approved the findings of their mandates commissions.

The second session passed two original laws, accepting the state economic plan and budget for 1963. Five other laws accepted the usual changes in government structure and made the necessary constitutional amendments, and approved amendments to the law on compulsory military service and the rules on privileges for workers in the Far North, postponed the promised removal of income tax from earnings, and changed the rules on infliction of fines by administrative procedure. Original decrees approved the audit of the budget year 1961 and a report by Mr. Khrushchov on foreign affairs and made one change in the Praesidium; nine confirmatory decrees accepted ministerial changes and new appointments. The Soviet of the Union decreed acceptance of some by-election results.

The third session again passed the original laws for the next state plan and budget and the confirmatory law on changes of

---

[1] A. M. Vasiliev in *S.G. i P.*, No. 8 of 1953, p. 25.

government structure (with constitutional amendments) and another on administrative fines, as well as four others approving the conferment on the police of the power to conduct preliminary investigations, the creation of a criminal offence of wilfully stopping a train, provision for transfer of experimental enterprises from local to central control and a transfer of territory between two union republics. Five original decrees accepted the 1962 budget audit and replaced two Praesidium vice-chairmen; four confirmatory decrees noted a number of government changes. Both houses decreed acceptance of by-election results.

The fourth session passed two original laws, on pensions for collective farm members and on pay rises for certain non-industrial workers. Four confirmatory laws changed the status of a government agency, increased the penalties for breach of fishing rules, stiffened the taxation on the private agricultural activities of collective farmers and confirmed the customs code. Five original decrees appointed a commission to recommend how collective farms should pay for their members' pensions, released Mr. L. N. Brezhnev as Praesidium chairman, appointed Mr. A. I. Mikojan instead, released Mr. Mikojan from the government and appointed a supreme court member. The houses accepted by-election returns and appointed officers.

The fifth session passed the 1965 plan and budget laws and confirmatory laws, setting up a ministry (with constitutional amendment), amending the law on education and adjusting a republican boundary. An original decree approved the budget audit for 1963; three others released Mr. Khrushchov from chairmanship of the commission for the new constitution, appointed Mr. Brezhnev instead and changed a Praesidium vice-chairman. Confirmatory decrees accepted the release of Mr. Khrushchov (two months earlier) from Council of Ministers chairmanship 'in connection with his advanced age and impaired condition of health', and appointment of Mr. A. N. Kosygin instead, and endorsed recent government appointments. The Houses confirmed by-election returns and appointed a standing commission member.

The sixth session passed a law restoring the administrative system to the pre-Khrushchovian ministerial basis and another making the consequential constitutional amendments. Ten confirmatory laws endorsed a seven-month-old edict converting six state committees into ministries and setting up a new ministry and other edicts, two to eleven months old, amending the law on military offences, proscribing crimes against peace and humanity, reducing the period of military service, regulating income tax payable by collective farms, establishing two public holidays, establishing a procedure for executing Yugoslav court orders, lengthening middle-school education in the Baltic republics, reinforcing the disciplinary regulations in the armed forces and making changes in the state pension system. Five original decrees made Mr. Brezhnev a member of the Praesidium, released his predecessor (on appointment as a first vice-chairman of the Council of Ministers) replaced a vice-chairman of the same body, released eight ministers and made certain appointments to the Council of Ministers. Four confirmatory decrees endorsed the seven-month-old appointment of another first vice-chairman and that (a month older) of a vice-chairman, the release of their predecessors and twelve miscellaneous ministerial appointments or releases. The Nationalities accepted two by-elections and made an appointment.

The seventh, and last, session passed four original laws, for the 1966 state plan and budget, for amendment of the much-amended article 70 of the constitution (composition of the Council of Ministers), and for restoration of the previous institutions of People's Control, and two confirmatory laws, one on ministry titles and statuses and one transferring part of a district from Kazahstan to the R.S.F.S.R. Seven original decrees accepted the 1964 budget audit, released Mr. Mikojan from chairmanship of the Praesidium and made him a member, appointed Mr. N. V. Podgorny in his place, appointed a chairman of the Committee of People's Control, a vice-chairman of the Council of Ministers and a member of the Supreme Court and approved the reply of the Minister of Foreign Affairs to interpellation on Vietnam (to which there was attached a resolution). Three confirmatory decrees recorded the abolition two months previously of the Khrushchovian device of personal ministerial appointments and the designation of a vice-chairman of the Council and heads of newly created government agencies.

Low-level soviet business seems highly resistant to change and even new legislation. A third instrument on the powers of village soviets, enacted for the R.S.F.S.R. in September 1957 and in other republics shortly after, and new laws at federal and republican levels ten years later have emerged from a continuous officially sponsored discussion in the journals which, broadly agreeing that they are undersized in relation to the farms—at best, on average about one to one, though without exact coincidence of territory—under-endowed and, by superior authority, under-regarded, has from time to time produced the suggestion that they be abolished. This is now declared false doctrine and rehabilitation may, or may not, have brought them means of transport of their own, and so have relieved their utter dependence on the farms which they are supposed to supervise, and the competent bookkeeping staff which previously they lacked. There are no indications, or probability, that it has provided heads of collective or state farms or any industrial enterprises which there may be in rural areas with cause to take much notice of anything which may be said in such soviets, although the extensive list of fields of concern in the model instruments approved by the 1968 legislation extends from oversight of the conformity of the actions of such organisations to legality and state economic plans down to the initiation of action for the conferment of decorations on mothers of ten children or courageous firefighters. Control of the farm in the interests of the state has by-passed the village; the interests of the members already have a voice—even if usually unheeded—in the farm's management. Services to non-members of the farms—a few years ago confined to the school teacher, a medical assistant, the few people who worked in the village shop, if there was one, and the officials of the village soviet itself, and even with recent consolidations hardly much extended—can do little to justify the soviets' existence. The cultural facilities which they are traditionally empowered and urged to provide—children's work out of school, libraries and reading huts and clubs—are such as the farm is often reported as providing for itself, and road maintenance, which they have long had in their lists, and for which some are now reportedly to acquire motor-rollers, has rarely ever been done unless an industrial enterprise or farm had the means and incentive to undertake it. Soviets can make rules, but rarely do, for good order and impose minor penalties for breach of them. Things done at their offices and in their name, but requiring little deliberation by them, include recording and authentication of small transfers of property and other legal documents and such assistance as their limited staffs allowed to the district tax agent. Seven years after the 1957 legislation taxation and the collection for the state of agricultural produce (milk, eggs, meat and potatoes) was said to be taking up 70–80 per cent of their working time. Whether 1968 can produce more effect remains to be seen.

Traditionally the regime has seen advantage in advertisement by meetings of elected or otherwise presumptively representative persons of its successive seasonal or occasional purposes, and, both under Khrushchov and subsequently increased emphasis has been placed on the co-operation of such bodies with more or less spontaneous organisations for social action. District soviets have generally found more to do in this respect; from the days of Stalin on these meetings have greeted the recurrent seasons with appropriate exhortations.

In town soviets which, with their industry largely run from the ministries, have a concern of longer standing with 'services to the population', the members have still often felt the hand of the machine heavy upon them; the organisers attempt to crowd the business into too little time, and the period for discussion is fully occupied by 'a small group of deputies and numerous guests, the representatives of the authorities'.[1] It is complained that they are told of the business to be transacted only two or three days before the session, and that on the budget, in particular, they have a mass of figures hurled at them without previous preparation, so that 'nothing remains but to raise a hand quite mechanically'. The same complaint is made of the work of republican Supreme Soviets. In Kazahstan, it was reported in 1956, it had been the practice to commission speeches long in advance. Deputies assigned the task wrote out their speeches and read them at the session. There and in other republics the work of the Supreme Soviet had the character of a 'parade'.[2]

Criticism of the administration has always been a purpose of the local soviets. The local leaders have to be kept up to the mark, men with ideas for getting results advertised and restrictive local alliances split open. The soviet provides one of the means by which this may be done and through which higher levels can get matters aired and keep themselves informed. Attempts to suppress such criticism are frequently denounced in the press and, in one form or another, are probably the rule rather than the exception. According to a report of 1956, the regional executive committees of Moscow, Leningrad, Khabarovsk, Krasnojarsk and Novgorod had not reported to their soviets for nine years. Only two regional executive committees in the whole of the R.S.F.S.R. had done so in the last year, together with 23.3 per cent of the district executive committees (as against 48 per cent in 1954), 46.6 per cent of those of towns (as against 7.05 per cent) and 24.6 per cent of the districts within towns (as against 64.7 per cent). The performance lower down was presumably better, since the all-over percentage was 67.5 (against 81.6).[3] Despite the approval of it in principle, to voice criticism is probably always a perilous activity, not to be undertaken without previous clearance from higher levels. Of the higher soviets, including probably all the Supreme Soviets, it can hardly be a real purpose; the leaders are too august, and their disgrace, if it comes, comes through other channels, unless authority wishes to reassure public discontent or teach some lesson.

Soviet deputies have some opportunity to make up for their passivity in the sessions by their intercession with the authorities on

---

[1] Letters from deputies of Voronezh town soviet, *Izvestia*, 18th May 1956.
[2] *S.G. i P.*, No. 3 of 1956, p. 7.
[3] *S.G. i P.*, No. 3 of 1956, p. 9.

behalf of their constituents. A Supreme Soviet deputy reports that since election (that is, in some sixteen months) he had received about a thousand appeals for help, most of which could be settled locally or through the appropriate ministry.[1] But even local soviet members do not find it easy. 'Your constituents ask, let us say, for the lighting of a street or the opening of a food stall. You go to the town executive committee office, and there they announce that "There is no provision for it in the budget". Deputies must often blush and admit their impotence to carry out the commissions of their constituents.'[2] Moreover, there are no residence rules for Soviet political representatives. In the local soviets—around the larger towns at least—it seems not uncommon for the deputy to live out-side the area of the soviet's authority altogether. Such limitations on local interest—which are not peculiar to the Soviet Union—prob-ably apply with even more force at the centre. The rigidities of plan and budget are probably more difficult to circumvent in Moscow than in the provinces, and it seems improbable that the generals and police chiefs and party functionaries, who make up a large part of the Supreme Soviet, have any deep roots in their constituencies. These factors, with the deputy's extreme impermanence, the in-frequency of his residence in the capital on Supreme Soviet busi-ness, and the fact that votes are committed in advance and so not available for trading, make it almost certain that they do not have a postbag of American congressional proportions. They are men of influence in a country where influence counts—the high proportion of Georgians and Armenians who have held leading posts under the regime is probably consequent, directly or indirectly, upon the presence of Stalin, Beria, Mikojan and others of their compatriots at the centre of power—but it is in their permanent professional capacities rather than in their transient character of deputies that it can best be exercised.

The soviets are also briefing conferences for their members in their capacity, which official writings emphasise, as organisers of popular effort. Membership of a soviet is an honour, a mark of favour from the government which alone in the Soviet Union can confer prestige, and which grants it only on obligation of service in the furtherance of its own purposes. The deputies are the leaders and instructors of the activists, charged to explain thoroughly to them, personally as well as by their ritual actions in the sessions, the nature and importance of the decisions of the soviet, its executive committee and higher authority, and to guide them in such purposes as carrying into effect the latest ideas on the permanent problem of

[1] V. Kositski in *Izvestia*, 23rd July 1955.
[2] Letters from deputies of Voronezh town soviet, *Izvestia*, 18th May 1956.

agriculture or local building work, by voluntary effort or otherwise. It is the practice for the soviets themselves to hold occasional meetings of their activists, and there has been some indication that confusion has developed in the minds of members and of the public as to the distinction between such meetings and the full sessions.

Service in the soviets is also regarded as a school of government, and this has been offered in explanation of the rapid turnover of members. It seems probable that this is largely humbug; at least in the Supreme Soviets the members are already too highly placed in the service of the system to benefit much from the distant view of government work which is there offered to them. The Supreme Soviet, however, is a highly artificial creation, and we cannot judge the whole system by it. It may be that there is some truth in the claim as applied to the lower levels. Service in a local soviet may offer experience of minor leadership in the local community which may lead to higher things, and the chance for the local leaders and promising new recruits to observe one another at work.

We do not have to seek for reasons why people attend the Supreme Soviet. Its membership comprises a selection of the most highly placed persons in the system. They probably find their activities there tedious, but they are no more likely to think them wrong than are the participants in the annual general meeting of a completely controlled subsidiary company—as is the Soviet State to the Communist Party—and they may well regard an occasional few days of boredom as a reasonable obligation of their station. For the more obscure minority the session is a chance to mix with the great, a chance to see and be seen; it is an outing with free transport to the capital, and at least as much excitement as attends party rallies and similar occasions in other countries. To the peasant there may be sufficient attractions of this sort even in service in a republican Supreme Soviet. In any case, the deputies have probably not much choice. Service in the Supreme Soviet or in a local soviet is an assigned duty like any other. To refuse it is to reject an important opportunity of securing a place in the establishment.

The Inner Bodies—How They are Formed

Since their earliest days the soviets have shown a persistent tendency to the formation of inner bodies, often at two or three removes from the directly elected bodies. These are commonly designated executive committees, praesidia and bureaux, usually in that order of remoteness from the elector. The last two take their names from the German and French terms respectively for the bench of chairman, vice-chairmen, secretaries and others appointed by deliberative bodies to direct their proceedings, though in fact in the Soviet system they do not perform these functions. Neither praesidium nor executive committee presides at Supreme or local soviet meetings—that is the function of the permanent or temporary chairman already mentioned.

The largest towns at least have more than one inner body. The terminology seems to be fluid; thus Moscow in 1937, when its soviet numbered over 2,000 members and its executive committee about seventy, had a praesidium of the executive committee of fifteen and a bureau of the praesidium of the executive committee of five. In the 1950s Moscow's executive committee was reduced to a chairman, a secretary, eight vice-chairmen and fifteen members; the first ten formed a praesidium (as also reported at Leningrad); in 1955, however, we hear that 'in the executive committees of the local soviets of toilers' deputies of Moscow and Leningrad, which are distinguished by the magnitude of their work, there have been established narrowly "collegial" organs, the bureau of the executive committee, consisting of the chairman of the executive committee, his vice-chairmen and the secretary. Without replacing the executive committee as a whole the bureau settles urgent questions.'[1] A decision of Moscow city executive committee of 24th March 1959 appointing its inner body of eight (chairman, two first vice-chairmen, four vice-chairmen and secretary) again called it a praesidium.

The inner body of a Supreme Soviet is designated praesidium, presumably because before 1936 the federal and republican representative bodies were themselves designated executive committees. It is chosen by the newly elected Supreme Soviet at its first meeting and, apart from replacements of individuals—not always made promptly on the occurrence of a vacancy—holds office until a successor is appointed four years later. It consists of a chairman, vice-chairmen, a secretary and members, all chosen from among the Supreme Soviet's own members with regard rather to representational considerations than to personal eminence. The chairman of the Praesidium of the federal Supreme Soviet must be chosen with special regard for the formal functions of head of state which fall more upon him than on his colleagues. The office has been held successively by the revolution's show peasant, who had the merit of having been also a worker, by a leader of the trade unions, by a widely respected soldier closely associated with the leadership since the revolution—though already clearly a spent force before he attained to the office—by a high-ranking but personally incon-

---

[1] V. D. Sorokin and Ju. E. Smelev in *S.G. i P.*, No. 6 of 1955, p. 11.

spicuous professional party secretary—though with a somewhat unusual combination in his career pattern of industrial macro-managerial and ideological, and apparently also military, special-isms, largely in a setting of the non-metropolitan territories—by one of the very few among the leaders with a continuous record of high office since revolutionary days, and since late 1965, by an-other professional party secretary with an apparently solidly con-ventional career in the oversight of mining and manufacturing in the Ukraine. The present incumbent's two immediate predecessors somewhat magnified the office—while the party first secretary was diminishing it by claiming for himself abroad the honours of a head of state; Mr. Brezhnev was unprecedented in visibly having fair prospects of effective influence still ahead of him, and Mr. Mikojan, though elderly and apparently somewhat outmanœuvred politically by Mr. Khrushchov, still seemed a more substantial figure than all but the last of his predecessors.

The function of the fifteen vice-chairmen (since abolition, in March 1958 of the additional post for the Karelo-Finnish union re-public) is to represent the sovereignty of the union republics. All are also chairmen of the praesidia of their republican Supreme Soviets; it is never suggested in Soviet sources that there is here an *ex officio* relation, and as election to the two offices rests with two different bodies it would probably be impossible to provide formally for this. But with party direction of all appointments this presents no difficulty in practice. Those appointed are usually secondary, or declining, figures in the party leadership of their republics.

The secretary of the Praesidium counts as a member of it, and usually speaks for it to the Supreme Soviet. The generous length of tenure suggests that it is not a crucial position of power, but it was apparently accounted sufficiently important to require its transfer on the death of Stalin to a secretary of the party central committee. The previous secretary, after a spell in an apparently personal post of assistant secretary, returned in September 1956. He went on in February 1957 to another high post as federal Supreme Court chair-man, being succeeded at the Praesidium by Mr. M. Georgadze, re-cently second secretary of the Communist Party of Georgia.

Besides these officers the Praesidium has a number of members —currently, since 1966, twenty and always within a range of ten about there—not appointed specifically in virtue of any capacity other than that of Supreme Soviet deputy, yet fall into a regular pattern. They always include a few of the leading figures of the party central organisation, a representation of the party regional first secretaries and of the armed forces (Marshal Budjonni, pre-sumably, as long as he survives). Others, often personally obscure, represent from time to time the autonomous units, the youth and women's organisations, science and learning.

In the union and autonomous republics the number of vice-chairmen and members differs. The R.S.F.S.R. has sixteen vice-chairmen, one for each of its autonomous republics; Georgia has two, who are specifically stated to represent its two autonomous republics; and Azerbaidjan one each for both its autonomous republic and its autonomous region. Uzbekistan, with only one auto-nomous republic, and Kazahstan, with none, have three vice-chair-men. Other republics, without autonomous republics have two. All autonomous republics have two vice-chairmen (except the North Ossetian, with one). Members, in both types of republic, number from five to fifteen.

Below the republican level, and so the level of Supreme Soviets, the corresponding organs are designated executive committees. According to Article 99 of the federal constitution they consist of a chairman, vice-chairmen, a secretary and members. Usually they seem to have some seven to fifteen members in all. The constitution also provides in Article 100 that for the smallest of the village soviets no executive committee need be appointed; the executive and administrative functions of the soviet are there performed by a chairman, vice-chairman and secretary elected by the soviet. It is not clear how this differed from an executive committee except in the absence of the obligation to appoint members other than the three designated office holders; Soviet writers suggest that in many such cases these 'in reality form an unofficial executive committee of the soviet'[1] with all its powers, and declare incorrect the view that in such cases all business must be taken in full soviet. It is suggested that absence of an executive committee sometimes en-courages personal rule by the chairman[2]—though this seems not uncommon even where there is one. In any case with the consoli-dation of the village soviets and an official campaign for executive committees this arrangement, formerly common—e.g. in 600 of the 882 village soviets in Tula region before the mid-'fifties—seems to have become a thing of the past.

Formally the election of the executive committee, including the designation of the chairman, vice-chairman and secretary, requires a vote of the soviet, with confirmation at the next higher level. Actu-ally, the chairman is appointed to office by the party committee at the immediately superior level (e.g. the region for a district chair-manship). In general social consequence he ranks immediately after the party first secretary at his own level—who, himself, appears to

[1] G. I. Petrov in *S.G. i P.*, No. 8 of 1955, p. 32.
[2] *Izvestia*, 29th July 1954.

be always a member of the executive committee—and it is a common occurrence for him to succeed to the party office. Apart from the obligation to include the vice-chairman and secretary—appointed by the party committee at the soviet's own level—he seems otherwise fairly free to choose, and dismiss, the other members of the executive committee; he evidently needs the confirmation of the next higher authorities in both the party and the soviet executive committee hierarchies, which if he is in good standing should cause him no trouble. For the most part he has looked to his departmental heads, but a drive over the last few years for more popular participation in local affairs is supposed to have, and probably has, produced some change in this respect. According to an early 1964 source,[1] 'If in the executive committee of Moscow regional soviet in 1961 there were 25 people, of whom only three (a carpet factory foreman, a village soviet executive committee chairman and a district executive committee chairman) were not heads of regional organisations, now of 36 people elected to the Moscow rural and industrial regional executive committees in 1962 eleven are employed directly in the sphere of material production.'

Objections by soviets to the list put before them for appointments for which they are nominally responsible seem to be rare and quite ineffective.[2] So submissive are they that it seems not to be uncommon for them to allow their executive offices to be given to persons not among their own membership, which is not only improbably generous but also plainly illegal. At the beginning of 1956, it seems, 534 persons were serving as chairmen of the executive committees of local soviets in the R.S.F.S.R. of which they had not been elected deputies, and a further 1,491 were similarly serving as vice-chairmen or secretaries. In 1954, 1,411 of the 13,311 chairmen of executive committees in the Ukraine and 1,643 of the equal number of secretaries were not qualified for their office by membership of the soviets.[3] It is not clear why the party did not have them elected to the soviet; lack of time is a possible explanation in view of the accounts which we get of the frequency of transfer of such officials, as of other managerial personnel. Another factor may be indifference to forms such as is expressed in the apparently common failure to hold by-elections to fill vacancies in local soviets.

[1] M. S. Sladkov in *S.G. i P.*, No. 2 of 1964.
[2] T. H. R. Rigby, *The Selection of Leading Personnel in the Soviet State and Communist Party* (London University Ph.D. Thesis, 1954), pp. 388–9, 390 (Work quoted in further references as Rigby, Thesis.) finds no case of objection to executive committee lists. *Izvestia*, 18th December 1954 reports one to appointment of a village soviet chairman, allegedy improperly motivated and badly handled.
[3] *S.G. i P.*, No. 3 of 1956, p. 9.

The indications are, then, that the chairman's control over his colleagues is far-reaching. Certainly according to the principle of one-man headship it is he who must take the blame for whatever goes wrong; but again, according to the equally emphasised principle of collegiality, he will lay himself open to censure if he does not consult his colleagues in the executive committee on all matters except those of the greatest urgency. It is probable that, in general, the executive committee is an effective deliberative body, as the soviet which elects it is not. But it is not a parliament; it is a cabinet composed predominantly, though not entirely, of departmental ministers engaged in full-time public service. They are not politicians but officials, of whom probably most look to make their way in the same branch of state service at higher levels; departure into such activities as the management of a collective farm may, however, diversify, and if successful probably materially advance any career, and full-time party office opens the way to the big prizes.

The union and republican praesidia were from the first deprived of departmental responsibilities by the creation of the Councils of People's Commissars, now the Councils of Ministers, and these latter are the true counterpart at these levels of the executive committees. Article 71 of the federal constitution and Russian legal writers refer to the federal Council of Ministers as the Government (praviteljstvo) of the U.S.S.R., though such analogies as this suggests with other systems are largely misleading. By Article 70 the Council of Ministers is composed of a chairman, an unspecified number of first vice-chairmen and vice-chairmen, ministers heading ministries designated in the constitution (fifty-five in May 1968), designated chairmen of boards (thirteen at the same date), the Head (nachaljnik) of the Central Statistical Administration and the fifteen chairmen of union republic councils of ministers. These last, added in 1957, serve ex officio; appointment of others is by edict of the Praesidium, with later confirmation by the Supreme Soviet, or occasionally directly by decree of that body if it happens to be sitting. In May 1968 there were two first vice-chairmen, and nine vice-chairmen (three also holding designated offices). This gives a Council of ninety-six (fourteen working outside Moscow[1]). Clearly even without other possible attenders, it is no cabinet.

In the Khrushchov period, when the number of designated Council of Ministers posts at the centre was approximately halved, extensive use was made of personal appointment as minister, which conferred membership. These appointments were terminated at the

[1] But at least two union republics (and probably all) have also a permanent representative attached to the federal council.

end of 1965, but the device could apparently be used again without formality.

The departments represented in the Council of Ministers are highly impermanent and their heads of small personal consequence. Most are specialists, risen through factory management, changing their designations from time to time, but rarely straying far from the range of business in which they have made their careers. If a change of administrative organisation sweeps away their ministerial office at federal level they commonly move to similar work at union republic or lower level or revert to deputy-minister status. Occasionally a reorganisation gives an opportunity to broaden out to a wider field of action centred round the same technical specialism; transfer for a spell to one of the co-ordinating and planning bodies gives wider career prospects. But in general it is not from such men that the general management of the Soviet Union is recruited. A career of party office more commonly forms the all-round man who is supposed to understand how the whole system meshes and is rewarded accordingly.

The relative obscurity of the subjects, with the opacity of Soviet affairs generally, allows us few rounded examples of such careers. One is the late Mr. I. A. Lihachov, who after twenty-four years as director of the country's largest motor vehicle factory became in 1953 federal Minister of Motor Transport and Highways, and on the abolition of the federal ministry in May 1957 removed to the similarly named post in the government of the R.S.F.S.R. The late Mr. I. I. Nosenko, who made his career, crowned with ministerial office, in shipbuilding, made two excursions into wider fields as Minister of Transport Machine Building and Minister of Transport and Heavy Machine Building during periods of ministry amalgamation. Mr. N. S. Ryzhov moved round a narrow circle of ministries—textiles, consumer goods and (twice) light industry—before being sent as ambassador to Turkey in February 1957. Mr. G. M. Orlov, came from a research background in paper to take charge of the timber, paper and pulp industry, under a variety of titles, at federal or, briefly, R.S.F.S.R. level from 1956 to the end of 1965; his successor came from chairmanship of the Council of the economy in the timber-growing economic district of Arhangelsk. Mr. A. N. Kosygin, who replaced Mr. Khrushchov as Chairman, is, unusually, a technical specialist in a top generalist post, having advanced from qualification in textile technology through factory management in the same industry. He showed, however, distinctive political sense in his willingness and ability in the Stalin period to adapt his field of industry to the low priority which the leader assigned to it.

Some, particularly those of the revolutionary generation or with considerable experience of party office—categories which have contained the most eminent—have been more versatile. The late Mr. A. P. Zavenjagin diversified a career in ferrous metallurgy with a period in Internal Affairs (i.e. police) when that ministry had a sizeable industrial empire of its own, and ended with responsibility for atomic energy under the title of Minister for Medium Machine Building. Mr. L. M. Kaganovich, who fell in the power conflict of 1957, held ministerial office in transport—which was considered his speciality—heavy industry, the fuel industry, foreign trade and the building materials industry. The Ministry of Foreign Affairs has been exceptional in requiring at all times an intimate of the leaders rather than a technical specialist, though with the appointment of Mr. A. A. Gromyko in February 1957 it has come nearer to the general pattern—perhaps only temporarily to meet a particular internal power situation.

In the rush of joint decisions of the party Central Committee, Council of Ministers and Supreme Soviet Praesidium upon Stalin's death there was one 'to recognise the necessity of having within the Council of Ministers, in place of two organs, the praesidium and the bureau of the praesidium, one organ, the Praesidium of the Council of Ministers of the U.S.S.R.'[1] There had been both an inner cabinet and an inner-inner cabinet, both undisclosed; only the former was to remain. The membership of this was defined as consisting of the chairman of the Council of Ministers and the first vice-chairmen. At the time Mr. G. M. Malenkov held the former office and there were four of the latter—the late Mr. L. P. Beria, Mr. Molotov, Mr. N. A. Bulganin and Mr. Kaganovich. There were then no vice-chairmen not designated 'first', though when the Supreme Soviet met a few days later Mr. Mikojan was so appointed, presumably without membership of this Praesidium. It is impossible to say whether for practical purposes such a body still exists and, if so, whether it has now grown large enough to have its own bureau, as under Stalin. The situation after the deposition of Mr. Khrushchov resembled the earlier transitional power situation in that there was again a formal separation of the highest party and state offices and some apparent attempt to establish a balance of personal authority between the two party officials occupying them. It is therefore the more probable—as it is in any case probable—that the orders which come from the party to the assembly of heads of department which is the Council of Ministers are first considered, at least for purposes of arrangement of business, by some inner group.

All eighty-four members of the federal government elected in

[1] Published 7th March, 1953 in *Pravda* and generally.

August 1955 were members of the Supreme Soviet—the republican chairmen divided, perhaps surprisingly, 10–5 in favour of the Soviet of the Union, the others with a majority of one for the Soviet of Nationalities. This was an unprecedented representation. In 1962 eleven government members—of fifty-six, other than republican chairmen—and in 1954 over thirty were members of neither house.

It does not, in any case, matter much. As is the practice in other countries of continental Europe, ministers who are not members are allowed to speak in either house in connection, though not always very close connection, with legislation or other business concerning their ministeries. Their appearance is particularly frequent in debates on the budget and plan. Since before the 1957 sessions the power under Article 71 of the constitution to put questions to ministers or to the government as a whole for oral or written answer was not exercised, general ministerial attendance was unnecessary. The contrived and restrained interpellations at the sessions of February and May 1957 and December 1965 suggest no change of substance in this situation. Nor, since the Supreme Soviet has no part in the making or breaking of ministers, does it seem that members need to have a close acquaintance with them, though their presence may be considered one of the metropolitan attractions for the senior shepherds, foreman weavers and trawler captains. Ministers of the U.S.S.R. are officials rather than politicians, as also are local executive committee members.

Governments of union republics and autonomous republics are similarly composed and readily responsive to changes of pattern or terminology at the centre. At all stages they have contained a substantial majority of members owing direct and manifest allegiance to a department—whether designated 'ministry', 'state committee' or by some other name—in a higher government. In the Khrushchov period they followed the federal practice of admitting heads of a variety of councils and committees personally appointed to ministerial rank.[1] They similarly followed in revealing the existence of an inner body, perhaps called a 'bureau' rather than a 'praesidium'.

What They Do

Apart from the acts of their several members, Councils of Ministers at all levels are, like the Tsars' Committee of Ministers, empowered to issue decrees (*postanovlenie*) and dispositions(*rasporjazhenie*) in their corporate capacities. The former category, issued

---

[1] Previously the usual membership had been about thirty. See, e.g., particulars for the Central Asian republics given by B. Hayit, *Osteuropa*, No. 2 of 1956.

over the signatures of the chairman and the head of the office, 'are, as a rule, normative acts'[1]—though they seem to include at least the more important official appointments—the latter, signed by a vice-chairman, deal apparently with particular cases. In principle such measures can only be in amplification of a law (*zakon*), but in fact the laws are few and vague, and, as we have suggested, the Council of Ministers is the principal source of Soviet legislation. Soviet writers insist on the inferiority of such acts in standing to laws, but 'The decrees and dispositions of the Council of Ministers are not subject to oversight in respect of their legality by any organs except superior organs of state authority. Acts of the government are obligatory for unconditional application by all, including the courts.'[2] Only the Supreme Soviet and its Praesidium can disallow, so that in practice such acts are equal in authority to laws. The Council is also responsible for approving the instruments (*polozhenie*) defining the organisations of the several ministries and for giving them general directions. Thus we find the Latvian Council of Ministers in June 1953 directing the Ministry of Housing and Civil Building to undertake important constructional work in one of the districts, and subsequently being called to account for failing to insist on progress reports from it. Councils are empowered[3] to disallow orders and instructions of the several ministers. The Praesidium of the Council of Ministers has not legislated in its own name; it has been concerned with policy, much as are cabinets in other political systems.

The legislation made by means of the Praesidium of the Supreme Soviet is less in volume than that of the Council of Ministers, but it is substantial, and much of it is important. Not all its measures need confirmation by the Supreme Soviet, only its appointments of ministers and 'those decrees which the Praesidium of the Supreme Soviet of the U.S.S.R. has made in the interval between sessions in the process of partial fulfilment of the obligations of the Supreme Soviet of the U.S.S.R.'[4] Such decrees may extend to the creation of new criminal offences, important changes in civil law and the establishment or abolition of government departments. Interpretation of laws, which the constitution leaves to the Praesidium, is a negligible part of its work. The granting of honours and awards and the movement of diplomatic staff form a large part of its published acts. Its ministerial appointments are made declaredly on the pro-

---

[1] Ts. A. Jampolskaja, *Organy sovetskogo gosudarstvennogo upravlenija v sovremenny period* (1953), p. 169.

[2] V. F. Kotok in Askerov et al., op. cit., pp. 295–6.

[3] Article 69 of the federal constitution.

[4] A. M. Vasiliev in *S.G. i P.*, No. 8 of 1953.

posal of the chairman of the Council of Ministers, which probably has a similar hand in its other acts.

We have what purport to be accounts of proceedings at meetings of the federal Council of Ministers, and presumably such bodies do sometimes meet in full session to settle inter-departmental problems in legislative and other operations, though perhaps not often. Meetings of the Praesidium of the federal Supreme Soviet, alleged to take place every other month, have since October 1967 been noted in general terms. This somewhat strains belief; the requirement that for representative purposes its members should be selected from geographically widely dispersed locations, and their very unequal functional and social consequence unfit it for regular work as a deliberative body. Some of the matters which it is declared to consider in session, such as election returns and ratification of international agreements, do not obviously admit of such treatment. Its edicts are signed only by chairman and secretary, with rare exceptions as when the chairman has been abroad or when the edict was to confer a decoration on the chairman himself; then a vice-chairman signed in his place. In the smaller republics the institution may perhaps work better. The Armenian Praesidium is said to have held regular sessions, hearing reports, from the chairman of the Council of Ministers among others, on action on suggestions from Supreme Soviet members, and taking action through its own instructors for the improvement of administrative methods in the republic at large. Even the Praesidium of the Council of Ministers, which looks like an effective cabinet, has not been a negotiation of diverse political forces, despite the presence of conflicts of personality. It was a co-optive team, and largely a form of action for persons with a real standing derived from their position and connections in the highest organs of the party. It is difficult and not very meaningful to determine whether at any given moment they were acting in their party or their state capacity.

These inner bodies play a constitutionally declared part in the Soviet system of multiple supervision. Under Article 69 of the federal constitution the Council of Ministers has the power to suspend decisions and orders of the Councils of Ministers of the union republics 'in respect of those branches of administration and economy which come within the jurisdiction of the U.S.S.R.', which in practice means any in which it is disposed to interest itself. Thereafter action would presumably be taken under Article 49, by which the Praesidium of the Supreme Soviet may annul decisions and orders of both the federal and the union republican Councils of Ministers if they do not conform to law. No details of any such cases of disallowance have been published; if there have been any they can only have been disallowances of republican, not of federal, measures. The Praesidium of the Supreme Soviet is obviously a weaker body than the Praesidium of the Council of Ministers, and probably than the Council of Ministers as a whole in respect of the importance of its members. Below, the government of a union republic, it seems, has as one of its major tasks systematic consideration of reports from the corresponding organs at the next lower level, Councils of Ministers of autonomous republics and executive committees of territories or regions—or districts if the republic is not divided into regions—on their work, usually accompanied by 'co-reports of persons who upon the instructions of the Council of Ministers have previously examined the activity of the executive committee concerned'.[1] The same happens at these lower levels. The republican Council of Ministers may disallow acts of a ministry, or local executive committee. It may suspend those of a local soviet.

It is a frequent charge against local administration in the Soviet Union that there is wasteful duplication of business between the soviets and their executive committees.[2] The executive committee does in fact seem to have rather more in common with its soviet than with the Council of Ministers in that it is largely trying to understand, assist and make popularly acceptable policies which have not only been decided on elsewhere but are largely being applied through other channels. Official doctrine denies the existence of any distinction between central and local government. The executive committee is the agent of the soviet at its own level and of the whole system of the state, and is accountable to the latter, through the executive committee at the next higher level, as well as to the former. Encouragement to concern themselves with the well-being of the local people, in compensation for the loss of their more effective agricultural powers—though not of all agricultural responsibility—may give new self-reliance to rural district executive committees, if higher authorities will allow use of resources for purposes in which they are comparatively uninterested.

Previously district executive committees have shown the same markedly economic bias as the higher levels. Checking on preparations for, and performances in, the successive operations of the farming year, and transmission of the approved sentiments upon them—often, it was alleged, without any very careful investigation of local circumstances—seem to have been the stuff of their work in the rural areas.

Another class of business mentioned as belonging to the soviets is

[1] Jampolskaja, op. cit., p. 208.
[2] See, e.g., M. A. Shafir in *S.G. i P.*, No. 10 of 1964, p. 27 (concerning village soviets).

the carrying out of the military call-up and the maintenance of records of defence obligations in respect of liability to provide horses and transport, as well as the certification and administration of the privileges and benefits belonging to the dependants of service men.

In the towns the work was already as it has lately been supposed to become in the districts, with most of industry under direct control of higher levels, and so limited scope for local action. Even in 1931 there were noted 'views that there is nothing for the town soviets to do, since all the most important measures pass them by'. They were reminded that there was scope for them in public works and the organisation of the food supply, and that 'the restaurant is a workshop of the factory'.[1] To the present day it is probably true to say that the activity of the town soviet and executive committee is probably nearer to that of West European local authorities than that of other soviets and executive committees, though the difference is one of degree only; economic affairs still remain prominent, at least in the form of a concern for the supply and marketing of consumer goods, and even social affairs are wider in scope than in other countries by reason of the very limited field left in the Soviet Union to private initiative of any sort. There we find executive committees heavily burdened with business on such matters as housing, the recognition of entitlement to accommodation and to various forms of social-service benefits, adoption orders and transfer of personal property. It has been complained that under present legislation they are obliged to waste time considering claims to benefit which on the basis of the facts as determined and reported to them by their officials they are not empowered to reject.

Executive committees are required to agitate with the appropriate ministry concerning any neglect of local interest, and slackness on the part of the ministry is not an excuse which will save them from denunciation in the press if nothing is done. As with higher soviet organs they issue formal acts of two classes: 'decisions' (*reshenie*) issued on the basis of collective deliberation, and 'dispositions' (*rasporjazhenie*) issued by individuals—at present, it seems, only the chairman, though it has recently been suggested that this should be extended to his deputies for the departments entrusted to them— though in the name of the executive committee as a whole. In 1953 the Leningrad town soviet gave 3,100 decisions and 1,736 dispositions; in 1954 the figures were down to 2,025 and 1,458 respectively as a result of one of the periodic offensives against bureaucracy. As in any other administrative system, there must be much business done in the name of the executive committee which it does not need

[1] Leading article in *S.G. i R.P.*, No. 1 of 1931, p. 3.

to discuss, and, as we have seen with village soviets,[1] this routine office work may well be seen by the authorities as the main practical justification for the soviets and their inner bodies. In eight months of 1954 the town executive committee of Millerovo (Kamensk region, R.S.F.S.R.) issued to citizens 6,000 certificates of various kinds and certified 4,000 entitlement books for state assistance, more than 3,000 forms for obtaining internal passports and 3,000 fuel books for railway personnel. It was suggested (by the secretary) that the number of such documents could be reduced by a half or two-thirds.[2]

District and town executive committees generally, it seems, meet two or three times a month, and those of villages somewhat less frequently. This is held to be sufficient for matters requiring collective consideration and, Soviet writers say, the distraction of a large number of meetings is detrimental to the day-to-day guiding work of the executive committee. Much of the detailed business, it is suggested, might be transacted out of the session by the chairman, secretary and others directly concerned, though this might require minor amendment of the law. Cases of meetings being held up to eight times a month are reported, and some are inordinately long. *Izvestia* reported in 1950 a meeting of Voronezh regional executive committee, which took twelve hours and covered seventy-five questions. The executive committees meet in private and do not publish minutes, but there are indications in the form of criticisms in the press to suggest that debate, though freer than in the soviet, is not free or always effective. In the usual fashion of soviet administration the chairman is liable to rebuke from higher quarters if he does not give due attention to his colleagues, but is held personally responsible, at peril of his own career, if plans are not fulfilled in good measure and time. The executive committee as a whole is often rebuked for failure to engage the members of the soviet or standing commissions in the conduct of its work; it 'severs itself from the masses and works in a rut'.[3]

The supervision exercised over an executive committee is not intended to be dependent solely on the zeal of its immediate superior. If the latter does not take action it is the duty of its own superior to do so. Regional executive committees are commended in the press for supervising carefully the direction of villages by districts.

[1] See p. 78.
[2] *Izvestia*, 6th October 1954.
[3] *Partijnaja Zhin* (No. 12 of 1947) complains that many members of executive committees consider that only the instruction department is concerned to see that all soviet deputies are involved in the work of the soviet, whereas it should be the concern of all.

Yet, in general, supervision remains inadequate. An *Izvestia* article of September 1955 complained that this had meant that the procurator's office had had to enter objections against 161 decisions and dispositions of local soviet executive committees in 1954 and 124 in 1955. The regional and territorial executive committees, it was complained, rarely took the trouble to check up on what their counterparts at district and village level were doing. Some higher executive committees merely added to the burdens upon their subordinates by insisting that the latter discuss at their meetings the higher level's latest decisions.[1] This is perhaps a residue of recent illiteracy, where the written word does not mean much unless read out and illustrated.

The praesidia and executive committees provide means by which the strictly managerial quality of the Russian political system may be reconciled with the myth of the supremacy of the soviets which is fundamental to the ideology. They are at best no more dependent on election than are most boards of directors in the British economy, and are selected for much the same tasks on the basis of much the same qualities, but it is in the name of the elected bodies that they act. This is exemplified in the gazette of Acts of the Supreme Soviet, which is filled almost entirely with decisions of its Praesidium. The myth is less strictly kept up at the local level, where the whole staff and organisation are ascribed to the executive committee and not to the soviet. Russian sources speak in general terms of the soviet structure, meaning the state as distinct from the party chain of command, but they always refer to the departments, or the officials, of the regional executive committee, rather than to the regional soviet.

Relations between executive committees and supposedly more direct offshoots of the elected bodies, such as standing committees, have latterly been subjected to press criticism. Unpromisingly, the suggestion has been made of a further body, a praesidium, to coordinate.

The Ministries and Departments

The U.S.S.R. constitution as at May 1968 declared the existence of the following ministries:

[1] G. I. Petrov in *S.G. i P.*, No. 8 of 1955, p. 25. The same writer (in *S.G. i P.*, No 6 of 1953, p. 62) stated that executive committees of district soviets rightly 'give guiding instructions' on the preparation and conduct of village-soviet sessions, 'but they must not themselves plan the conduct of the sessions', since this is constitutionally a responsibility of the village chairman. Such fine distinctions between educative guidance and maniulation must make life very difficult for the soviet official.

All-Union:[1]
External Trade
Maritime Fleet (i.e. merchant-shipping)
Ways of Communication (running the railways)
Automobile Industry
Aviation Industry
Chemical and Oil Machine-building
Civil Aviation
Construction, Road-making and Public Works Machine Building
Defence Industry
Electronics Industry
Electrical Engineering Industry
Gas Industry
General Machine Building
Heavy, Power and Transport Machine Building
Instrument Making, Automation and Control Systems
Machine Building
Machine Building for Light and Food Industries and Domestic
    Appliances
Machine-tool and Appliance Industry
Medical Supplies Industry
Medium Machine Building
Radio Industry
Shipbuilding Industry
Tractors and Agricultural Machine Building
Transport Construction

Of these only the first three had been in existence at the time of
Mr. Khrushchov's departure from office, though State Committees
of similar title, and probably similar function, to the others had
been operative.

Union Republican:[2]
Agriculture
Communications (i.e. posts and telecommunications)
Culture (concerned with forms of intellectual influence other than
    formal education)
Defence
Finance
Foreign Affairs
Health Protection
Higher and Specialised Middle Education
Chemical Industry

[1] Article 77 of the constitution.
[2] Article 78.

Coal Industry
Commerce
Construction
Construction Materials Industry
Construction of Heavy Industrial Enterprises
Education
Ferrous Metallurgy
Fisheries
Food Industry
Geology
Industrial Construction
Installation and Special Construction Works
Land Improvement and Water-resource Management
Light Industry
Meat and Dairy Industry
Nonferrous Metallurgy
Oil Extraction Industry
Oil Refining and Petrochemicals Industry
Power and Electrification
Preservation of Public Order (i.e. general police)[1]
Rural Construction
Timber, Woodpulp and Wood-processing Industry

Of these the first eight came down from the Khrushchov era. Again, concentration on the form may exaggerate the extent of the change; most of the functions covered by these ministries had been fairly obviously the responsibility of State Committees or other identifiable bodies under the previous order. Clearly, however, ministries were again the favoured instruments of administration as much as in the high Stalin period; the list was somewhat changed, with a similar array of various types of machine building under unrevealing but traditional names; (Medium Machine Building, for example, was usually responsible for atomic energy), more emphasis on construction, in which area four new ministries were created in February 1967, and fewer non-economic agencies.

Other Departments and Agencies of Ministerial Rank:[2]

The State Planning Committee of the Council of Ministers of the U.S.S.R. (Gosplan SSSR)
The State Committees of the Council of Ministers of the U.S.S.R.
for Building Matters (Gosstroi SSSR)
for Material and Technical Supply (Gossnab SSSR)

[1] Reverted at end of 1968 to its former, more evocative, name of Ministry of Internal Affairs (MVD).
[2] Article 70 of the Constitution.

for External Economic Relations
on Labour and Pay Questions
for Science and Technology
for Vocational and Technical Education
The State Committee for Agricultural Deliveries of the Council of
Ministers of the U.S.S.R.
The State Committee on Forestry of the Council of Ministers of
the U.S.S.R.
The Committee of People's Control of the U.S.S.R.
The Committee of State Security attached to the Council of
Ministers of the U.S.S.R.
The All-Union Agricultural Machinery Association (Sel'hoztehnika)
The State Bank of the U.S.S.R.
The Central Statistical Administration attached to the Council of
Ministers of the U.S.S.R.

Agencies not of Ministerial Rank:[1]

In addition to the bodies named in the Constitution as represented by their heads (Ministers or others) in the Council, others mentioned in early 1968 as answering directly to it were:

The All-Union Bank for Financing Capital Investment (Stroibank)

and the following economic agencies with names suffixed 'attached to the Council of Ministers of the U.S.S.R.':

State Committee for Industrial Safety and Mine Inspection
Committees for: Matters of Invention and Discovery; Standards, Measures and Measuring Equipment; Cultural Relations with Foreign Countries; Cinematography; The Press; Radio and Television
The Chief Administration of the Microbiological Industry
The Chief Administration for the Hydrometeorological Service
The State Commission on Reserves of Useful Minerals

This last category is unlikely to be exhaustive, and it would be surprising if it, or any other part of this administrative structure, should prove to be in any substantial sense permanent. The Council of Ministers has always reflected the fluidity of the system, both in its own composition and in the list of commissions, committees and chief administrations, surviving from disbanded ministries, not yet incorporated in projected ministries or, like the long-standing and

[1] *Ekonomicheskaja Gazeta*, No. 10 of 1968.

apparently still extant Commission on Religious Affairs, unlikely ever to make ministerial status. Nomenclature, while broadly indicative of standing, does not usually seem to aim at a precision which the nature of the system would be likely to frustrate. The distinction between being 'of' and being 'attached to' (*pri*) the Council of Ministers seems to be broadly indicative, but the placing of the Council in the titles of the various bodies which are of it is probably rather aesthetic than administrative, and the choice of 'committee', 'council' or some other designation for a new body may owe more to the moment of its inception than to the intended function.

Some names are, to at least a limited extent, under the protection of tradition; the short title of Gosplan seems to be safe, though the long title is not invulnerable, and tradition has not availed to protect the agency from some abrupt discontinuities in its functions. Usually concerned with the whole operation of planning, it has sometimes been relieved of responsibility for the shorter term, but briefly in 1962 its name was used for a body concerned exclusively with short term planning. In the latter phases of the Khrushchov reign, when the unity of the several industries was being reasserted against the claims of regionalism implied in the sovnarkhoz structure it apparently fell to Gosplan to be the principal agent of that aspect of co-ordination.

This late-Khrushchovian period produced, in organisational titles and in occasional formal expositions, rather more explicit indications of hierarchic structure at the centre than the system had ordinarily been accustomed to give. Of the State Production Committees—broadly, the industrial management ministries then re-emergent under another name, and now restored to their traditional style—and other State Committees which then formed the apparatus of government, some, particularly concerned with construction, were declaredly 'attached to' Gosstroi; others, mostly specially involved in technological innovation, answered to the apex bodies of the structure of Councils of the Economy, then represented in the Council of Ministers: most answered to Gosplan. The present arrangements for co-ordination seem not to have been thus formally proclaimed, but it seems very probable that some of the agencies under the Council still exercise this function on its behalf and that for Gosstroi at least this remains the main task.

Distinctions between all-union and union-republican agencies, traditional—and constitutionally declared—among ministries are made between state committees also, but with reservations. All-union ministries are those which exist only at federal level and manage directly all their concerns wherever situated throughout the

U.S.S.R. 'Union republican ministry', by an inconvenience of
terminology which exists in Russian as well as in English, means
not a ministry existing at the level of a union republic, but one
which exists both at that level—not necessarily in all fifteen union
republics—and at federal level. A third category, republican ministries, are those at republic level which have no direct superior in the
federation; relatively few and unimportant under Stalin, their range
has latterly been somewhat extended. Again, the Khrushchov period
having to explain the adaptation of this convention to a structure
predominantly of State Committees rather than ministries shed some
rather unsurprising light on manner of operation. A committee of
all-union character might then perform some of its functions
through agencies in the republics not under its direct jurisdiction;
one of union-republican character might in different republics work
through agencies of different status. The return of the ministries
may well bring back much of the administrative particularism
which was declared to have earned them their previous abolition.
The General Instrument on Ministries issued in July 1967 by the
Federal Council of Ministers and concerned only with the ministries
formally so designated, to the exclusion of the remaining State
Committees and other government bodies, makes no provision for
co-ordination at any level below the Council itself. The size of this
body, in itself, makes it seem very probable that there is in fact
some other machinery for that purpose, and it seems likely that
Gosstroi at least retains something of its former second-tier function
for agencies in its field. The tradition of the administrative system,
however, in this part, as in the whole, has been one of *ad hoc*
arrangements rather than of the ingenious but fragile institutionalisa-
tions which sprang so readily from the former leader.

By May 1968 the R.S.F.S.R. Council of Ministers contained all
the union-republican ministries existing at federal level except
Defence—which no republic has formed—Construction—which the
R.S.F.S.R. had in April 1967 removed from its Republican list but
not yet re-opened as Union-republican—Construction of Heavy
Industrial Enterprises, Industrial Construction, Installation and
Special Construction Works, Power and Electrification, the
Chemical and Coal industries, the two oil industries, the two
metallurgical industries and the Preservation of Public Order. The
title of the timber ministry was simplified to Ministry of Forestry.
Republican ministries then were:

Education
Grain Products and Animal Feeds
Local Public Works (*komunalnoje hozjajstvo*)

Motor Transport and Highways
River Fleet
Social Security
Fuel Industry
Public Amenity Services (*bytovoye obsluzhivanje naselenija*)

The first six of these dated back to the Khrushchov period, though with some change of title and functions for Grain Products—concerned with procurement and marketing of agricultural produce. The R.S.F.S.R., like the Union government, had its Gosplan, Gosstroi, State Committee for Vocational and Technical Education, Seljhoztehnika and Central Statistical Administration, as well as a State Committee of Council of Ministers rank for Use of Labour Reserves (training and placement of young technicians). Committees existed for Cinematography and the Press, and among chief administrations attached directly to the Council of Ministers were:

Supply and Disposal (i.e. procurement of materials for industry
    and provision of outlets for products)
Transport and Supply of Oil
Viticulture and Wine making

The ministries and other administrative organs of autonomous republics have not been divided into categories corresponding to the distinction between union-republican and republican ministries; all have been subject to some ministry or similar body at the level of the union republic, which might itself be of either type.

The departments and administrations to be formed by local executive committee have been presented in republican constitutions. For territorial and regional soviets in the R.S.F.S.R. the list as prescribed in June 1967, when something like traditional order was restored after the extreme complexities introduced by Mr. Khrushchov's 1963 splitting of industrial and rural soviets, was

Departments:

Finance
General Affairs
Health Preservation
Popular Instruction
Social Security
Building and Architecture
Organisation and Instruction (general administrative inspectorate)

Administrations:

Commerce
Culture

Local Industry
Local Public Works
Agriculture
Building and Repair of Motor Roads
Construction Materials Industry
Food Industry
Fuel Industry
Meat and Dairy Industry
Preservation of Public Order
as well as a Planning Commission.

Other agencies might, with approval of the Council of Ministers of the republic, be formed to provide for special features of the local economy.

Towns were to form Planning Commissions and bodies corresponding to the first five in the first and the first four in the second of the above lists (Local Industry only where appropriate and with approval of the Council of Ministers, and Commerce and Culture as Departments). Departments or Administrations as appropriate might be sanctioned for Militia (operative police force).

District executive committees seemed at that stage to have a departmental structure closely resembling that of the towns without the provisions for local industry or for establishing some of their agencies at the higher level of 'administrations'—though what, in any case, the distinction means in terms of the administrative resources available on the local scale of operation is by no means clear.

For all categories of executive committees the prescribed external organisation has changed little over the whole post-Stalin period, though the number of committees (or soviets) themselves has changed considerably, and the upper tier have seen their organisations divided—though with retention of some common departments —and re-united in the course of the Khrushchov experiment. The towns and districts did not in general suffer this form of disruption, though the latter had still not, by May 1968, recovered their agricultural administrations which had once been one of their principal organs and which, not for the first time, they had lost during that period of upheaval. They continued, as they had throughout, to be held responsible for the functioning of agriculture in their areas, but without administrative means of doing anything effective about it.

For the village soviets, for which this experience of responsibility without means had long been familiar, no organisation was prescribed and in most areas staff continued to be scarce, ill-distributed, untrained and grossly underpaid,[1] despite widespread amalgamations over the last few years.

The central establishments of the several federal ministries are, by the general instrument of July 1967, to be determined by the Council of Ministers, and within them the ministers are empowered to make their own dispositions. The establishments, and apparently the powers, of the republican levels of ministries of union-republican type are to be prescribed in an instrument (*polozhenie*) approved by the republican Council of Ministers in concert with the corresponding Ministry at federal level. Ministers are required to have a number of deputy ministers—like themselves specialist officials rather than politicians although a few of them appear in the Supreme Soviet. Six or seven—with one or more designated 'first'—seems a common provision. With other officials appointed by the Council of Ministers they form the minister's collegium, in agreement with which he is supposed to work, subject to their right of appeal to the Council of Ministers.

Appointments of ministers and of chairmen of bodies conferring *ex officio* membership of the Council of Ministers are made by edict of the Praesidium of the corresponding Supreme Soviet. Appointments of deputy ministers, vice-chairmen and members of such bodies and of all members, including chairmen, of other state committees are made by act of the Council of Ministers itself. Appointments of heads of soviet executive committee departments are formally made by the executive committee with confirmation by the head of the corresponding branch at the next higher level (the minister for regional appointments). In fact it is not concealed that the most important—those likely to carry membership of the executive committee itself—are made and confirmed by the corresponding party committees.

The structure of a Soviet ministry was always more closely comparable to the head office of a large firm than to a ministry as known in most non-socialist countries. The general instrument on U.S.S.R. ministries sets their tasks firmly in economic terms—the general development of the several branches of the economy entrusted to them, fulfilment of plan tasks, improvement of productivity, of technology and the use of capital, personnel development and improvement of labour conditions.

The two classes of acts issued by ministers, as distinct from, and subordinate to, those of the Councils of Ministers, are called instructions (*instruksia*) and orders (*prikaz*). They differ in that the former are, in principle, normative—binding upon all—while the latter are

---

[1] E.g. Article by a *raion* ispolkom chairman in *Sovety deputatov trudyashchihsya*, No. 2 of 1967 pointing out that most village soviets in the Ukraine had not even a book-keeper or cashier.

addressed to a particular quarter. The titles quoted in Soviet sources do not suggest much real difference, except that the order is perhaps more limited in its scope of application—in time or in space—and that appointments and dismissals of individuals always fall into that class. A major purpose of ministerial instructions seems to be to prescribe rules for the economical use of scarce materials and adoption of new practices. The federal minister of a ministry of the union-republican type is also empowered to issue directives (*ukazanie*) binding upon the corresponding ministry at republican level. In practice there are frequent instances of his acts taking effect directly upon organs subordinate to the ministry below. Whether the charge laid upon federal ministries in the new general instrument to respect the rights of ministries at union-republic level will make any difference remains to be seen.

Though far-reaching, however, the authority of the ministry seems to have been strangely limited in content, in that the need seems recurrently to be felt to confer on the minister powers to exercise the most basic controls over the disposal of funds on his budget. Probably, however, the lack is not in fact of legal powers but of the physical ability to check on all that is going on.

It seems unlikely that any minister is now substantially limited by his collegium. The responsibility for whatever is done or omitted is his, and the 1968 general instrument on ministries affirms that in the event of any dispute his decision prevails pending any appeal to the Council of Ministers; it may be surmised that that body would ordinarily be more likely to find for their colleague than for his subordinates. However, there is no reason to suppose that ministers habitually reject the advice of their departmental heads in this more than any other system. The collegium seems to have an important part to play in the perpetually difficult task of keeping watch on what is going on at lower levels, checking on performance by the ministry's own departments and by republican ministries and other subordinate organs—and like the Councils of Ministers sending out their own teams to gather material for a co-report by which the report of the subordinate body may be checked. It also participates in the drafting of the more important instructions and orders, and in the selection of personnel, and considers and agrees to official criticism of the ministry. It considers ways of promoting new processes and 'socialist emulation'—the officially sponsored competitive bidding-up by enterprises and organisations of production targets and commitments generally—and, like other deliberative bodies, is expected to draw into its work a wide circle of activists—specialists, directors of enterprises and learned institutions and inventors of new techniques. Like all such, it is expected to be a show, an inspiration, a conscience and a watchful eye; unlike some, it is probably the scene of real, though often limited, discussion. It seems normally to meet at least monthly, though attendances are apparently sometimes poor and discussion narrowly departmental and overburdened with petty detail. Like other directing bodies, collegiums are apt to be slack in checking that anything is done about their instructions and to word these in such vague form as to make such checking very difficult.

The limitations on the freedom of action of ministries at republican level and the administrations and departments of local soviet executive committees are more obviously predominantly imposed from outside. Ministries of republican—as distinct from union-republican—type are a minority which in most phases tends to diminish, and even they are often subject to limitation by State Committees and other organs of the federal government, as by their assignments under the planning system. The more numerous agencies having a direct hierarchic superior, from union-republican ministries of union republics downward, are evidently more concerned with implementing than with initiating, though the federal general instrument on ministries repeatedly charges ministries at the higher levels to evolve their decisions in consultation with, and with respect to the rights of those in the republics. The degree of discretion left to subordinate organs varies considerably from time to time, from place to place—with the local resources as well as with the degree of enlightenment of the supervisor—and from one field of administration to another. Clearly, however, initiating enterprise is not a quality which commonly withstands the pressure bearing down on most district executive committee departments.

In the Khrushchov period, when particular concern was expressed for the maintenance of spontaneity at the lower administrative levels, though without providing an environment consistently conducive to it, recourse was had to a long-standing soviet tradition of tempering bureaucracy by the introduction of non-professionals. Apart from the local standing commissions and a wide range of other quasi-voluntary activity organisations, this found expression in the non-staff (*neshtatny*) departments of local executive committees, manned by part-timers, as also were certain posts of vice-chairman. In early 1964 there were stated to be on the territory of Stavropolj rural regional soviet twenty-three organisation and instruction departments so staffed, twenty-two commerce departments, three housing departments, two local public works and housing departments and two industry departments. These had the services of 710 workers, of 6,500 engaged in such work in the R.S.F.S.R. as a whole. The quality of their work is not indicated.

CHAPTER IV

The Party

Structure

Within the multiplicity of regulatory machinery in the U.S.S.R. a duality is particularly emphasised—between the state (or soviet) structure and the party. All tasks of any importance imposed by the leadership are laid, with full responsibility, upon both.

The party structure closely resembles that of the state at all levels from the district upwards. Changes of terminology and territorial delimitation are frequent, but if—as after the Khrushchov reform of the management of agriculture in March 1962, by the institution of the production administrations and the removal of the party body to that level—one of the systems gets out of line the other rapidly conforms. There is, however, one persistent and significant terminological difference: autonomous republics have party organisations designated not 'republican' but 'regional'. More formal regard is shown for the dignity of the union republics; their parties have their own names—e.g. the Communist Party of the Ukraine or the Communist Party of Georgia—and congresses and central committes, as at federal level, instead of the conferences and committees of the lower levels. In operation, however, their position does not differ greatly from that of the organisations in the autonomous republics or regions.

The Eighth Congress of the party, in March 1919, explicitly denied that the recognition of separate soviet republics implied federal rights for their parties. The present rules indicate no change in this policy; republican communist parties are throughout mentioned in the same paragraphs as the organisations of territories and regions, and no indication is given of any distinction from them except in point of terminology. Officials are posted as freely to republican communist party posts as to posts in the regions of the R.S.F.S.R., and some manage in the course of a career to serve in the party organisations of several different republics.

The R.S.F.S.R. is unique in not having a party organisation of its own. The Twentieth Congress, in February 1956, established for the first time a bureau of the Central Committee on party work in the R.S.F.S.R. It survived until the Twenty-Third Congress of April

1966 and functioned much as the executive body of a republican party, but without either central committee or congress or any forms of election from the party structure over which it presided. No substitute for it was provided upon its abolition. This is a discrimination not against the R.S.F.S.R. but in its favour. The Communist Party of the Soviet Union is in fact the Russian Communist Party, and the parties of the other republics are its branch organisations.

Another Central Committee bureau, to supervise the parties of Central Asia (Tadjikistan, Turkmenistan, Uzbekistan and Kirgizia) was operative from 1962 to 1963. This, however, did not displace the existing republican structure. Again abolition—this time within the Khrushchov period—left no trace of the innovation.

The party rules (*ustav*) adopted by the Eighth Party Congress in 1919 remained in force with incidental revision in 1922, 1925, 1934, 1939, 1952 and 1956, until the Twenty-Second Congress, of October 1961. Even the rules then adopted show a less marked break with the forms of the past than is represented, in the history of the state, by the 1936 constitution; they appear to change the institutions very little and to be more concerned with increasing the emphasis laid on the rights and obligations of members. In its own mythology the party, alone understanding the laws of history, has not needed to change or to make concessions to expediency. Its rules do not purport to describe the sort of order known in the West as democratic, but one based on the quite different principles of 'democratic centralism'. Changes in them have therefore been confined to inessentials and points of emphasis.

Among these has been the party's name. The Bolshevik section of the Russian Social-Democratic Workers' Party took at the Seventh Congress in March 1918 the name of Russian Communist Party (Bolsheviks) in dissociation from the reformist Social Democracy of the West. On the formation of the Soviet Union it became the All-Union Communist Party (Bolsheviks). In 1952, at the Nineteenth Congress, it dropped the long-unnecessary word 'Bolsheviks' and assumed its present name 'The Communist Party of the Soviet Union'. In the titles of rules from 1922 to 1939 it was also styled 'Section of the Third International'.

The absence from the party's history of the formal constitutional break of 1936 is reflected in its structure of representative machinery. The system of multiple indirect election formerly underlying the congresses of soviets is there still in operation, and the double set of inner bodies which formerly existed in the All-Union Congresses of Soviets still exists in the party at all levels. As the party has not had to compromise with the demand for federalism there is no 'senate-type' second chamber at the top, and as it has not had to compromise with traditional methods of administration the excrescence of the Council of Ministers finds no counterpart in the party structure.

The primary organisations of the party, until the 1939 revision of the rules known as 'cells', are not based on territorial units as are the lowest organs of the soviet system, but on units of economic activity —the factory, the government office, the military or naval unit, the state farms and nowadays the collective farms (formerly rather the machine tractor station). As a last resort a few primary organisations have always been formed on a territorial basis in areas where the economic units have been too small to form organisations of their own, and the 1961 rules allow specifically of their formation in residential areas (village and house administrations). This may be largely intended to meet the objection that the system did not fully engage the services of members retired or not otherwise in employment.

Apart from the general assembly of members, required to be held monthly, primary organisations with fifteen or more members form a bureau, and all, regardless of membership, have a secretary and deputy secretary. Above a normal minimum of 150 members one or more officials may be paid; otherwise they combine their duties with other employment. In factories with over fifty party members or candidate members the primary organisations may, with district, area or town committee approval, be formed in the several shops or sections instead of the factory as a whole; in any case party groups, under the direction of the primary organisation, may be established in the working brigades. Where the factory has over 300 members and candidates—in some special cases over 100—and the regional or equivalent party committee approves, there may be, over the organisations in the sections, a party committee for the factory as a whole; either the committee or 'several' sectional organisations may demand a general meeting. A similar two-tiered structure is allowed in collective farms with over fifty members.

Originally the party cells were financed locally by the soviet executive committees, but from early in 1920 the practice was adopted of financing them from the centre, to make them independent of any local control and amenable to party discipline.

Party groups are combinations of three or more members in soviet, trade union or other organisations to maximise their influence in the party's interest by concerting in advance their action on the basis of its policy. Their formation is obligatory wherever there are sufficient members, and they answer for their work to the next-higher party committee.

From district to region the outermost of three rings of party organisation is the conference; in the union republics it is called, for its greater dignity, a congress, as at the centre, but with no difference in substance. Alternatively, below region, a general meeting of all members may be held. At all levels the rules empower the body to elect its next inner ring, the committee, and also the checking ('revision') commission—its audit and review body—and to hear reports from both, and discuss matters of party, economic and cultural development. It elects delegates to the conference or congress at the next higher level. Such bodies are to meet on demand of a third of the members in their areas; otherwise they should meet at least once every two years. Congresses of republican parties in republics which are not divided into regions are also required to meet once every two years; those which are so divided need have a congress only once in four years. Over the years the requirements as to frequency of meetings have been relaxed. Conformity with them, as at all-union level, seems to have been imperfect. Neither the rules nor so much information as we have about the practice give much support for the declaration in the former that the conferences and congresses are the 'supreme directing organ' of the organisations at their levels.

The committees, or at republican level central committees, hold office from one conference or congress to the next, and during that time, like the bureau of a primary organisation, 'conduct all current business'. Specifically they supervise the work of the next lower level, systematically hear reports on it and, at district or town level, 'keep a record of communists'. They 'confirm' the appointments of their heads of departments, of editors of newspapers (at regional level 'party newspapers and magazines') and, for regions, of chairmen of party commissions (party judicial tribunals). Regional and equivalent bodies have power to appoint 'secretariats'—apparently specially high-powered administrative departments—for current matters and for checking performance, while for district and town committees stress is laid—as contemporarily in the soviet system—on the power to appoint part-time workers (non-staff instructors or commissions). The rules no longer emphasise as formerly the responsibility of district committees for promoting Marxist-Leninist education, nor is their special concern for the control of party groups in external organisations now mentioned, though the importance of such groups in general is still stressed.

Nothing done by the 1961 rules revision adds much to the apparent importance of the committees as such as operative bodies. The rules make no provision as to their size but they seem to be quite large: in the larger towns and districts within them fairly uniformly forty-five to fifty, in rural districts possibly a little smaller. They are required to meet at least once in three months at district-town-area level and once in four months at region or republic. These intervals, like those for the conferences, have been increased over the last few years (for the higher levels in 1956, and for the lower in 1961). For committees at all levels the main function clearly remains the election of a further and, as far as we know, ultimate inner body, the bureau.

Under the rules of 1961 there are no limitations on the numbers either of members of bureaux or of the committees' secretaries (who are to be included in the bureaux). Until then the former were fixed at 7–9 for districts and towns, 9 for areas and 11 for regions, territories and republics; before 1956 the secretaries were everywhere limited to three. Since approval by the next higher level is required for appointment of district, town and area secretaries (and party practice suggests that this extends in fact to all levels) some control of numbers is probably retained. Five years' party standing is required for secretaries at the higher level, and three years at the lower.

The post of first secretary is probably the most powerful single office at any given level throughout the Soviet state, and at regional level he is the heir to the full authority of the pre-revolutionary governor. There is also a second secretary responsible particularly for the internal organisation and sometimes for the propaganda-agitation departments of the party machine, though the junior secretaries often include a propaganda specialist.

Congresses of the Communist Party of the Soviet Union are now required to meet once every four years. This requirement was placed in the rules in 1952, and the Twentieth Party Congress in 1956 met within the time prescribed. The Twenty-First 'Extraordinary' Congress of January-February 1959, the status of which was not made clear, somewhat confused the record, but the next regular congress, the Twenty-Second, did not meet until October 1961 or the Twenty-Third until April 1966. The confusion of the times, with the leadership long at issue and ultimately transferred—to a coalition which may well have required some skill in the structuring —could account for this last relatively short delay, but some cause more intrinsic to their nature and function must underlie the persistent irregularity of recurrence. From 1925 to 1956 the party had never managed to comply with its own changing rules in this respect; while they prescribed annual meetings the interval became in fact two, three, four, five and finally thirteen years (1939–52). The Seventeenth Party Congress, meeting in 1934 when annual sessions were long a thing of the past, changed the requirement to once in three years, and so it remained, though unobserved, until 1952. It may be that the party's reformation in this respect will prove to be permanent, but it is hardly to be expected that congresses will be effective in making party policy. They are too large (in 1966, 4,620 representing full members and 323, without votes, representing candidates; in 1961, 4,408 and 403 respectively and in 1959, on a less generous scale of representation, 1,261 and 106); they are still too infrequent and they would have a long party tradition of passivity to overcome. The rules of the party define the functions of the congress as consisting in hearing and confirming the reports of the Central Committee of the party and the Central Checking Commission, both of which it also elects, and other central organisations of the party, reviewing and amending the programme and rules of the party, and determining the practical line of the party on the main questions of current policy. In practice they are used almost entirely for the announcement by the leaders of important new developments of the party line, and there is no effective discussion. With the rise of Stalin and his elimination of Trotski, which, we have already seen, was completed by the time of the Fifteenth Congress in December 1927, debate vanished from the party congress. Previously an occasional vote had gone against the official leadership, but thereafter all decisions have been unanimous and in the desired direction. The congresses are numbered in series from the first in Minsk in 1898. The next four were all held abroad, the sixth was held in Petrograd in July-August 1917, between the revolutions, the seventh in the same place in March 1918, and all subsequent congresses in Moscow. Until 1936, from 1939 to 1952 and since April 1966 the rules have provided for conferences also at federal (and now republican) level. Traditionally they differ from congresses in that delegates have been supposed to represent party organisations rather than members. They were smaller bodies, although subject to the same laws of expansion as most Soviet deliberative bodies. When they last met they had come to have about a thousand participants. They became increasingly rare after 1926, being held only in 1929, 1932 and 1941. Unlike the congresses, they had no authority to decide issues of policy, but were merely advisory to the party Central Committee—to which arrangements for their post-1966 role are now again left. The business transacted by them was nevertheless similar in kind to that of the congresses, and the 1922 revision of the party rules was in fact made by a conference, the Twelfth.

The inner body of the congress of the party as a whole is, as in the union republics, designated the Central Committee. At both levels the Central Committee is in theory the supreme authority when the congress is not in session, but it seems to have followed the usual course of increasing numbers and declining powers. Unlike most bodies, in fact, the Central Committee seems never to have experienced any reversal of the tendency to expansion. From a membership of fifteen, together with eight 'candidates' or probationary members—all full members of the party—at its first post-revolutionary election in March 1918, it had, as elected at the Nineteenth Congress in 1952, grown to 125 and 111 respectively. The death of Stalin brought no reversal of this growth trend; the 1961 Congress elected 175 and 155, that of 1966, 195 and 165. The full members then included all members and candidates of the Central Committee's inner body, the politburo, and all the secretaries, as usual. The rest of the membership also followed a well-established pattern, with a strong representation of both the federal government (sixty-one ministers or heads of state committees and eleven vice-ministers among the members and candidates together in 1966) and the 'apparatus' of holders of full-time posts as party officials. In 1966 apart from the eleven central committee secretaries places were found for eleven heads of central departments, all the union republican first secretaries, thirteen other republican secretaries (three, and one other republican central committee inner body member, from the Ukraine), first secretaries of fourteen autonomous republics, fifty-two of fifty-seven territories and regions in the R.S.F.S.R. and twenty-one of fifty-six in other republics, those of the cities of Moscow and Leningrad and five second or other secretaries (all from those two cities or their surrounding regions). One first secretary of a district (in Moscow city) was included—and brought the number of women in this party group to three (all from Moscow city or region). Local soviet executive committee chairmen had five representatives from the R.S.F.S.R. (Moscow and Leningrad cities and regions and one other region and one from the Ukraine). Republican governments had thirty (eleven from the R.S.F.S.R. and four from the Ukraine); republican supreme soviet praesidia seven. One interest always strongly represented, and latterly increasingly so, is the military; in 1966 they had thirty-five (with an overlap of seven with the government category). The police had two (a federal and a republican minister), as previously, and the law—in the form of the procuracy—one. Ambassadors numbered thirteen in 1966— five up on 1961. Other interests represented were the press with a markedly increased presence (the head of TASS, nine editors and four others), and, on a modest scale, the *Komsomol*, the trade unions, the co-operatives, science, learning and literature (or the literary bureaucracy). As usual there were a few persons of lower status—four plant managers and a chief designer from industry, heads of one state and one collective farm, ten industrial and two collective farm workers.

Members and candidates of the Central Committee alike are entitled to attend meetings, though the candidates have no votes, so that it is already a somewhat unwieldy body for the taking of decisions. In fact it is used mainly to publicise declarations of policy, and to hear progress reports and exhortations to improved perform-ance. This role it shares with the congresses, and even the Supreme Soviet, though it is a rather more flexible instrument, easier to call and less burdened with either a routine of business to be performed or members of little personal significance. For this, however, a large attendance, within reason, is an advantage. To the members and candidates are usually added the members of the Central Checking Commission and—notably in the Khrushchov period—experts and others in the area under discussion—with right of speech.

In consequence of this development, as with other bodies, plenary meetings became infrequent. They were originally required to be held twice monthly, and then from 1921 once in two months, from 1934 once in four months, and from 1952 once in six months. To this last requirement they at present more than conform. Evidently this has not always been so. Mr. Khrushchov is reported to have said that in the last fifteen years of Stalin's life plenary sessions were hardly ever called, and that during the war there was none at all.[1] The published record bears him out only in part; one such session is supposed to have been held in 1939 and two in 1940, and the decisions in January 1944 to adopt a new national anthem in place of the Internationale and to allow union republics to main-tain armed forces and establish direct foreign relations were announced as having been taken at a recent plenary session;[2] but certainly only one is clearly recorded between the end of the war and Stalin's death (held in February 1947).

The party's principal decisions are promulgated in the name of the Central Committee, sometimes jointly with the state authorities, and the central staff acts in its name. Its members include the chief advisers of the top leadership, but as a body it seems to have little life of its own, and according to the common pattern its powers have passed to an inner body elected by it. In June 1957 Mr. Khrushchov seems to have brought its forgotten powers into play as part of a manoeuvre, probably resting also largely on control of the army and the publicity system, to rid himself of a hostile majority in that

---

[1] Khrushchov, closed-session speech, Twentieth Party Congress.
[2] *KPSS v Rezoljutsijah i reshenijah s'ezdov konferentsi i plenumov Ts. K 1898–1953* (Moscow 1953), II, 1018 (work quoted in further references as *KPSS v Rez.*); *Pravda*, 28th January 1944.

inner body, but this seems to be a device not readily repeatable. The Central Committee seems to have played little part in the continuing struggle for power of the succeeding months, and in his next, and ultimate moment of need, in October 1964, Mr. Khrushchov was apparently not allowed to use the tactic again.

The federal Central Committee and that of the Ukraine have for most of their history differed from other party committees in having two bureaux, for policy and organisation, known as the politburo and orgburo. Immediately before the October revolution a body by the name of politburo was instituted with seven members, of whom Lenin was chairman, with the task of preparing for action, but it does not seem to have functioned effectively, principally because the ease with which the revolution was achieved obviated the necessity. The two-bureaux structure came into being by a resolution of the Eighth Congress of the party in March 1919. A politburo of five members was set up to decide on questions which did not admit of delay and to report fortnightly to the regular plenary sessions of the Central Committee. The orgburo, also of five, was similarly to report fortnightly on 'organisational work'. In respect of influence the politburo early drew ahead for obvious reasons. Lenin at the Ninth Congress explained that any question at all could be considered one of policy upon the request of a single member of the Central Committee. The politburo could and did expand its competence to cover the whole territory or organisation belonging in principle to the orgburo, leaving the latter body only to fill in the details of its decisions.[1] The politburo was independent of any organ in party or state, although much doubt was expressed by foreign observers in Stalin's lifetime whether even its members had any effective influence with Stalin on matters of policy. Mr. Khrushchov has since confirmed, if we may trust the accuracy of the record and discount the desire of the speaker to dissociate himself from the past, that on many matters of substance they were not only not consulted but not even informed.[2] Of Stalin's six fellow-members of the politburo at the time of the death of Lenin only one survived the purges of the period of his rise to full power, and that one, Bubnov, soon lost his influence and, apparently, his liberty. Those who took their places were of Stalin's choosing, and themselves had an insecure tenure both of office and of life, and no certainty of being consulted on any particular issue that might arise. Mr. Khrushchov has apparently explained how the greater part of the work of the politburo was in fact performed by various small working parties

[1] See instructions of Lenin quoted in Khrushchov, closed-session speech, Twentieth Party Congress.
[2] Ibid., pp. 9, 32.

chosen from among its members by Stalin, and how Mr. Voroshilov at least was interdicted from attendance at full sessions unless with Stalin's specific permission for each occasion.[1]

At the Nineteenth Party Congress in 1952 the politburo was abolished and replaced by a new body called the Praesidium of the Central Committee, with a greatly enlarged membership. Instead of eleven members and one candidate there were now twenty-five members and eleven candidates. This was generally interpreted at the time, probably rightly, as an attempt by Stalin to apply at the highest level of the party the technique of weakening by swamping which he had applied to other organs and to the party as a whole. One full member of the old politburo, A. N. Kosygin, was reduced to candidate membership of the new body; another, A. A. Andreev, who had already had to take the blame for faults in agricultural policy, was dropped altogether, being reduced to candidate membership of the Central Committee; the rest, including Shvernik, became full members of the Praesidium. The additional members brought into the Praesidium were mostly younger men of the generation which Stalin himself had trained, ministers, first secretaries of party regional committees, ideologists and others. The orgburo vanished in this reform without trace.

Immediately upon Stalin's death, however, in March of the following year the position was in fact reversed without the formality of calling another party congress. The name of 'praesidium' was kept, but the membership was reduced to the proportions of the old politburo, with ten members and four candidates. Thirteen years of apparently unchanged operation later the Twenty-Third Congress restored the name of 'politburo' on the stated grounds of providing a better indication of the work done by that body and as part of a package of revisionary reforms—including resuscitation of Stalin's title of 'General Secretary'—valued perhaps rather for their un-Khrushchovian than for their more positive and earlier associations. No suggestion was made of restoring the orgburo.

The politburo as restored in substance in 1953 contained all its old members less the deceased (Stalin) and the already demoted (Kosygin and Andreev) together with two of the new men of 1952 (M. Z. Saburov and M. G. Pervuhin); its candidates were Shvernik, reduced again to that long-familiar status, P. K. Ponomarenko and L. G. Meljnikov, also full members of the 1952 body, and M. D. Bagirov, new in 1953. As restored in name at the Twenty-Third Congress of 1966 it contained none of these men of 1953, though A. I. Mikojan and Shvernik—a full member again since June 1957—survived to attain apparently honourable retirement on that occasion.

[1] Ibid., op. 31–2.

With eleven full members and eight candidates it was two larger than at any time under Stalin—apart from the 1952–53 departure—having attained a maximum of twenty-four between June and October 1957. However, over the whole post-Stalin period, forty-six persons had had their moments, of varying lengths and apparent initial prospects, of play in what seems to be the great arena of Soviet political contest: one (O. V. Kuusinen) had died in office after a run of some seven years (1957–64); one (F. R. Kozlov) had retired in November 1964 on apparently genuine health grounds (dying two months later). The others who failed to stay the course seem to have succumbed to the hazards of life at the top. Only one, L. P. Beria, an intial member bearing the odium and suspicion of dangerous advantage of head of the police power in the acute phase of the struggle for the Stalinian succession is known to have been killed by his colleagues immediately after removal from office in June 1953. At the other extreme were some impressive recoveries. A. P. Kirilenko, appointed candidate in June 1957 and dropped in October 1961, reappeared in April 1962 as a full member; Kosygin, re-entering with the same class of candidates, suffered no further setbacks, was promoted to full membership in May 1960 and ended second in the hierarchy, in virtue of his office as Chairman of the Council of Ministers after the deposition of Khrushchov; V. V. Shcherbitski, dropped after a very short run as candidate (October 1961–December 1963), reappeared at that level in April 1966. There were fourteen direct promotions from candidate to full member— after very markedly varied terms of service—and one demotion. Seven first appointments were made at the level of full member without previous candidate service. In accordance with the general style of Soviet political life, fitness for appointment was not indicated, returners were not publicly welcomed back and failure, or protracted non-advancement was in general not explained. The main exceptions were Khrushchov's registration of the defeat of his principal rivals—Molotov, Kaganovich and Malenkov—and their supporters in June 1957, his rejection in October 1957 of Marshal Zhukov, one of his main allies on that occasion, and the fall of Khrushchov himself in October 1964. In the first of these incidents the losers were attainted, in the press and in the speeches of their victor, of anti-party conspiracy; in the second the regime's characteristic suspicion of military ambition—suspended during the quite exceptional year of military presence at this level of power—was given uncharacteristically explicit expression; the third was allowed to happen as quietly as the situation allowed—on grounds of old age and ill-health—but subsequent reference to the quality of Khrushchov's planning and style of leadership were not flattering, or perhaps unjustified. His fall did not in itself remove any other member of the Praesidium, probably because few if any who had enjoyed his patronage showed any disposition to come to his aid.

It is this shifting balance of personal connections which has chiefly attracted attention outside the Soviet Union, providing a form of gauge of political forces and trends which often cannot be directly observed. The men who attain to membership of the politburo (or praesidium) are, however, not shadows, but men of some substance, professionals crowning a successful career in the party, usually predominantly in its field service. Recent experience in the more sensitive non-Russian republics is usually looked for, commonly among their native peoples—always the Ukraine, but usually also Central Asia and the Baltic republics. The ideological profession and other headquarters services need to be represented—security and economic planning in particular—and usually produce some members whose recent career has proceeded through the central apparatus and the secretariat. The head of the government must be included, and he may well, as now, be rather a manager with an industrial specialisation than a first-secretary generalist. But managers as such are few in this body. No career military figure, as they prominently do in the Central Committee—apart from Zhukov (1956–57); no editors—apart from Shepilov (1956–57); no career diplomats; no women—apart from Furtseva (candidate, 1956, member 1957–60). Nor is there here room for the purely symbolic member, except perhaps the occasional old man to recall past idealisms. Pelshe, first elected to membership in 1966 at the age of 69 may come into this category, but he is also a still working republican first secretary from the Baltic. Any tendency of this element to raise the average age unduly is counteracted by such appointments as Shelepin—in 1964, to full membership from a career in the control of the youth movement and security—at 45; it remains at a little over 50.

The Ukrainian party, still following federal practice, had a praesidium after 1952 when all others still had a bureau. A by-product of the changes made by the Central Committee resolution of November 1962 dividing the party into industrial and rural organisations was the loss of this prestigious difference in a new uniformity of republican terminology. A bureau was instituted for each function and a praesidium to tie the whole together. With the reversal of the 1962 resolution by the Twenty-Third Congress the bureaux were removed, and the republican supreme body remained a praesidium. The Ukraine later got back into line with federal terminology. Federal example has in any case prevailed in scale and structure of membership and in apparent function, though the military, still excluded from the federal politburo since Zhukov, now again appear at republic in the person of the commander of the forces there. As required in the 1961 rules, still in force, they contain all republican Central Committee secretaries—usually first, second and three others. Previously it had been Ukrainian practice, as it still is at federal level, to have some secretaries who were neither members nor candidates of the praesidium (or politburo).

The commitment of the party to operative management put great power in the hands of whoever could manipulate its internal administration. It was upon realisation of this, above all, that Stalin built his power. At the Ninth Congress, in 1920, the secretariat, instituted at the same time as the politburo and orgburo, was greatly strengthened by the appointment of three full-time secretaries and acquisition from the orgburo of all 'current questions of organisational and executive character', including the patronage for staffing the state system with reliable men. In April 1922 Stalin first achieved secretarial office, by decision of a newly elected Central Committee, and, unlike any previous holder, was given precedence over his fellows by the addition after his name of the words 'General Secretary'. In any case he could hardly have failed to dominate his companions, the recessive figures of Molotov, who alone of the three had been appointed a secretary already in the previous year, and Kuibyshev. It was probably not then intended to make this office one different in kind from its fellows. Stalin continued throughout his life to sign the party decisions as 'secretary' of the party and not as 'General Secretary'. Nevertheless the distinction was made and was justified. As far as his office was concerned the rapid changes of the previous years were at an end for the rest of his life. In contrast, the other secretaryships changed hands with fair frequency, though no longer as the result of faction conflict in the party; they came to be held by young and promising men whose claim to the office was evidently the favour of Stalin himself. The 'apparatus', or official staff, of the party continued to be ascribed officially to the Central Committee, but in practice it was directed by the secretary general and the secretariat, itself nominally an organ of the Central Committee. In the reorganisation of the top structure of the party in 1952 the orgburo was abolished at the federal level and in the Ukraine; the secretariat took over its functions.

The death of Stalin on the 5th March 1953 provided some test of the strength of the office. Malenkov, who among the secretaries of the party had seemed the most obviously intended by Stalin as his successor, especially since the death of Zhdanov in 1948, was relieved of his secretaryship on the 14th March and so was left with only the state office of Chairman of the Council of Ministers, which by Soviet tradition was the lesser post—one which until 1940 Stalin had left to one of his subordinates—and seems so to have remained. Khrushchov had a week earlier been relieved of his duties as first secretary of the Moscow party organisation to concentrate on his work in the Central Committee, and in the list of secretaries published on the occasion of Malenkov's resignation his name was placed first, followed by four others. On the following 12th September he was formally designated 'First Secretary', and under this changed title he seems to have continued to fill Stalin's role. Possession of the first place in the party administration had been shown not to give power of itself, but the example of Khrushchov suggests that it is a position which a strong man can use with great advantage. Like Stalin during the greater part of his career, Khrushchov held no state office other than membership of the unimportant Praesidium of the Supreme Soviet so long, apparently, as he felt he could safely leave detailed administration to men of lesser standing. In March 1958, however, intensified competition in the leadership induced him to assume the chairmanship of the Council of Ministers from Mr. Bulganin, who had held it since Malenkov's resignation in February 1955. On his fall the offices were again divided, Mr. Brezhnev taking the party first secretaryship and Mr. Kosygin the chairmanship of the Council of Ministers, with the traditional relative ranking.

The Twenty-Third Congress, in keeping with its other measures of reversion to the less ferocious aspects of the Stalin style, replaced the title of First Secretary—with its associations, from local practice, of team relation with a second and other secretaries—with the previous, more monarchically associated, title of General Secretary. Mr. Brezhnev, who was continued in the office, was obviously strengthened by the change of title; he did not thereby become a Stalin. Nor was his predecessor very obviously inconvenienced by his humbler designation.

Formally there has never been a second secretary at this level, though Mr. Suslov, alone surviving from the time of Stalin after the fall of the original First Secretary, would have a good claim to that title. The other secretaries, from three to ten in number (seven in May 1968), remained comparatively transient. Thirty-one persons have held secretarial office (including the First) in the five years from Stalin's death. Two died in office and one (Kozlov again) shortly after release from it. Two relinquished it to act as head of state—of whom one resumed, to become the present General Secretary. Several early tenures and one later one (October 1961–April 1962) were of only a few months, though their holders were thereafter diminished rather than destroyed (the last continuing in the state post of chairman of the Soviet of the Union).

Twelve of the thirty-one have not been members or candidates of the politburo (or praesidium) at any time during their secretaryship. Seven others had periods of secretaryship during which they were not of the politburo (praesidium). For only four has their tenure of both offices been coterminous.

Latterly it has been possible to identify some of the secretaries as having charge of particular departments of the central administration of the party. Such departmental responsibilities appear to fall chiefly on the secretaries not members or candidates of the politburo, leaving the members or candidates with a more general co-ordinating role. With a somewhat fluid team answering for the activities of a not entirely, though apparently rather more, stable headquarters organisation, it would probably be unrealistic to define the portfolios held by the secretarial group, but a reasonable coverage of the several fields of the economy and other party work seems to be attempted.[1]

Party congresses elect another continuing body, the Central Checking Commission, charged by the rules to maintain a check on 'the expeditious and proper conduct of business in the central organs of the party, the funds and enterprises of the Central Committee...' It reports to the congress on such matters as the collection of revenues and local, not central, efficiency in tasks of propaganda, party education, etc. Its membership has grown from an original three to thirty-seven in 1952, sixty-three in 1956, sixty-five in 1961 and seventy-nine in 1966. In broad categories of interests represented the structuring is much as in the Central Committee, with central, republican and local party officials, generals, diplomats and representatives of the state apparatus, predominantly central. It is, however, very clearly a second team; republican party officials are second, rather than first, secretaries and the regional first secretaries usually come from markedly less important regions; republican supreme soviet praesidium chairmen are predominantly in this body, but the more important category of council of ministers chairmen finds its representation entirely in the Central Committee, with (in 1966) only two deputy chairmen in the Checking Commission; industrial managers are exclusively in the Central Committee, but their agricultural counterparts are as likely to be in the one body

[1] See, e.g. Boris Meissner in *Ostenropa* 7/8 of 1966 pp. 453 and 455–6, showing at the time of the XXIII Congress four chief secretaries (politburo members) two co-ordinators (candidates), two external relations secretaries and three for internal matters (party organisations, agriculture, heavy industry).

as in the other. Until the introduction of the chairmen of the republican Councils of Ministers into the federal Council of Ministers the
latter had no members on the Commission; the reform brought in
three. Now that they have moved up to the higher body departmental ministers (six in 1966, plus two deputy ministers) have taken
their places, but not from the most crucial ministries. Cultural
workers are rather strongly represented. In practice, the Commission
seems, particularly in the practice of its members' regular attendance
at plenary sessions of the Central Committee, to operate less as a
check than as a third, supplementary, category of members of the
latter body, permitting completion of the representation of union
republic Supreme Soviet praesidium chairmen, autonomous republic
first secretaries and other small measures of rounding out.

    Another central organ is the Committee of Party Control—from
late 1962 to the 1966 congress called the Party Commission. This is
now 'attached to', and to be elected by, the Central Committee
(before 1939 by the congress) and charged to maintain a check over
members and candidates for the avoidance of breaches of party or
state discipline and the hearing of appeals against sentences of
expulsion or other party punishments imposed by the next subordinate level. The 1925 rules, which first mentioned it, and those
of 1939, presented it as a supervisor of institutions—party, state or
economic—rather than of individuals, and all such functions may
not yet be extinct. The 1952 rules, as a new departure, provided for
representatives of the central body at the republican-territorial-
regional level, independent of the local organisations, but the 1956
congress, at a time when over-concentration and duplication of
supervision was somewhat out of favour, removed this provision.

    Since early days there has been latent in the system the idea of a
regular way of progress at the higher levels of the party: from
candidate member of the Central Committee to full membership,
thence through the orgburo, or a junior secretaryship, or both of
them, to candidate membership of the politburo, and so to full
membership of this higher body. The relative status of the Central
Checking Commission has always been rather indefinite; its members
seem to rank with, but after, the candidates of the Central Committee, though a fall from the latter to the former status is by no
means irredeemable. At times such as the years of relative stability
between the end of the purges and the death of Stalin the pattern
became fairly clear. But stability in the Soviet Union is never more
than relative. The rigidly status-conscious party bureaucracy with
its probationary layers of 'candidates' is something of a vision of the
less troubled world which may be but is not yet—like the constitution, though more fully realised. The aims and character of Stalin

made the selection process highly personal, and the rates of progress
of different individuals have varied greatly; it seems that the
manoeuvrings among Stalin's principal successors and their retainers,
to preserve a balance or establish a hegemony, have since operated
to the same effect. Thus Mr. Shvernik, who was elected a candidate
member of the politburo in 1939, remained in that position until
October 1952 and from March 1953 to June 1957 before achieving
full membership. Some more fortunate in their connections or their
moment—including, among present politburo members, Mr.
Suslov and Mr. Shelepin—have served only very short terms, or
none, as candidates before advancement to full member status. The
situation at the lower level is equally fluid. The 1956 congress
elected fifty-two new full members to the Central Committee; only
twelve were taken from among the candidate members and three
from among members of the Central Checking Commission; the
rest were completely new to the central elected bodies of the party.
The 1961 congress elected 111 new full members, twenty-eight from
among the candidates and one former candidate dropped in 1956,
and five from the Central Checking Commission. The 1966 congress
was more conservative, it elected only forty-five new full members,
and again twenty-eight of them were promoted candidates and five
from the Central Checking Commission. Of the seventy-five new
candidate members in 1956 four had been demoted from full
membership, five transferred from the Central Checking Commission, and the rest were completely new. In 1961 there were 123 new
candidates—three demotees and five transfers from the Central
Checking Commission—in 1966 ninety-four, with one demotee and
seven transfers. These elected directly to full membership are usually
recent appointees to major first secretaryships—ten of the twelve
such appointments in 1966—central party posts and key ministerial
offices. Their survival prospects do not appear to differ materially
from those of members arrived in more ordered fashion. The candidate's distinction from the outsider in this respect is as vague as, in a
system where votes count for little, is his formal distinction from the
full member. The real distinction seems to be one of probability; in
a quiet period the full member at any level is more likely than not
to survive re-election, while the chances are against the candidate.
Membership of the Central Checking Commission never seems to
provide much security. Even in the relatively conservative congress
year of 1966 it had sixty-one new recruits in its seventy-five members
—three transferred from Central Commission candidacy (one to be
chairman of the commission) and the rest new to the central bodies,
as against the twelve advancements from its old membership to the
Central Committee.

The most striking innovation of the 1961 rules was the provision
made for rotation in office at all levels including the Central Committee and its Praesidium, designed allegedly to bring in new forces
and remove those 'who have become convinced of their own indispensability' in a given office. Provision was, however, made at all
levels for the exemption of those who had been able to transmit that
conviction to a sufficient number of their colleagues. By the time of
the 1966 congress the author of the reform had already been
persuaded of his own dispensability and, on the ground that the
normal process of election made adequate provision for turnover,
the rule was dropped.

Staff

The party rules of 1934 and 1939 specified the departmental
organisation of the staff at the centre and the various subordinate
levels, but in 1952 these provisions were dropped, and they were not
restored in 1961. We therefore have no complete account of the
present position. The organisational structure has in fact been subject to variation in response to the course of a debate of the party
with itself, characteristic of many which may be observed in the
Soviet system and evidenced, as usual, not by open differences between individuals but by repeated changes of the single official
policy. The issue was whether the departments should be organised
principally on the basis of the several fields of economic activity to
the advancement of which the party (as almost everything else in
the Soviet system of government) is directed, or according to the
nature of the services—indoctrination, staffing, technical guidance
and general supervision—which it provided for all alike. Thus the
1934 rules provided that the Central Committee staff should be
organised into seven departments: for agriculture, for industry, for
transport, for planning, finance and commerce, for the political and
administrative machinery, for the leading party organs, and for
culture and propaganda of Leninism, and also the Marx-Engels-
Lenin Institute, having the status of a department, and two 'sectors'
for office business and for special business (police). Republican
parties and territorial and regional committees were to have the
same functions divided out among four departments. In the 1939
rules, however, the divisions of the Central Committee organisation
were given as the 'cadres' (i.e. staffing) administration (*upravlenie*),
an administration of propaganda and agitation and departments
(*otdel*) for organisation and instruction (i.e. for keeping a watch on
lower party organisations and improving their methods), for agriculture and for schools; lower committees had departments for the

first four functions and also military departments. The function of these last bodies was defined in the rules as 'giving help to military organs in connection with the maintenance of accounts of liability to military service, organisation of the call-up, mobilisation in the event of war, organisation of anti-aircraft defence, etc.' It was prescribed that there should be separate secretaries at regional, territorial and republican levels for propaganda and agitation. In 1948 the propaganda and agitation administration was demoted to the status of a department, and the separate departments within it for the press and other media of propaganda were renamed 'sectors'. Organisation by services rather than by the industries served seems to have been the favoured principle during Zhdanov's ascendancy, but since his death in August 1948 there has been a return to the 1934 pattern, with the abolition of the cadres administration and the transfer of its functions to departments responsible for the several industries, including agriculture, and for (state) administrative organs. Formation of the bureau on the R.S.F.S.R. brought further disruption—bipartition of the industrial departments and the department for party organs ('organisation and instruction', extending to *komsomol* and trade-union activities). Its abolition restored their unity. Apart from party organisation work and propaganda and agitation, departments then existed for eight industrial categories, for agriculture, for administrative organs, for science, and educational institutions, for culture, for military matters (political education in the forces), for four categories of international business (mainly relations with communist parties abroad), a special section (police), a department for general affairs and the office services.

A part of the central organisation which has never been specified in the rules is the system of party schools under the control of the federal and republican central committees and the committees of territories and regions. By a decision of the Central Committee of the 2nd August 1946, designed to remedy the excess of small and inadequate training courses, schools were to be established at federal level and at the level of region, territory and republic, or in the first instance at a limited number of such centres. The federal school was to have two 'faculties' (*fakultet*), one to train leading party workers —secretaries and heads of departments of regional and territorial committees and republican central committees and secretaries of area committees and the town committees of the larger towns, and the other to train leading soviet workers—chairmen, vice-chairmen and heads of departments of regional and territorial executive committees, chairmen and vice-chairmen of Councils of Ministers of union and autonomous republics, and chairmen of executive committees of town soviets in the larger cities, as well as the corresponding officials of the youth organisation. There was also to be a separate department (*otdel*) to train editors and deputy editors of regional, territorial and republican newspapers. The school was to provide a three-year course—reduced to two years in 1956, when a correspondence course was also started—and a nine-month refresher course. At the regional level the schools were to have the same two faculties, though only a selected few of them were to have the department for newspaper editors. They were to train—since 1956 in a four-year course—officials of similar categories but at the level of districts, primary party organisations and village soviets. For all of them middle-school education was prescribed as a condition of entry, and there was to be an entrance examination. At the end of the course there was to be a further examination which in the federal school might lead to the conferment of the academic title of 'candidate', the Soviet equivalent of the master's degree, or rather more, otherwise conferred only by institutions of university status. In addition, there was established by the same decision an Academy of Social Sciences, which is also under party management, training ideologists for the party organisations, universities, learned institutions, and specialist journals in a three-year course, and this was given power in suitable cases to confer the doctor's degree. The decision required that within the next three to four years the 'basic leading cadres' at all levels of the party and soviet machines should be passed through the full or refresher course of such schools. Students could be recommended by their party organisation, but it was also open to them to make applications themselves.

Work in the Forces and with Youth

The rules make provision in general terms for the formation of party groups, each with its own secretary and with responsibility to the local district or town party organisation, to work in all congresses, consultations and elected bodies of soviets, trade-unions and other organisations where there are three or more members of the party for the purpose of maximising the party influence. In addition, provision is made for the special circumstances of work in ministries and in the armed forces. For the former it was provided before 1961 that secretaries of primary party organisations required confirmation by the Central Committee of the party; this is now omitted. It is still provided that such bodies in ministries are not there to check the work of the administration; they must, however, 'firmly combat bureaucracy' and 'inform the appropriate party organs in good time of inadequacies in the work of the institution and also of individuals. . . .' Published commentaries do not make the distinction much clearer. In the armed forces organisation is rather more distinctive. Rules provide for a Chief Political Administration under the Central Committee: the military department of that body's staff fills this role. Though independent of the local organisations, political administrations and departments subordinate to the Chief Administration are charged to work in close co-operation with them. Full-time officers of this service, holding military ranks but exempt from general military duties, are posted to all units down to company level, this lowest level being added only at the beginning of 1950. The origins of the office go back to the earliest days of the regime when technical military competence and political reliability were not to be found in the same hands and the military commanders were consequently held, like factory managers, to need watching. Political commissars, reliable party men not usually skilled in the military arts, were appointed with authority co-ordinate with that of the commanders and power of veto over their orders, as well as general concern for the state of loyalty and morale in the unit. The title of political commissar was felt to be inappropriate once the regime had built up its own military profession and the principles of one-man headship had been established there as in industry, leaving to the party officer mainly educational duties, and after some two years of hesitation and repeated reversal of policy connected with the varying fortunes of the Finnish and German wars the designation was abandoned in 1942, in favour of the present designation of 'deputy to the commanding officer for political matters' (*zampolit*). Many men of the old type remained, but with the changed character of the work it became the practice to recruit persons of superior educational standard from among serving officers and men. Latterly the policy seems to be to recruit among those who have been through the normal officers' training. This is a network which has no counterpart in civil life. Primary party organisations with their own party organisers (*partorg*), and party bureaux with their own secretaries, exist in the forces much as outside, at company, or sometimes platoon, and at battalion level respectively, but they are subordinate to the political administration network, and their full-time officials are a little lower in rank than the *zampolit* at the same level and form part of his staff. Until 1956 the rules of the party provided for a special organisation of the party bodies in the country's transport services corresponding to that in the armed forces and subject to political administrations in the ministries of ways of communication, the maritime fleet and the river fleet. The Twentieth Party Congress of 1956 abolished this special provision in respect of transport.

A special section of the rules provides for the work of the party among young people. The All-Union Lenin Communist League of Youth (the *Komsomol*) is described in an official publication as 'a mass non-party organisation uniting in its ranks the broad strata of progressive Soviet youth'. Despite the use of the term 'non-party', the same source adds that the organisation 'is connected with the party, and forms its reserve and its helper in the work of the communist education of the young generation',[1] and the party rules state that it 'carries out its work under the direction of the Communist Party of the Soviet Union'.[2] Its central committee is subordinate to the Central Committee of the party, and its local organisations are 'directed and checked' by the corresponding party organisations. The structure of the league consequently corresponds to that of the party at all levels from the primary organisation upwards to the All-Union Congress, which, like that of the party, meets once every four years. It is, however, appreciably less restrictive than the party in its admission policy, though it seems to have been more so than the junior organisation for children of the ages of nine to fifteen, the Pioneers. It presents itself as both a preparation and a test of fitness for admission to the party, and so helps to build up the prestige of the latter as an élite organisation. Apart from this eliminating process there also appears to be much voluntary abandonment of the race to show political worthiness. Despite the increased comprehensiveness of party membership of latter years this relation between the two organisations seems likely to continue, for according to the official figures the *Komsomol* also has grown vastly in membership with 9.3 million members at the time of its Eleventh Congress in 1949, which was already more than that of the party, and almost twice the party's membership—23,000,000 as against 12,500,000—by the Fifteenth Congress (1966). By party rules *Komsomol* membership lapses when the members join the party 'unless they occupy directing posts in the *Komsomol* organisations'. This provides for the requirement made in the rules of the *Komsomol* that organisations of that movement shall each have a leader who is a member of the party, as the *Komsomol* itself provides leaders for the organisations of the Pioneers. The work of these organisations consists largely in political education and indoctrination, but the years of eligibility to the *Komsomol* (fifteen to twenty-eight) cover a sufficient stretch of adult life to make the league a useful auxiliary to the party in practical tasks. *Komsomol* members form joint organisations with members of the party where the latter are few in number and take their share in the recurrent campaigns of political action among the masses and in such arduous

[1] *Spravochnik propagandista i agitatora* (1955), pp. 29–30.
[2] Rule 62.

and valuable manifestations of enthusiasm as the development of new towns or of the virgin lands of Kazakhstan, the building of factories, and drives for the improvement of production in town and country.

Membership

The rules provide (Rule 1) that 'Any citizen of the Soviet Union who accepts the programme and rules of the party, participates actively in the building of communism, works in one of the party organisations, carries out the decisions of the party and pays membership dues may be a member of the Communist Party of the Soviet Union'; but the suggestion of a more restrictive admittance policy which we see in the constitution is in fact supported by the persistent practice of the party. The rules of the party themselves provide (4b): 'The question of admittance to the party is considered and decided by the general assembly of the primary party organisa- tion, the decision of which enters into force on confirmation by the district committee, or, in towns where there is no division into districts, by the town committee of the party.' This process has to be gone through twice. Recruits are first admitted as probationary members or, in the party's terminology, 'candidates', and only when they may be supposed to have acquainted themselves with the aims and methods of the party, as full members. Clearly this is something that one cannot just join by turning up at the meeting with an initial subscription in one's hands. A 1956 reiteration of the official doctrine on the point declares that 'the party does not chase after quantity of accessions, understanding that its strength consists not in the quantity of members but, above all, in their quality. . . . The party regulates the business of admission with regard to the tasks which lie before it at this or that stage of activity'.[1] The principles on which the selection is made have therefore varied considerably from time to time in the party's history.

Though appropriate in a period of conspiracy, the selective and severely disciplined party which Lenin created in the Bolshevik faction after the split of 1903 was less so in the period of revolution, when concealment was no longer in question and the concern was rather to secure at least the acquiescence of as many people as possible and, where occasion offered, to mobilise them for action. By the time of the first ('February') revolution of 1917 the Bol- sheviks probably had not more than 40,000 members, which put them well behind the Constitutional Democrats (that is, the liberal party), the Menshevik wing of their own Social Democrat Party,

[1] *Pravda*, 6th April 1956.

and the Social Revolutionaries, who were dominant in the rural parts.[1] The rules adopted by their Sixth Congress in August 1917 prescribed the conditions of membership on much the same terms as Lenin had tried to have incorporated in 1903, but the specific requirements for admission were liberal. Any person might be admitted on a recommendation of two persons to the party organisation, subject to confirmation by the next general assembly of members of the organisation. Estimates of membership in the succeeding months vary widely, but by January 1918 it had risen to 115,000 members,[2] and for the first time the workers' party had acquired a solid mass of worker supporters. The peasants were still few.

The circumstances of the civil-war period intensified the motives for attaching to the party all who were not committed against it and also provided an opportunity of gaining a foothold in the rural areas and undermining the Social-Revolutionary influence there. An appeal at least to that class of peasant from which the committees of the poor were recruited was clearly both advantageous and possible. Thus by the beginning of 1921 the membership of the party had risen to substantially over half a million,[3] while the proportion of the members classified as workers had declined markedly since the immediately post-revolutionary period (January 1918) from 56.9 per cent to 41 per cent, and the proportion of peasants had risen from 18.5 per cent to 28.1 per cent. The office workers and others showed a smaller but still appreciable rise from 28.6 per cent to 30.8 per cent.[4] The Tenth Congress in March 1921, however, recorded concern at the combined effect of losses of worker members in the civil war and the removal of the majority of the survivors from work in the factories to organise the new society and the admission of 'lower-middle-class intellectual and semi-intellectual elements, petty-bourgeois and not yet worked over in the spirit of communism, whom the party has not yet digested'.[5] Such further intensive drives to get people into the party as did occur before the final consolidation of Stalinism in 1939 were associated, unlike that

---

[1] 'A. Uralov' (A. Avtorhanov), *The Reign of Stalin* (1953), p. 17. But by May, according to the present official data, the figure was 80,000 (*KPSS v Rez.*, I, 332). I. Deutscher (*Stalin, a Political Biography* (1949), p. 143) gives the February figure as '30,000 at the most', and quotes a Soviet source for a figure of about 76,000 for May.

[2] M. Fainsod, *How Russia is Ruled* (1953), p. 211, quoting 1930 edition of Large Soviet Encyclopaedia. *KPSS v Rez.* (I, 403) gives 'not less than 300,000' for March, though allowing that only 170,000 were represented at the party conference of that month.

[3] Fainsod (op. cit., p. 211) gives 576,000. *KPSS v. Rez.* (I, 514) gives 732,521 for March 1921.

[4] Fainsod, op. cit., p. 213.

[5] *KPSS v Rez.*, I, 520.

of the civil-war period, with attempts to alter its social composition in the direction of a more marked proletarian element. These latter movements were the so-called Lenin Draft of 1924, the successful attempt—ostensibly in honour of Lenin, who had just died—to recruit by an intensive three-month campaign the force of not less than 100,000 'workers from the workbench' which a party conference some ten days before had set as the target for the next year, a further less successful attempt in the following year and a similar drive in 1927 in honour of the tenth anniversary of the revolution. In reality these were all part of Stalin's drive to power, the attempt to swamp the membership of the party as it existed at the time of Lenin's death under a much greater volume of new recruits of a type who would be readily manipulable to his purposes. The worker could be used both against the intellectuals, whose influence in the party was still strong in Lenin's lifetime and whose theories diverged from those of Stalin in a manner inimical to his aspirations after monolithic solidarity, and against the peasants, whose loyalty was not to be relied upon in the period of mass forcible collectivisation.

These occasional drives to get people in were superimposed upon a more constant and increasingly severe policy for keeping people out, and periodically for weeding out those who were in. Already in March 1919 the Eighth Congress ordered a re-registration of the membership, with a special check on all who had joined since October 1917. In December 1919 the Eighth Conference of the party stiffened the rules concerning admissions. The two sponsors for each new recruit were now required to be of at least six months' standing in the party, which in a period of rapid expansion was more severe than it seems. Moreover, the requirement of probationary service as a 'candidate' was then introduced into the rules for the first time, and here there appeared a point of discrimination against the intellectuals, in that while workers and peasants were required to serve for two months, six months were required of persons of other social origins. The figures of membership for the period indicate that these principles were not so rigorously applied as to exclude at least the lower strata of the non-manual workers and intellectuals. The Tenth Congress of March 1921 raised to one year both the six months' standing required of sponsors and the six months' probation imposed upon the less-favoured class of recruit, and inaugurated a purge which in twelve months reduced the total membership (with candidates) by over 200,000 to some 532,000, according to present official figures.[1] But it was only on the con-

---

[1] *KPSS v Rez.*, I, 514, and I, 599. As there was no cessation of new admissions the number of exclusions was larger. But purges were at that time still non-violent.

clusion of the civil war that the party was able to indulge in the luxury of discrimination on class grounds between the workers and their peasant allies. The Twelfth Party Conference of August 1922 produced some tightening up all round, raising the minimum period of probation from two to six months and the number and standing of the sponsors required to three of three years. For the first time the requirement of confirmation by higher authority was incorporated into the rules. Here new elements of discrimination appeared. Admission upon the minimum terms so defined with confirmation by the next higher party committee, that of the *uezd*, was confined to workers and Red Army men of worker or peasant stock. Other peasants required similar sponsorship, but were to serve as candidates for a full year and required confirmation by a still higher party committee, that of the governorship. People with other social backgrounds were subject to this last rule as to the confirmation, but were to find five sponsors of five years' standing—a very difficult requirement to fulfil in the circumstances—and were to serve two years as candidates. Former members of other parties might be accepted only upon approval by the Central Committee—a provision which remains in the rules to the present day, though pending further territorial acquisitions, it can now hardly apply to anyone except perhaps a few refugees from other countries. Subsequent successive revisions of the rules continued the trend of increasing discrimination on class grounds by adding to the number of categories and defining more and more narrowly the most favoured one. The Fourteenth Party Congress in December 1925 distinguished among the workers those engaged permanently in physical work for wages, while other workers and Red-Army men of worker, peasant or farm-labourer stock formed a separate and lower group. The Seventeenth Party Congress at the beginning of 1934 reformulated the distinction among the workers; those who had been so engaged for five years or more now alone constituted the first category, and all other workers were placed in the second together—by a development which foreshadowed future change—with engineers and technical workers, who had previously been in the lowest. Within the categories the formulation of the terms of entry for all except the least-favoured category, the intellectuals, was somewhat eased in 1925. The first category required only two sponsors of one year's standing, the second two of two years' standing, and peasants three of two years. But here, too, the 1934 rules produced a drastic stiffening: the most favoured workers required three sponsors of five years' standing and were to serve a year as candidates; the other workers required five sponsors of five years' standing, and the peasants required, in addition, the recommendation of the heads of the political departments of their machine-tractor stations or district party committees. All other applicants required five sponsors of ten years' standing. All except the new privileged first class had to serve for two years as candidates. At the same time there was instituted a category of associates inferior in status even to the candidates. These were the sympathisers' groups, described as 'the nearest to the party of the non-party activists who have shown in action, in production, their devotion to the party, but are not yet fitted to join the party'.[1] The factory and similar party committees and political sections of machine-tractor stations might admit people to such groups on the recommendation of two members of the party. The sympathisers were required to attend all open party meetings, and might speak but not vote. There was no specific provision in the rules for their ultimate reception into the party as there was for candidates; but, nevertheless, that was the intention. The Central Committee at a plenary meeting of the 21st–25th December 1935 described the groups as 'the most important reserve for filling the gaps in the ranks of the All-Union Communist Party (Bolsheviks)'. They took party organisations to task for superficiality in the treatment of the sympathisers and failure to screen them carefully with this end in view.[2]

These latest developments were an obvious manifestation of the forces of their period: that of the purges. These in the form of private calumniation of most, public inquisition of all and summary expulsion of many had arisen early in the party and had largely done their work before they reached their climax in the state at large in 1937. A resolution of the Sixteenth Party Conference in April 1929, based on a recommendation of the Central Committee and the Central Control Commission meeting in joint session earlier in the same month, had decreed a general purge, and a further wave of this protracted process was initiated by another resolution of the last two bodies in January 1933. In the phase initiated by the murder of Kirov, the Central Committee by letters of December 1934 and May 1935 ordered the general withdrawal and the reissue after due checking of all party cards and a revision of the party records. One result of this was that the new stringent admission rules of 1934 did not come into effect until November 1936, for all admissions and advancements had been suspended since the end of 1932; and despite the professed intention of the congress and the Central Committee to get them going again,[3] it was not until then that anything

[1] Rules 15–17 of the party rules as formulated by Seventeenth Congress, 1934; *KPSS v Rez.*, II, 778.

[2] *KPSS v Rez.*, II, 329.

[3] *KPSS v Rez.*, II, 822–31 (resolution of plenary session of Central Committee, December 1935).

was done. By that time the total membership, including candidates, was down by a million and a half from its pre-war peak at the beginning of 1933 of three and a half million, and in consequence of continued expulsions accompanying the new recruitment a further slight wastage continued until about the beginning of 1938, when it stood at 1,920,000.[1] As was to be expected in the circumstances of the period, the main victims had been the peasants and the new workers with strong rural connections, but in the process Stalin had also got rid of most of the leading 'Old Bolsheviks' (pre-revolutionary party members). In 1939 only 20,000 of the 1917 members were still in the party—according to one reasonable estimate only about 10 per cent of those who must have still been living,[2] the rest having been pushed out to the bleak life of the ex-member. Another observer calculates that by that time the ex-members already numbered a million more than the members,[3] though this, perhaps, over-estimates the expectation of life of the ex-member. The membership by this time was just under 2,500,000 members and candidates together,[4] that is to say, a million less than in 1933, but already half a million more than in 1938. The wastage was being made good, but with a different sort of material. The members were better educated on average; some 127,000 (5.1 per cent) had had a higher education and 335,000 (14.1 per cent) a secondary education as against 9,000 and 110,000 in 1928.[5] But few had been educated in any tradition other than that of Stalin. Of the members 70 per cent had joined since 1929[6] and these were in no obscure positions; already they provided 43 per cent of the congress delegates. These new recruits were predominantly young men.

By the time of the Eighteenth Party Congress of 1939 there were thus few motives for discrimination left. Stalin's power and the collectivisation of agriculture were accomplished facts. The regime had at its disposal a managerial class of its own creation on which it felt it could rely. The traditional criteria of class origin had ceased to be significant in the new society where function alone—utility to the regime as manager, as maintainer of prestige, morale or security, or as exemplary worker in production or other approved purposes—

[1] Fainsod, op. cit., p. 224.

[2] G. Bienstock, S. M. Schwarz and N. Yugow, *Management in Russian Industry and Agriculture* (1944), pp. 28–9.

[3] A. Avtorhanov in *Vestnik Instituta po Izucheniju Istorii i Kultury SSSR*, No. 12 of 1956, p. 12.

[4] *KPSS v Rez.* (II, 877) gives the figures as 1,588,852 and 888,814 respectively.

[5] Malenkov's report to Eighteenth Party Congress, *XVII S'ezd V.K.P.(b)*, p. 148.

[6] Malenkov's report, p. 149.

was important. Consequently that congress abolished the social class categories regulating the entry of new recruits, and with them the short-lived sympathisers' group. By the new rules all aspirants to party membership required three sponsors of three years' seniority in the party and were to serve for one year as candidates. The only special provision, apart from that concerning former members of other political parties, applied to persons between the ages of eighteen (the minimum age for candidate membership of the party) and twenty. Entry at such ages was restricted to members of the *Komsomol*. Any member of that organisation might present the recommendation of its district committee as equivalent to the recommendation of one party member. These regulations remain unchanged.[1] The period of the war of 1941-5, however, brought certain temporary concessions. A decision of the Central Committee of the 19th August 1941 provided that soldiers should require only three sponsors of one year's standing, and another decision of three months later provided for those who had distinguished themselves in battle a reduced candidate stage of three months. Wartime concessions were allowed to continue until 1947, though they were less generously applied after the cessation of hostilities. There occurred a rapid rise in membership. This was not entirely a product of the circumstances of the war period. In the society as refashioned by Stalin recruitment to the party had obvious attractions for both recruit and regime; the advisability had been discovered of bringing all persons of importance within the party where in exchange for privileges and prospects they could be induced to accept obligations and a degree of supervision greater than could conveniently be imposed upon ordinary citizens, though it was realised that a watch must be kept for the arrant careerist. Early after the resumption of admissions, and repeatedly, local party organisations had to be warned against recruiting drives pressed as ends in themselves and to the neglect of individual fitness. Nevertheless recruitment went on apace, and during the war it seems that the party so far overcame its objections to seeking members as to persuade the officers and recipients of decorations to join, presumably in order that it might have the benefit of their prestige. At the beginning of the war the membership (with candidates) was just under 3,900,000.[2] By September 1947 it was 6,300,000,[3] far higher than ever before, and in consequence of war casualties or other cause only some 2,000,000 pre-war members (i.e. about half) survived among this number.[4]

---

[1] Rule 5 of the current rules.
[2] *Bolshevik*, No. 3-4 of 1941, p. 56; speech of Shatalin.
[3] *Pravda*, 9th December 1947.
[4] Rigby, Thesis, p. 131.

This development gave rise to the expectation outside Russia that
a weeding-out of the unsuitable would follow, and some colour was
lent to the supposition by authoritative hints of revision of the
membership rules to be introduced at the Nineteenth Congress in
1952. In fact, no general purge has occurred, though there have
been local checks, with expulsions, sometimes on a fairly large
scale. There is evidence of this from Belorussia, Kirgizia, Esthonia
and Moldavia up to 1952, and in 1948 the Georgian party, in re-
action against previous over-generous recruiting, seems to have
expelled more than it admitted.[1] Some local party organisations
apparently put a stop on all recruitment in this period, but this has
been ruled incorrect.[2] At the Nineteenth Congress Malenkov
claimed that the party had since the war been applying a policy of
restricting admissions and devoting more attention to training, and
would continue to do so. But the only material change then made in
the rules in this respect—and none was made in 1956—was the
insertion of a provision limiting to one year the additional term
which an unsatisfactory candidate could be required to serve. If
thereafter he had still not justified himself he was to be expelled.
Previously some aspirants had been allowed to cool their enthusiasm
for the cause through protracted periods of probation. As usual the
change of policy does not seem to have produced any immediate
change of practice. In 1954 some party candidates in Armenia were
reported to have remained as such for twelve years, and more than
half of those in Georgia and Belorussia, as well as 45 per cent in the
Ukraine and Lithuania, to have exceeded the official term.[3] Some
success, however, as well as the non-occurrence of the purge in the
grand manner, is reflected in the proportions of the membership as
announced at the 1952 and 1956 Congresses. At the former it was
given as 6,013,259 full members and 868,886 candidates; at the
latter it was 6,795,896 members and 419,609 candidates.[4] The subsequent record—1961: 8,872,516 and 843,489; 1966: 11,673,676 and
797,403 is inconclusive.

Over the country as a whole party members in 1961 were just over
4 per cent of the population. Russians still have a significantly larger
proportion of the membership than of the total population, though
the disproportion is no longer gross as before. Of the other nationalities all except the Georgians are somewhat under-represented.

[1] Ibid., pp. 120–1.
[2] D. Bahshiev, *Partijnoe Stroiteljstvo v Uslovijah Pobedy Sotsializma v
SSSR* (1954), p. 84.
[3] Rigby, Thesis, pp. 126–7.
[4] *KPSS v Rez.*, II, 1096; *Pravda*, 15th February 1956 (Khrushchov), 17th
February 1956 (Aristov).

Of recent years, however, in contrast to the remoter past, non-Russian names predominate in the central committees of the republican parties and, as far as the evidence takes us, among regional first secretaries in the republics. Nevertheless, there are always a large number of Russians as well, while there is not a corresponding contingent of non-Russians in office in the R.S.F.S.R.

It is still, on the whole, a man's party. Reports at recent congresses have shown a steady rise in the proportion of women members, but they are still only about a fifth of the total. Women do not hold many of the leading offices, though there have latterly been cases of service as regional first secretaries and, in 1959–61, as a member of the Praesidium. They are more prominent in such lesser offices in the party's gift as those in the trade unions and the youth movement. That they should be in a minority is not surprising. The party is a party of active participants in politics, not one of supporters, and the most actively influential offices in the Soviet state are still held by men.

In general character the party seems to be, as it was becoming before the war, a form of co-optive aristocracy of the new society, representing primarily the managerial element of the system. About 30 per cent of members and candidates have some form of specialist training of higher (university) or middle (secondary) standard. Over 90 per cent of secretaries of regional and comparable organisations and three-quarters of those of districts had higher education. As early as 1936 it was stated that nearly 99 per cent of the factory managers were members, and the position was apparently similar in the higher ranks of the army. On the other hand, a report of 1939 indicated that the rural areas, with 65 per cent of the population, did not contain 20 per cent of the membership, and of these members only half were on the collective farms. Here there has been some change, partly because as a matter of policy recruiting has latterly been directed towards the rural population, and particularly the rural intelligentsia, and partly because of the intensification of the long-standing practice of posting urban communists to rural areas, mainly in the attempt to provide agriculture with managers capable of achieving the results which Moscow believes possible. By the Congress of 1956 the total rural membership had increased, but the balance within it was much the same. The rural districts, Mr. Khrushchov reported, had more than 3,000,000 party members and candidates, but less than half of them were working directly in the collective farms, the machine-tractor stations or the state farms. At the time the heads and senior officials of those institutions could have accounted for most of that number, but the position has probably somewhat improved since then, if only because larger units of management may be more economical in top staff. In the coal industry Mr. Khrushchov had similarly reported 90,000 communists, but only 38,000 of them working underground.

In the local soviets we have seen the party diluting its élite, which even now it has to some extent to limit in numbers in order to preserve its quality, with less satisfactory though still serviceable non-party material in the remoter places and less important posts for which considerations of economy and public relations require local recruiting. But, as we have suggested, the degree of dilution does not indicate the degree of party control. Nor perhaps do the same particulars indicate who is who in the party. Since the soviets, as distinct from the executive committees which are supposed to be answerable to them, do not ordinarily exercise much influence on the course of events, the members of the party assigned to serve in such bodies are not necessarily of more consequence socially or in their political influence than those engaged on the party's business in some other capacity which does not require them to stand for popular election. About party representation in the inner bodies, such as the executive committees, we have little direct information, but all the signs are that it is very high.

As in the Supreme Soviet, so also at the local level there is some interlocking of membership of party and state deliberative bodies. The first secretary of the party committee is normally a member of the soviet executive committee, and the chairman of the soviet executive committee is normally a member of the party bureau. An article of February 1956 declared that, in consequence, 'in the recent past . . . leading workers of region and district spent almost their whole time at sessions. Scarcely had a meeting of the bureau of the regional committee of the party been concluded after several hours, and not infrequently after several days, when a meeting of the executive committee of the regional soviet began.'[1] It was claimed that this position was now somewhat eased by the reduction in the frequency of meetings in both types of body, but it seemed that it remained usual for the local leading officials to serve in both. They are, however, few in number and, in their executive functions, either in one hierarchy or in the other. To entrust office in the two systems into the same hand—to appoint, for example, the same person as both party secretary and soviet executive committee chairman—would surrender to administrative detail the position of detached supervision which the leadership has hitherto sought to preserve for it, though the Yugoslavs in their Stalinist days seem often to have overlooked this objection. Only at the very top has there been effective merging in the simultaneous tenure by the same

[1] P. Doronin in *Kommunist*, No. 3 of 1956, p. 63.

person of office in the Praesidia of the party Central Committee and of the council of ministers. The effective cabinet, alone of all bodies in the Soviet structure, was not checked by a parallel body within the party structure but was merged with it. It is, however, now more common than it used to be for officials to move from one to the other in the course of their careers, and those who reach the top in the state structure seem usually to have held some party office at some time.

What Membership Means

The revisions of the party rules in 1952 and 1961 gave marked attention to the duties of members—declaredly directed against the disposition of members, and in particular of holders of leading offices, to regard their position as one of privilege, and the failure of organisations to call them to order for this. The existing obligations were brief: to master the foundations of Marxism and Leninism, to obey party discipline and participate in party life, to be a model progressive worker in one's own trade, and to keep in touch with the masses, explaining the party's purposes to them, and their worries and needs to the appropriate authorities. To these were added in 1952 references to obligation towards the state as well towards the party and the application of both to the leaders as well as to the ranks. Members were declared bound to preserve the unity of the party, not merely to acquiesce in but actively to promote the fulfilment of party decisions, to promote self-criticism and criticism from below, to inform the higher authorities, up if necessary to the Central Committee, of the shortcomings of others without respect for persons, to keep no secrets from the party, to be watchful in the preservation of all party and state secrets and always to follow the party's personnel policy in any field without regard for friendship, kinship or personal inclination. To obstruct a member in his duty of delation, or to transgress in any of these respects, were stated to be serious offences, specifically declared in the case of the two requirements last mentioned to be inconsistent with continued membership of the party.[1] The 1961 rules stressed technical progress as an object of members' solicitude and the obligation to active political work and to the promotion of friendly relations among different peoples, in the Soviet Union and internationally (though also to strengthen the U.S.S.R. militarily).

Since 1939 the rules have also specified certain rights of the party member. These were not affected in 1952, but were extended in 1961.[2] They are the right to discuss policy at party meetings or in

[1] Rule 3 of current party rules.
[2] Rule 4.

the party press (provided that no decision has been reached), to criticise any member at its meetings (the 1961 rules adding specifically that this should be regardless of rank), to elect the party organs and be elected to them, to be present when his own conduct is under discussion, and to put questions or declarations of views to all party authorities, up to the Central Committee. But in practice the obligations of a disciplinary character operate so as to negate these rights. According to the principle of democratic centralism issues of policy are subject to discussion only until the party has made up its mind, and since 1934 the party rules have made it clear that discussion and criticism were to be offered only as invited. To discuss important issues in all the party primary organisations, Stalin declared in 1923, would be to carry them out into the street, to reveal plans to the enemy and lose the advantage of surprise over him, to be involved in the endless debate,[1] and this the conspiratorial tradition of the party precluded. Criticism in this, as in any other rigidly organised hierarchy of authority, can always be represented as breach of discipline. The evidence which we have suggests that a member will normally only venture to criticise a leading official at his own level or at any superior level if he has or thinks he has the support of persons of still higher status in the direct line or in any parallel line of authority. Thus when, as before the 1956 Congress, the transport system had its separate party organisation, it was apparently possible to play off higher levels in this and in the ordinary territorial organisation of the party against one another. It is presumably possible to criticise without having obtained prior support in the hope of rallying such support later, but this is a somewhat perilous undertaking. The right to an open trial for party offences was certainly not observed in the purges of the 'thirties, when the presence of the accused was commonly required only for purposes of self-criticism. Whether this is true of normal times it is impossible to say, since the Soviet Union and its party have never known normal times. Of self-criticism and criticism from below, which always go together, as in the rules of the party, the former is the obligation to public confession of guilt in respect of any charge brought against a member with the authority of the party. Its object is apparently to enable the authorities to point moral lessons for the edification of the members and the public at large, and particularly the basic moral that all that goes wrong is the fault of an individual and not of the system. In consideration of this service such self-criticism is apparently commonly accepted in mitigation of the offence, real or fictitious. The term 'self-criticism' is also frequently used of organisations as well as of individuals, in which connection

[1] Speech at Twelfth Party Congress, April 1923.

it comes very close to the sense of criticism from below. The latter is the denunciation by subordinates of their superiors in the party or state hierarchy. The suppression of criticism, the attempt to prevent news of such denunciation reaching higher authorities, and refusal by the person denounced to acknowledge his own fault, are among the offences most commonly reprehended in the press, and visited with some degree of party reprimand, but it has been pointed out that the prevalence of the practice itself argues that an official in an important office has normally reason to suppose that he has a good chance of getting away with it. There is evidence that the ability to recognise when a criticism has official authority is one of the great techniques of the art of Soviet official living. The obligation to the payment of membership dues is mentioned separately in the rules. These are assessed according to a progressive scale on the basis of the members' or candidates' salaries from $\frac{1}{2}$ to 3 per cent, payable monthly. There is also an entrance fee of 2 per cent of the monthly salary on admission as candidate. The greater part of the cost of membership lies in less material burdens. On joining the party a citizen forfeits many of his personal freedoms, even those guaranteed by the constitution. Thus 'if religion is a private affair as far as the state and the citizens of the Soviet Union are concerned, it is not a private affair so far as the party and its members are concerned. The Communist Party is not indifferent to its members' attitude, for the outlook of the party is dialectical and historical materialism which is irreconcilably opposed to religion and idealism'.[1] He is obliged to be respectable according to the rigid ideas currently held by the authorities and scrupulously honest. As his party standing is likely to bring him into contact with persons of influence he may be in a better position than others to avoid censure for lapses from such standards, but if detected in them his condemnation is likely to be greater. Also he is required to give heavily of his time, not only to work hard in his own calling but to be available to assist in any of the numerous campaigns and drives instigated by the authorities, and not only to be obedient but to display an active, constant and quite inhuman zeal. 'Proper channels are for official business. If I'm a communist absolutely everything concerns me,' says the elderly overworked doctor in Ilja Ehrenburg's novel *The Storm* to the party organiser who seeks to persuade him that there is no need for him to add to his burdens by acting as an unofficial housing agency. More than any other Soviet citizen he is liable to find himself uprooted from his home and work. In one case of 1953, typical of many, a thousand members are reported to have been sent by party and *komsomol* committees for permanent work in a steel-works

[1] *Kommunist Tadjikistana*, 27th June 1954.

construction trust in the north-west. Repeatedly there are similar drafts to points in the agricultural system, to posts which are often important but often also far away. Even if allowed to stay in one place, he is likely to be involved in various forms of party service to an extent which leaves him very little free time—as, for example, the woman worker, mentioned by the trade-union newspaper in February 1956, who was a deputy to the Minsk town soviet, a member of the party bureau of the combine in which she worked, and a member of the workshop committee of her trade union. In addition, she had latterly been appointed a delegate to the Twentieth Party Congress, and was also overfulfilling her work obligations under the plan in honour of that occasion, as presumably were all good workers. Even if he avoids any sort of office he cannot fail to put in an appearance at a variety of party or other meetings in support of, or in protest against, or for information about, things remote from his interests. If he attempts to evade his responsibilities, as obviously many members do, he lays himself open to censure.

The party member is also subject to special dangers which do not confront the ordinary citizen. Prominence in the Soviet Union, and especially perhaps party prominence, involves a special liability to blame, since the system never takes the blame for anything, and to sudden unexpected presentation in the role of scapegoat. In the party records a member's career is documented in detail as that of a non-party citizen is not. This may be to his advantage in securing for him early consideration for any of the many posts to which the party has the presentation, but it could be turned against him. In addition to the sanctions of the law he renders himself liable to party disciplinary measures, reprimands of various degrees or ultimately expulsion, which can blight his career. The state of the ex-communist, it is said, is appreciably worse than that of the citizen who has never been a member. As in other fields of Soviet penal action, there is apparently more thunder than lightning. Ministers are criticised in the press for serious party offences yet remain in office,[1] and at least one writer of memoirs claims to have been expelled from the party three times and on each occasion to have argued himself back.[2] But if a Soviet citizen refrains from joining the party when he has the opportunity—as it seems that many do—it is of such inconveniences that he is likely to be thinking. It is improbable that he wishes to dissociate himself from the official philosophy or current policies or, unless perhaps he holds strong religious views, from any part of them.

The incentives to assume these burdens are no less obvious than

[1] e.g., the case of Mr. Dygai mentioned below, p. 178.
[2] G. A. Tokaev, *Betrayal of an Ideal* (1954).

the burdens themselves. A party card is almost indispensable for advancement to the highest posts in all walks of life. Without one probably no army officer could hope today to get beyond junior rank, no worker in industry or commerce to attain a managerial post in an enterprise of any size and significance, unless his technical abilities were quite exceptional, and even then considerable material inducements and moral pressure would be applied to persuade him to join. Latterly, the peasant who is not prepared to associate himself with this product of the townsman's political speculations has as little hope of ever being chairman of a collective farm. For a post of any effective influence in the administrative organs of the Soviet system the requirement is the same. For the really ambitious there is the prospect, at the price of accepting even greater restrictions and even greater risks, of paid full-time office in the administration of the party itself. Apart from these more tangible attractions the social cachet of belonging to a unique élite organisation of which the prestige is built up by all the resources of official propaganda must count for something.

For the ordinary member, who is not prepared or able to make a career as a full-time party official, influence within the party is probably very narrowly limited. The large issues of policy never come up for discussion, and as regards decisions of detail the principal local party officials bear too much personal responsibility for it to be at all probable that they will stand much interference from the rank-and-file members. The power of election, too, is probably not much more effective within the party than outside it. At the beginning of March 1937 the Central Committee ordered that the party's electoral practices should be brought into accordance with those of the state as established by the new constitution. Secret balloting upon individual candidates was to replace open voting on a list. The practice of co-opting, instead of electing, a large part of the membership of party committees, which was declared to be widespread, was condemned, and regular holding of elections was prescribed. Nevertheless it was not intended to give the local organisations an entirely free hand. In August of the following year the appointment of all first, second and third secretaries down to district and town level was placed in the gift of the federal Central Committee, though without removing the local power of election.[1] Since the war there have been further complaints of neglect of the electoral principle. In 1947 it was complained that there had been no party elections at district, town or regional level in Belorussia since

[1] *Partijnoe Stroiteljstvo*, No. 19–20 of 1938, p. 78, quoted in Rigby, Thesis, p. 338, who suggests that the requirement has probably lapsed. See p. 181 on appointment and election to party and other office.

the war. In any case, since all appointments by whomever made require confirmation by higher authority, the scope of selection of the local bodies must at least be limited by knowledge of what would be acceptable. Moreover, the cadres secretary of the next higher level attends all election meetings and apparently always has a candidate to recommend as secretary or head of department, who is always elected. He is supposed to persuade rather than to coerce; the cadres secretary who informed a conference that 'In the practice of party work it is not the accepted thing to nominate for the list of candidates for secret voting any candidates in excess of the number which it is necessary to elect to the membership of the district party committee',[1] was held to be at fault. Nevertheless he is expected to get the right man in, and does. We have accounts of posts of first district secretaries being as a general practice filled from among the junior secretaries and departmental heads of the regional party organisation. The ordinary party member generally has his reward in the form of influence, but outside the party, not within it.

For the party office-holders the position is very different. Their place is one of real influence and real personal responsibility. In particular the first secretary of a party organisation from district upwards is the general agent of the government for his area. The success or failure of that area in fulfilling the assignments set it by current government policy, particularly in agricultural production and deliveries, is set to his account. To succeed he must know the resources of his area and the character of the people with whom he has to deal, take decisions and exercise persuasion. Instructions from above can never be sufficiently detailed, and a regular target of attacks in the Soviet press is the party secretary or other party official who spends all his working hours in his office, or in meetings passing on the instructions which he has received, and issuing commands instead of developing and applying a sense of circumstance and personality in the field. The advice is much the same as that given to prefect or district commissioner in other systems of government. How far his influence can be exercised on those above as well as those below, to urge a slower or more rapid process of local industrialisation, better supplies to consumer goods or the commitments of a large proportion of the country's resources and attention to the exploitation of a promising industrial or agricultural technique of interest to his area, it is hard to say, depending as it must on the personalities involved. It is possible that Mr. Khrushchov may have discovered for himself the possibilities of maize cultivation, but it may also be that the idea was conceived by an official who thought he could earn credit by growing it well in his

[1] *Partijnaja Zhizn*, No. 1 of 1948, pp. 27–8.

own area. Clearly in the Soviet Union as elsewhere it is impossible for any one mind to know all things, and to think out all things, without influence from outside. Even Stalin must have needed to consult at least the politbureau on some matters, and it is highly probable that he was obliged to accept the word of regional party first secretaries and of the Central Committee members drawn largely from their ranks, as well as of the ministers and heads of other principal agencies on the state of affairs in their own areas or fields of action, though not necessarily without corroboration. With his probably less self-confident successors the need may well be the greater; merely to meet the top leaders or their immediate advisers is to have some influence.

The number of officials on the paid establishment of the party was stated in the report of the checking commission to the Twentieth Congress in 1956 to have diminished since 1952 by 24.7 per cent, but it has not been officially stated what the figure then was. A common, though not very confident, estimate at that time was a little under 200,000,[1] which would give some 150,000 in 1956. The chairman of the commission reported that the great preponderance of the established party workers belonged to town or district committees and primary organisations; that is to say, the levels at which the greater part of the operative work is done. The establishments of regional and territorial committees and republican central committees, it was stated, did not amount to more than 12.2 per cent of all the local staffs (i.e. of our hypothetical 150,000 less perhaps some 800 in Moscow). This gave these widely varied units an average of 108 officials each. Districts (some 4,000, each with a staff of two or more secretaries and some dozen department and sector heads and 'instructors' for work in the field) must have at least 60,000 'responsible workers'. These may include many of the 30,000 working in May 1955, presumably as full-time paid officials, in the party instructor groups in the machine-tractor stations, though some have gone to farm directorships or chairmanships. Towns of various sizes and the largest primary organisations—they are mostly small enough to have only a part-time secretary—can easily make up the further 60,000 or so—if these figures mean anything. With closer party control of agriculture—since early 1958 no longer through machine-tractor stations—and of industry apparently surviving from the Khrushchov phase there can be little room for cuts.

There is little certain evidence of how one rises into and through this select corps within the party, for the careers of the leading officials generally become known to the outside world only when they have well established themselves; the significant earlier stages

[1] e.g., Fainsod (op. cit., p. 178), suggests 194,000.

are missing. It has been stated that organs of the party and soviet systems and the economy are staffed largely from among secretaries of primary party organisations, and the duty laid by the Central Committee in February–March 1937 upon every secretary to select and train two deputies for possible advancement to his own office is still quoted as actual, and probably applies in the sense that all leading officials are supposed to keep an eye open for talent. Readiness in a member to give largely of his time and self-advertisement to those in whose gift the post lies are probably the usual ways to these and equivalent initial appointments. Formal educational attainments now evidently play a large part in the selection, and the party's own training schemes are related to them. It has been suggested of late that this criterion is over-emphasised to the exclusion of consideration of character and organisational ability. In 1954 24.3 per cent of the district-committee first secretaries, 14.7 per cent of the junior secretaries at the same level, and 14.6 per cent of the chairmen of district soviet executive committees, who for obvious reasons are commonly put in the same category in Soviet writings, had a full higher education; for incomplete higher education and middle-school education together the figures in the same three categories were respectively 70.4 per cent, 79.1 per cent and 69.6 per cent for 1952, the latest year for which details were available. In all cases this was a marked increase over the figures for 1946 or the pre-war years.[1] Given the necessary educational standard, or even without it, since it is likely that quite a number of exceptions are still made in the formal requirements, work as an ordinary member or unpaid official, particularly in connection with some successful campaign, is probably the best way of showing the requisite qualities of character and organisational ability to obtain a permanent place in the party administration, and to procure advancement within it. Similarly, association with failure, inability to raise production, a tendency to antagonise unnecessarily and produce resistance must have undone many officials and returned them to their places in factory or collective farm. Typically, it seems, the party official is not a technician, a master of any particular process, even of the propaganda process for which the party is peculiarly responsible, but an organiser, a mover of men, able to secure results in any field of activity. Whereas there are specialisms in wide variety developing in Russia, and a man can live out his life and obtain distinction, and probably even ministerial rank, in a single industry, the type of official in whose career party office has a large place is distinguished by ability to move from one field to another, within the party or

[1] Particulars for 1954 and 1946 in article in *Partijnaja Zhizn*, No. 9 of 1954, pp. 6–7. Those for 1934 and 1939 are in Fainsod, op. cit., p. 321.

outside it—as chairman of the local trade-union organisation, as
chairman of the soviet executive committee and particularly latterly
as chairman of a collective farm—or as a party first secretary to
marshal all fields. Territorial, as well as functional, mobility is a
feature of this career, though less markedly so than formerly when
there seemed to be fear on the part of the authorities of their
establishing a local connection. Now rational posting considerations
probably rule—that the best men should be available to man the
trouble spots, of whatever kind. It is apparently a perilous career,
but for one who can play it properly may be brilliant. If he
can rise to the status of a regional first secretary he will receive
emoluments and perquisites and influence such as are rare in any
system, perhaps obtain a place on the Central Committee, and
collect an Order of the Red Banner of Labour—or, even in the
recent comparatively ungenerous phase of decorations policy, perhaps the higher Order of Lenin—upon his fiftieth birthday.

The Party as Administrative Machinery

The function of the Communist Party of the Soviet Union is
comprehensive, as the constitution itself indicates, and it has repeatedly been said, in one form or another, that its concern extends
to the whole life of Soviet society. This life is conceived mainly in
economic terms by those who have most influence in shaping it, so
the economic motive predominates in definitions of the business of
the party. 'Party committees as organs of political leadership,' it
was said in a *Pravda* editorial (5th January 1955), 'are responsible
for the condition of the economy. The party appraises the work of
its local agencies on the basis of actual economic result.' It added,
however, 'the solution of economic tasks should be approached by
methods characteristic of party organisations. Party workers cannot
narrow their work to the sphere of economics only. They are first
and foremost social and political workers. What is required of them
is the ability to combine political and economic work.' For the
performance of this administrative or managerial function the party
has one of its most valuable means in its individual members, many
of them placed in the key positions in ministries and soviets, in the
factories and the intermediate bodies between them and their
ministries, and in the similar links in the chain of agricultural
management from the collective farm upwards. All of them are
indicated by the very fact of their membership as among the most
ambitious in the community, and a number of them zealots. Such
as are not holders of office are thus likely to be contenders for office
in the party or elsewhere, and accordingly watchful for faults among

those above. Such considerations of interest are supported by the voice of duty as expressed in the party rules; and though evidently the lower office-holders often make the task difficult and sometimes perilous, the higher management is not sparing in its efforts to circumvent them. The more enthusiastic and even the merely intermittently enthusiastic party members form a band of trusties with a stake in the established order.

It is not enough that members should be energetic and intolerant of sloth and inefficiency in the part of the machine with which they are charged. They are concerned not merely with expeditiousness of performance but also with the correctness of the decisions taken, and of that correctness the party itself is the measure.[1] Consequently, for example, it is reasonable that 'the party gives the soviets directing instructions determining the political line and orientating their work'.[2] It is not a matter of a few general guiding principles laid down at the centre. The party repeatedly insists that the correct decision must be 'concrete' and based on knowledge, both 'scientific' (i.e. theoretical, or Marxist-Leninist) and practical. It is to provide this concreteness, to relate the central policy to local circumstances—though, the centre in practice always insists, without rejecting any part of it—that the chain of local party organisations exists, and it is consequently from them that the soviets receive the 'directing instructions', and as elaborated by them that these are binding upon the soviets. It is suggested that this should be achieved 'not by commanding but on the basis of the influence exerted on the activities of these organisations by the communists working in them'.[3] This influence, however, in a matter of such importance cannot be left to individual conscience and public spirit. We find the Drogobych regional party conference in the Ukraine criticising two of the regional party secretaries for failure to attend sittings of the regional soviet executive committee of which they were members. In their work, we have seen, they are required to operate in disciplined groups. Such practices are not peculiarly Soviet, but it is evident that the process sometimes takes peculiarly direct administrative forms. Thus we find *Pravda* (7th January 1953) reporting without any indication of disapproval that the bureau of the Primorski (Litoral) territorial party committee, in the far east of the R.S.F.S.R., had twice charged the head of the territorial soviet executive committee's commerce section to attend in one of the

---

[1] 'To decide a question rightly means to decide it in full accord with the policy of the Communist Party and of the Soviet government...' (G. I. Petrov in *S.G. i P.*, No. 8 of 1955, p. 23.

[2] V. Borisov in *S.G. i P.*, No. 12 of 1947, p. 11.

[3] Borisov, op. cit., p. 10.

towns of the territory and help local organisations with reforms, and had censured him for doing nothing about it.

There exists also another form of supervision which is distinctive of the Soviet system: a standing inspection—not ideological but mainly economic and organisational—conducted by paid officials of the party with acknowledged right of access to the records. Committees of the party, or their bureaux, are required to exercise a constant supervision over the soviets and their executive committees at their several levels, and to report to the next higher level of the party up to the centre. There the ministries have their own party committees, with a similar right of supervision vested in a secretary paid from party funds and so independent of the ministry payroll and of any influence exercised from within the ministry. In a case reported in May 1954 the secretary of the party organisation in the federal Ministry of Building was found to have been receiving pay from the ministry for filling a fictitious post of deputy minister. 'Minister Dygai,' it was reported, 'irresponsibly fixed rates of payments to party officials, and by thus corrupting them tied their hands.'[1] The Central Committee of the party removed the party secretary from his post; and others, including the minister himself, received reprimands. He nevertheless retained his ministry until the reforms of May 1957 and subsequently, after a period of high planning office in the R.S.F.S.R., returned to federal level, and died in office.

Locally, too, the party, in so far as it acts institutionally rather than through its individual members, does not confine itself to the general regulatory organs of the state, the soviets. The party committees in the larger enterprises have their own officials enjoying a separately financed independence similar to that of the corresponding bodies in the ministries. 'The party exercises strict supervision to see that the independence of party officials is not infringed, that nothing hinders them from developing self-criticism and criticism from below. Party officials who are excused from production duties, as is known, are paid from party funds and are forbidden to receive payment under any pretext from economic organisations. The party Central Committee most strictly forbids economic executives to award bonuses or otherwise reward party officials. Party officials are similarly forbidden to accept any bonus or emolument from economic organisations.'[2] Secretaries of smaller party organisations who continue to hold productive posts—often it seems as foremen or in similar capacities—seem to have the same duties as paid secretaries. These officials answer to the industrial department of

[1] *Partijnaja Zhizn*, No. 3 of 1954.
[2] Ibid.

the party organisation at the appropriate level. In 1939 this link and
the departments themselves were abolished as detracting from the
management's authority, but in 1941 they were restored. They seem
to form an essential link in the industrial-administrative structure.
The party organisations should not, however, wait passively for the
reports of the factory committees and their secretaries. Party organisations at the responsible level and in all higher levels are empowered and expected to carry out regular inspections and to give
directions. The Soviet press regularly complains of bad planning of
such inspections so that the management is troubled by visitors
from too many levels within a short time, superficiality of interest in
some places and a tendency to keep entirely to the managerial level
instead of combining the inspection with political work among the
workers at large. All that one enterprise has seen of the party officials during the past year had been one visit from the first secretary
and two or three from the secretary for the industrial department,
which, it was implied, was not enough. They had been concerned
merely to collect facts for production at the next meeting of the
party bureau, plenary session of the committee or conference, and
had not taken the trouble to check the accuracy of the information
which they had been given. Here, as in all fields, the standard which
the authorities have in mind is the constant retention, by various
means, of a finger on the pulse of activity in the area, not an occasional inspection.

In the local councils of the economy as originally set up the party
as such was given representation without nice regard to objections to
its direct intervention in management. The reform was to 'increase
immeasurably the responsibility of party organisations' at region for
economic affairs.[1] Regional first secretaries reacted happily in print;
neglect of their instructions could no longer be justified by a plea of
ministry orders. Yet orders still came, first from the planning bodies,
soon also from the new state committees. Mergers of economic
districts and institution of higher tiers of councils of the economy—
reaching finally to federal level—took command away from the
regions. The chairmen of the councils—recruited from industry,
from the party or elsewhere—themselves proved to be men of substance—usually of republican central committee standing. Restoration of the ministries faces the secretaries with a contest which is at
least more familiar.

In collective agriculture the party's involvement has been of a
peculiarly direct administrative kind. As the principal body of
experts the Ministry of Agriculture, acting through the machine-
tractor stations, had a strong claim, but the undeniable lack of

[1] *Pravda*, 11th January 1954.

success in that sector of the economy weakened it as compared with the industrial ministries and, as principal organ of general contrivance, the party was invoked to overcome the enmeshed resistances, both natural and human. Especially of recent years it has tightened its hold through a variety of experiments. In September 1953 the party Central Committee set up in each machine-tractor station—in so far as they could be induced to reside there—a group of party workers headed by a supernumerary secretary of the party district committee to supervise the farms in its area. With the dissolution of the machine-tractor stations from early 1958 the district committees resumed control from the district centre, but were still probably stronger than they had been before 1953 by the concentration of the collective farms into fewer units, by the loss by the Ministry of Agriculture—as by other ministries—of much of its managerial function and by the increased 'instructor' staffs in their own organisations. The production administrations still have the party similarly at their elbow, and such control of this crucial economic field is likely to continue under any order. On the division of the party in 1963 rather more of the leading party officials seem to have gone into agriculture than into industry, and with its reunification have apparently resumed control.

A principal concern of the party from the first has been staffing, or, as the terminology has it, cadres work. This is not merely the provision of a civil service. The party's concern with cadres extends to the political posts, both representative and administrative, as known in other countries, to managerial and technical posts in industry and to key posts in all other walks of life and, to some extent, to lesser posts as well. The Soviet Union is best regarded as a single concern with vast commitments and limited resources of educated manpower. The party is not the sole agency concerned with this problem. Ministries and enterprises have their own cadres departments, and in fact it is usual for the responsibility for appointment or election to any important office outside the party's own staff to be divided among as many as four authorities: the soviet or economic organ to which the appointment is to be made, the appropriate ministry or other superior authority and the party committees, or the responsible departments in them—at present, as we have seen, divided according to the kind of activity rather than united in a single cadres department—of both levels.[1] But the party as the 'leading nucleus' bears, as in other business, a greater responsibility than the other organs. We find the good district party secretary moving his party forces about 'to the decisive sectors of production', and also the bad party secretary exercising misplaced

[1] Rigby, Thesis, p. 367.

ingenuity to keep his failures in jobs at the level of subordination to which they are accustomed.

The party committee at each level has a schedule of appointments (*nomenklatura*), for which it is responsible as appointing or confirming authority, including those of leading officials of manufacturing and other business enterprises, banks, state and collective farms and agricultural procurement agencies as well as official posts in the soviets or in the party. Like most other organisational matters in the Soviet Union, the allocation of responsibility for appointments varies with time and place according to a debate in the party mind between the voice of necessity, which demands centralisation, and the voice of conscience, which speaks for decentralisation. For instance, until early in 1954 appointment to posts as chairmen of collective farms was apparently in the gift of district party committees, but perhaps because these were evidently apt to be moved by improper considerations such posts were then removed to the regional *nomenklatura*.[1] Vice-chairmen, field-work-gang ('brigade') leaders and livestock-farm managers were left to the district.[2] At a moment of large-scale emergency recruiting for such work the district seems still to have been important as a provider, if not as appointing authority. Thus it is reported that in the Smolensk region, 'In the spring and summer of 1954, 825 district and regional workers were sent to leading work in the collective farms. Among those recommended for posts as chairmen of collective farms were fifty-six secretaries of district party committees, more than 200 heads of departments of district committees of the party, and deputy chairmen of executive committees'. Under such special circumstances there may even have been some public consultation to learn of suitable persons: 'In all towns and districts of the region assemblies of the party activists have been held. At them selection was made of the most authoritative and experienced comrades for work in the capacity of chairmen of collective farms',[3] but it seems clear that more normally such appointments are made by the party as a routine administrative matter. On the basis of reports submitted by

[1] *Pravda*, 6th March 1954, decision of a plenary session of the party Central Committee in February-March 1954.

[2] I. V. Pavlov (in N. D. Kazantsev, I. V. Pavlov, A. A. Ruskol (eds.), *Kolhoznoe Pravo* (1955), p. 305) speaks of this assignment of the presentation to posts of chairman and vice-chairman as if it were a devolution down the administrative line 'to raise the responsibility of local party organs'. It may be that there is now less interference from the centre, but the recent mass drafting of suitable people from the towns into agricultural management hardly suggests it. On the concern of party organs with the appointment and dismissal of the lower office-holders on collective farms, see H. Dinerstein, *Communism and the Russian Peasant*, p. 89.

[3] *Kommunist*, No. 3 (February) of 1956.

their own inspectors, examination of subordinate officials, and reports from the public the responsible departments at all levels are expected to maintain records of persons suitable for appointments to any post which may occur within their *nomenklatura*. These are not confined to members and candidates of the party, though they are an important and flexible resource. As the composition of the soviets suggests, non-party men may be used in positions of considerable prestige and even, it seems, of real importance. At the least the district *nomenklatura* seems to have included some hundreds of types of posts and that of a union republic some thousands.[1] As usual, however, party responsibility is not limited by formal assignment, so that party organisations at any level are required to keep a general eye on all cadres matters, and are liable to blame for failure to draw attention to suitable persons for even the less important posts which are not formally theirs to fill. Nor can they count on being left alone to exercise their power of presentation. The source quoted on Smolensk region reports that 'in 1955 upon the call of the Central Committee of the Soviet Party of the Soviet Union and the Council of Ministers of the U.S.S.R. a further 380 persons were selected for the region and sent by the Moscow party organisation for work as chairmen of collective farms', and it is probable that such assistance by the centre is general. Probably the principal party posts of all levels—secretaries, from primary organisation upwards, and heads of all the main departments—are on the *nomenklatura* of the next higher level with or without higher confirmation. The appropriate party authority is held responsible for the quality of those whom it appoints. Its reconciliation of its own responsibilities in connection with appointments with the rights of others—the members of a soviet or its executive committee in the appointment of their officials, the members of a collective farm in the choice of their chairman and a ministry in its selection of staff— is a matter for its own tact. Here, as in many other fields, the party evidently values the ability of an official to enforce the party's will without causing avoidable hard feelings, and will not long tolerate one whose action in this respect repeatedly raises a storm.

Similar considerations of tact and also, it seems, a reluctance to waste the higher organising and co-ordinating abilities of the party officials in matters of detail which can safely be left to a lower grade of staff in soviet or other organs, are evident in official criti-

---

[1] Rigby (Thesis, pp. 332–3) gives about 220 for districts and towns in Kirgizia, about 800 for regions and 2,700 for the republican Central Committee (quoting *Sovetskaja Kirgizia*, 21st September 1952, as the basis of his calculation). Kirgizia, as one of the less-developed republics, probably has fewer categories than most.

cism of other aspects of party work. Stalin's dictum that 'The party is the nucleus of ... [state] authority, but it is not, and cannot be identified with, state authority'[1] has been quoted or paraphrased time and again as a ruling that it is incorrect for party organs to displace organs of the state, though exception is made for times of emergency such as the war and, apparently, for areas of special urgency, such as agriculture now seems to be. They should in principle develop, encourage and assist the latter, arrange for the training of their officials, keep them informed on policy and, above all, keep them under supervision. But they must not use them as their mere agents, and they must not involve themselves needlessly in details. Thus two periodicals of April 1948 criticise a regional party committee for employing the chairman of the regional party executive committee upon work in one of the districts for months at a time and a district party committee for issuing detailed instructions to a village soviet upon the procurement of wood, the repair of club-houses, and the cleaning of seed. At the end of the previous year it was held unsatisfactory that a district party committee should be in direct telephone communication with a collective farm whereas neither the district agriculture administration nor the district executive committee was so provided, so that for information about the affairs of the collective farm they had to get into touch with the party secretary. Such a case might not now incur criticism. There is an occasional complaint that the party is too much involved in economic matters generally, but this is hard to avoid in Russia's circumstances of permanent crisis.

These administrative functions demand of the party administrators qualities which, whether admirable or not, are certainly rare, and it is evident from criticism in the press that they are not always up to the required standard which their party requires. The offence of 'familyness', readiness to do a deal for personal advantage or an easy life with those whom they are supposed to be supervising, apparently exists even in the élite, where it is particularly reprobated. Indeed the system of appointment which virtually makes all the principal functionaries in an area clients of the local first secretary, probably tends to promote it. Against this vice the supreme virtue of 'partyness' seems to have a hard fight. Moreover, officials of the party, and especially the prominent, show a human resentment of criticism which at times clearly takes the form of extreme vindictiveness. The party, apart from any concern which it may feel for justice, is interested that they should not get out of hand, and to that end it enforces upon them an obligatory humility. In view of

[1] Stalin, *Voprosy Leninizma* (Problems of Leninism), 11th Russian edition (1954), p. 124.

the very substantial power which the system places in their hands,
this is difficult; it involves a complexity of supervision which is very
wasteful of manpower and a severity of retribution which, because
many cases are never known to the higher authorities, cannot but
appear arbitrary. This is hardly conducive to the smoothness of
operation of the political system.

Even without avoidable fault this maintenance of a duplicate, and
rather higher-powered, administration is a substantial addition to
the cost of running a country which is still poor by the measure of
its ambitions. The cost is somewhat diminished, presumably by the
contrivance of the system so as to attract much voluntary unpaid
service from the ambitious in the hope of future advantage, but this
can only cover part of the field. The desire of the authorities to keep
this area of enthusiasm and voluntary action as large as possible,
and consequently the field of bureaucracy as small as possible, is
understandable. So is the desire of the established officials in both
state and party—or, to put it in more realistic terms, in the general
state service, and in that select corps of organisers within it which is
called the party apparatus—to widen the area of established procedures and of predictability.

The Party as Organised Faith

Probably even now some of the Soviet leaders are so far imbued
with the principles of primitive Marxism that they would prefer to
concentrate on the indoctrination of the people and then leave to
them the 'administration of things'.[1] But certainly in practice they
lack sufficient confidence in the force of indoctrination to influence
action, and with good cause. Nevertheless ideology is still evidently
felt to have a place of first importance in the system. Russian official
pronouncements repeatedly insist that 'party work is, above all,
work with people', even in its administrative aspects, and, as we
have seen, the inspection of factories and the direction of collective
farms alike are supposed to be combined with 'political work', the
promotion of right views. The party retains from its conspiratorial
days the function of all political parties, even of those in parliamentary countries, of keeping the ideology up to date, bending it to
fit developments of circumstances and of the faction fight, reconcil-
ing divergent interpretations of it, proving its consistency with its
alleged principles and winning support for it. It differs from parliamentary parties in its monopoly of power and, by reason of its
control over the machinery of state, its penal sanctions extending

[1] This is, in principle, the position of the League of Communists of Yugoslavia.

beyond expulsion even for purely ideological offences, and in being the authorised and sole agency of the state for such work. Though the several ministries, especially those concerned with education and culture, have propaganda functions in their own fields, there is no ministry charged with propaganda or information work in general. The practice of some local party organisations in earlier days of turning over their agitation functions to the soviet executive committees at their several levels was denounced as an error and would almost certainly be so regarded now. Here as elsewhere it is pointless to discuss whether the party has taken command of the state or the state of the party; they are integrated so that the party is merely a specialised agency of the whole system by which the society is organised. As we have seen, it does not, like parliamentary parties, have to campaign as such for election.

The process of reaching agreement—that is to say, the political process as we have defined it—is obviously easier if all accept the same things as good. Thus ideology is an important political institution. If it is generally accepted within the political community it will enable the leadership to silence criticism by the unanswerable argument, and often to convince inconvenient persons of their own error and guilt, which for its exemplary effect on others is better than merely persuading them of the advisability of professing it. The evidence which we have of Soviet purges, 'self-criticism', and criminal proceedings, suggests convincingly that the official ideology is thus deep-rooted. Ideological exercises, like military drill, instil the habit of ready response to orders, and keep the mind occupied to the exclusion of other ideas. Because the official ideology of the Soviet Union offers a complete explanation for all the circumstances of life and is taught in a vacuum of other ideas, those educated in it have great difficulty in entirely rejecting it at any time.

Ideological uniformity, however, has its cost. The minimum responsiveness of all is purchased at the cost of apathy in a part of the intelligentsia, a lack of initiative among those whose business is the understanding of human affairs. This is evidenced by the constant complaints of the failure of Soviet playwrights and other literary men to produce works which, besides being ideologically unobjectionable, are also reasonably interesting. Further, the Soviet intellectual world at large is often denied the opportunity to take account of fruitful trends of thought in the non-Marxist world, though it is apparently also saved from the temptation to explore some philosophical and other intellectual dead ends there in fashion. Moreover, the propagation of the official faith is a further burden upon the administrative system, in this case primarily upon that part of it which is known as the party.

The most important method by which the member is kept in touch with the latest trends in the party line is the regular meeting of his primary party organisation and of any conferences at higher level to which he may be elected, but also all members are supposed to devote some attention to their own political education. Since 1947 regular attendance at ideological meetings has not in principle been compulsory, but all members who do not attend are apparently expected to undertake some course of private study. It is evident that they do not always do so in any form acceptable to party authority, and that in particular they try to avoid the investigation of political themes which might conceivably involve them in trouble. An article by Mrs. Furtseva, then candidate member of the Praesidium, published in February 1956, complained of a preference among members for the study of remote periods of history, and particularly singled out for criticism the party members in the Ministry of the Fuel Industry of the R.S.F.S.R. who had elected to study medieval history. The ministry party committee, she suggested, should have directed them to some course of study more relevant to their work. The same article directed attention to the lack of local political schools in one of the districts of Moscow and to the poor attendances. The report of the central checking commission at the Twentieth Party Congress in the same month, however, stated that short courses and seminars run by regional and territorial committees and republican central committees had in the course of the year been attended by 50,000 propaganda workers, and the party's 288 evening universities of Marxism-Leninism by 149,000, 80,000 of them party members, 33,000 komsomol and 36,000 non-party, apart from the work of the major training institutions. In addition to such means of education there are also the party publications, which include Pravda, the principal national daily paper and critic and leader of the rest of the Soviet press, together with a large proportion of the provincial daily press, and a number of specialist organs, including in particular the Central Committee's theoretical and political journal, Kommunist and its organisational journal Partijnaja Zhizn. In the contents of these the practical nature of the system's concerns is clearly indicated. Discussion of concrete tasks in the organisation of industry and agriculture is much more frequent than are speculations on the nature of society in general. Comments on foreign affairs, where the scope of manipulative action by means which can be publicly discussed is more limited, make a greater use of the categories of Marxist theory. Even there they are very obviously directed to striking home the lessons which happen to fit in with the latest turns of practical policy. The daily press in particular, and to some extent Partijnaja Zhizn, devote much of their attention to shortcomings on the part of individuals in the fulfilment of the tasks assigned to them. To the foreign observer it must remain something of a mystery why anybody regularly reads some or perhaps most of these journals, in view of their very poor and very inexplicit news coverage. It may be assumed that the career party official, those who hope to be so, and persons in leading positions in other fields, will wish to know what themes are particularly engaging the party mind at any given moment, so that they may give due attention to them in their own writings and utterances. Since it is practicably impossible to keep a watch on everything which is supposed to receive their attention, they must seek to show themselves particularly watchful against the shortcomings of others in those fields where slackness on their part is, for the time being, particularly apt to involve themselves in official censure. The total circulation of the Soviet press is limited by the standards of other countries. The total circulation for one issue of each of the 7,537 newspapers, ranging in frequency of appearance from the unique seven issues of *Pravda* a week and perhaps 500 others which may roughly be called dailies, to the weeklies, is given in 1957 as 53,500,000. Issues are usually of four pages each. Publications of periodical form are given as over 2,500 and their total annual circulation as 418,500,000.

The activities of propaganda and agitation named in the designation of the responsible branch of the party's administration are distinguished in official terminology. Lenin quoted with approval Plekhanov's statement that 'a propagandist presents many ideas to one or a few persons; an agitator presents only one or a few ideas, but he presents them to a mass of people'. This distinction fits in with the regime's recognition that different ideological standards are appropriate for the leaders and for the people at large and even the general run of party members. The rules of the party now only require members to 'recognise' (*priznatj*) its programme. A previous requirement, that before admission as full members they should 'assimilate' (*usvoitj*)—that is, fully understand—it, was dropped in the revision of 1939 on the authority of a statement of Stalin in 1937 that its application would 'leave only intellectuals and learned persons generally in our party. Who wants such a party?'[1] Zhdanov, introducing the revision, pointed the contrast with the leaders who still needed to 'assimilate'.

Doctrine need play only a small part in the thinking of those who are not professionally committed to it as propagandists or in similar capacities. But whatever is presented must be swallowed whole.

[1] Stalin in *Vlastij Sovetov*, 6–7 of 1937, pp. 26–7, quoted in resolution of the Eighteenth Congress of the party, 1939; *KPSS v Rez.*, II, 912.

The admission of disagreement on points of doctrine which diversified party life in the early years after the revolution ceased with the rise of Stalin to power and has not been revived with his death and partial denunciation. If the cult of personality is now proscribed, the cult of infallibility of a collective management apt, as the Khrushchov experience showed, so lapse into personalism, remains.

The department of propaganda and agitation under the Central Committee of the party is much more an operative agency in itself than are most of the other departments which are concerned to supervise the work of the ministries in the state structure. It included, according to an analysis of 1950, twelve sectors: central press, local press, publishing houses, film, radio, fictional literature, art affairs (including theatre and music), cultural enlightenment institutions (i.e. mass education), schools (i.e. formal education), science, propaganda and agitation.[1] This structure, like most in the Soviet Union, has changed from time to time, but the total range of functions remains much the same. The structure at the lower levels is simpler, but always includes as an important part of its organisations a press section and a section for schools.

The party control of the press extends beyond the publication of its own journals. A number of the ministries, and also the youth organisation, and such approved specialist and learned organisations as the Writers' Union, produce their own newspapers and periodicals, but all are under the supervision of one or other of the press sectors of the party Central Committee and subordinate levels. Editors of all journals, party or otherwise, are appointed on the *nomenklatura* of some party committee, as are most other officials in positions of influence. As we have seen, special attention is devoted in the organisation of the party schools to the training of editors at all levels down to the local, and emphasis is laid upon the necessity of a regular guidance of them in the course of their work. 'The increased role of local newspapers in economic and cultural work wholly depends on the level of party guidance of the press,' said an article of April 1955, adding, with an echo of Lenin, 'Where this guidance is competent, the newspaper is a true propagandist and agitator, a militant organiser of the masses. . . . The party Central Committee persistently demands that local party agencies work with newspapers not as occasion arises but systematically and fundamentally, and direct their work from day to day'.[2] The local party committee should examine the editorial plans for some time ahead and suggest

[1] Louis Nemzer, 'The Kremlin's Professional Staff: the "Apparatus" of the Central Committee of the C.P.S.U.', *American Political Science Review*, No. 1 of 1950, p. 72.

[2] *Kommunist*, No. 2 of 1955, p. 13.

subjects. The same article, however, criticised the uniformity of style in Soviet newspapers, a theme which is constantly recurring in official pronouncements, and to the eye of the foreign observer obviously provides ground for criticism. Where the whole of the press is geared to the single machine of the state and party this fault is probably inevitable. Failure of local newspapers to devote attention to the principal themes which for the time being the government is seeking to propagate is another regular theme of criticism in the national newspapers. Specific instructions are from time to time issued to the press, as for instance the instructions from a plenary session of the party Central Committee of September 1953 to direct attention to socialist emulation and experience of progressive techniques. The demand that editorial plans should be inspected some time in advance can only be understood in the circumstances of the Soviet press, which is not bound by consideration of competition to publish news at the earliest possible opportunity, but can and does keep it for days or even for weeks. How far any individual editor can defy the instructions of a particular party official clearly depends upon much the same considerations of relative influence with higher authorities as determine other situations of power in the Soviet Union. We read of regional party committee officials in Gorki region, the assistant director of the industrial department, the director of the press department and the secretary of the Gorki town committee, allegedly seeking to prevent publication by the local newspaper of a satirical article on misappropriation of funds in a local factory. In the last of a number of telephone calls to the editor the town committee secretary said, 'I don't forbid it but I don't recommend it. I advise you to be more precise and weigh the pros and cons.' Apparently the newspaper did not publish; but *Pravda*, with which the editor was already presumably in touch, did, and the officials earned a rebuke.[1]

It is a frequent subject of complaint that the party is neglecting the ideological side of its work to concentrate upon its administrative, and particularly its economic, tasks. This, though reprehensible from the point of view of a party which has always laid much emphasis upon ideology as the foundation of its claim to sole power, and which makes no concessions to the limitations of human capacity, is nevertheless quite understandable. Officials are aware that failure in their more material tasks will the sooner be detected and visited upon them, and therefore they tend to concentrate on them. Many of them, it is frequently complained, bring to their ideological work the same trust in 'results' which can be set out statistically in the report of the party committee to its conference—

[1] Feuilleton in *Pravda*, 31st March 1955.

'so many propagandists and agitators were selected, so many reports, lectures, talks and readings (even readings!) were carried out, so many thousand persons were "covered" '.[1] One town, the commentator noted, had the impressive record of one agitator to three inhabitants; but it was not explained at the conference that none of them had done any explanatory work.

The Party as Symbol

An important function of the Communist Party is to be the embodiment of the Leninist revolutionary tradition, the link with the ideals of primitive Marxism, and the living justification of the authorities' claim to have possession of a philosophical method affording a unique insight into the causes of things. It is a mark of distinction from the outside world not favoured with this insight, a badge of the special holiness of Russia, and the embodiment of orthodoxy in a country which has always had, and appears still to need, a comprehensive official creed. For this reason, if for no other, the party must continue to be represented as something with a life of its own and not merely a part, however essential, of the state's administration.

The party has also an international significance. It is the embodiment of the hope of world revolution—of the hope, expressed in the heading of all the principal Soviet newspapers and periodicals, that the proletarians of all lands will unite. The Comintern, the Third International which until its abolition on 22nd May 1943 was specifically charged with this side of Soviet policy, and the Informburo, or, as the West knew it, to emphasise the continuity of aims and methods, the Cominform, the organisation of certain European Communist Parties formed in 1947 and dissolved in 1956, were comparatively unimportant bodies. The work could, did, and presumably still does go on even without their existence. Their purpose was symbolic, to remind foreign countries that they had Russia's friends in their midst, and in the case of the later organisation that Russia now had dependencies. In fact the party itself, even as a symbol—apart from its material contacts—has probably always been more important in this respect. It provides something with which communist parties abroad can feel kinship, as perhaps they could not with the Russian state, an inspiring vision of what it is like to be in power. Even so, it is unlikely that any very great weight is given in the minds of the Soviet leaders to this aspect of the party's role. It is essentially a practical instrument of rule.

[1] *Kommunist*, No. 18 of 1955.

CHAPTER V

The Web of Management

Soviet government has from the first been dominated by the problem of running and developing the total national firm, of taking economic decisions without benefit of the guidance which market forces provide for operators in established and more traditional economies. It has evolved a distinctive system of management, consistent and capable of extreme concentration of effort, but inflexible, constantly deficient in initiative below the top and, at the same time, afraid of the disruptive consequences of such initiative as evolves. In particular the system has so far shown itself incapable of satisfying the manifold and changing requirements of the ultimate consumer, though latterly increasingly aware of the need to do so, or of coping with the inescapable localism of agriculture. To its needs have been geared, in a more direct way than other societies find tolerable, the provision of education, housing and other social services. On its successes, favoured by a long-term trend of economic upsurge of which it was not the originator, has been built the Soviet Union's position of consequence in world affairs; from its inadequacies, and the ambitions of those who think themselves capable of making them good derives the instability of form and operation which has characterised the system throughout its life.

Organisation in Industry

Industrial enterprises (*predprijatie*), factories, mines, oil wells, chains of shops, etc., are, like towns, classified according to their 'subordination'. The pre- and post-Khrushchov categories are: Union (under ministries at federal level), Republican (under ministries at republican level) and local (under executive committees of local soviets, usually regional). In principle the distinction is one of importance; in practice it sometimes becomes a little thin—as, for example, with two fisheries trusts reported in 1954 to be in business at Rostov, buying up fish from collective fisheries in the Sea of Azov: one coming under the federal and one under the republican ministry of fisheries.[1] At the local level, Rostov region executive committee in 1957 had a hand in the management of some of the

[1] *Izvestia*, 17th July 1954.

region's breweries and confectionery factories, but its wine-making factories and bakeries and other enterprises were run from Moscow.[1]

Local industries have, in general, been concerned with consumer goods, to which, with very occasional exceptions, the authorities have given a low priority. The favoured heavier and extractive industries have shown a constant tendency to move up the line into the direct management of federal ministries and commonly, though not necessarily, into the all-union category. Even Stalinist centralisation allowed some mills and other minor enterprises for the processing of agricultural produce and enterprises for the production of bricks and tiles and other building materials to be run by collective farms, themselves generally comparable to enterprises of local subordination, and these were 'not forbidden to dispose of their surplus production to the local population'. This concession has latterly been widely extended.

Under the 1957 reorganisation there were to be only two subordinations: to the council of the economy at (originally) about regional level and to a local soviet executive committee. In fact, over the next few years the local category was almost extinguished; subordination to council of the economy (for a consolidated area) remained, though exercised under increasingly close central supervision.

The traditional system provides for enterprises to be grouped in a trust (*trest*), integrated industrial site (*kombinat*) or federation (*federatsia*) where the local situation requires it. Such bodies are regarded as, like the enterprise itself, legal persons acting under authority of the ministry but with some independence of action and legal responsibility of their own. The word 'trust' appeared in the Soviet terminology during the period of the New Economic Policy at a time when there was some imitation of the practices of the private-enterprise economy and an attempt to suggest competition with it. When in 1927 a new basic law on trusts was enacted this suggestion was dropped, and the trust became an administrative organisation subject, like all others, to the national economic plan. Above this local level the enterprise or group of enterprises might be connected with its ministry through a number of intermediary bodies: sectors (*sektor*), departments (*otdel*), administrations (*upravlenie*) and chief administrations (*glavnoe upravlenie*, commonly called *glavk*). Few chains of command had all these links, but it was stated in 1954 that such cases could then be found in the wood, coal and oil industries. Reshuffling of the organisation to find something more easily operable and more responsive to changing needs was a constant activity well before the Khrushchov reforms. One article in

[1] *Pravda*, 20th March 1957.

such a campaign of 1956 stated that 'the structure of many ministries and authorities on the three- or four-link system (chief administration—administration—department—sector) has given rise to an enormous number of small subdivisions and has led to an inflation of the staff, an increase of the cost of its maintenance, irresponsibility, formalism and an office-minded approach to the business'.[1] The ministries particularly mentioned were non-industrial—the Ministry of Agriculture, the Ministry of State Farms, the Ministry of Agricultural Procurements and the Ministry of Commerce, but the same applies to industry.

The main economic causes of the reorganisation in 1957—and undoubtedly the politics of personal connections was also a factor— seems to have been high-level concern at the disposition of ministries to keep everything within the firm, from the making of screws for their machinery to the operation of their own telephone services and ships and, above all, to maintain their own supply and constructional organisations, duplicating those of other systems. Saving of labour was mentioned as an important element of the reform plan, but was from the first unconvincing; in administrative staff at least the councils of the economy were soon massive bodies. Typically they had administrations for all industries in their districts including consumer goods, and departments for such common services as economic planning, capital development, engineering and power, labour and wages, personnel and training, housing, accounts and finance, a variety of inspectorates and their own arbitration tribunal (*see* pp. 208–9). Even the chief administration was still found at least in the network maintained by the planning bodies for arranging the supply of materials and disposal of products between economic districts. Even in so far as the complications resulting from the quest of ministries for self-sufficiency were overcome, the sin of localism (*mestnichestvo*) appeared to take its place, and in pursuit of it to urge on local interests the claims of the economy as a whole and to transmit to industry in each area the experience of other parts of the same industry elsewhere, came a further complex of chief administrations and other agencies under the planning bodies and the state committees. The changes of title were usually made of the same terminological bricks, with little disruption of underlying reality. Reversion was thus facilitated.

From the manager's point of view that reality presents itself in terms of diversity of instructions and paucity of tangible information. Planning of production and allocation of materials are usually functions of different authorities, costs are largely unknowable and accounts, as officially required to be kept, of little assistance. From

[1] E. V. Shorina in *S.G. i P.*, No. 8 of 1955, p. 17.

the point of view of higher authority the constant problem has been to reconcile the paper fulfilment of production plans with the manifest deficiency of the goods which the users require. Of latter years, however, there have been some signs of increased respect for rationality, particularly connected with the proposals of Professor E. G. Liberman of Kharkov to give enterprise managers more incentive to work the system by linking their bonuses to profit. After extensive debate in the press relaxation of output plan requirements for a large section of the clothing and textile industries to permit them to become more readily responsive to consumer demand was approved in January 1965. Extension through the industries of traditionally low priority was rapid, but by early 1968 the effect on the institutional structure remained limited.

The Khrushchov period produced a new borrowing, at local level, of capitalist forms and terminology—the firm (using the English word). This, originally, it seems, adopted by the footwear industry in the Lvov area, is a group of factories under common management with specialisation of production. It does not appear to differ much in its subordination position or the laws under which it works from previous attempts to avoid the usual rigidity of communist management.

Even in established tradition the enterprise manager is personally commissioned to obtain and maintain the equipment and materials, to engage and discharge staff, raise financial resources, handle moneys, conclude contracts and agreements and conduct legal proceedings as necessary to discharge the firm's production task, and the responsibility for shortcomings is his. But he is under considerably more restraint than his counterpart in a private-enterprise economy. Apart from the party organisation in the factory and the oversight of his ministry, with more specialised supervision by other ministerial and equivalent networks, his discretion is limited by the financial conditions decreed in the state economic plan, by the rigidities of the system of allocation applying to many of the raw materials which he needs to complete his assignment and by wage rates and provisions of specialist staff to his departments fixed at higher levels. Articles by enterprise directors published in *Pravda* in 1955 complained that applications for materials were required to be submitted before precise instructions had been received from higher authorities on the range of goods to be produced in the following period, that the annual planning period was too short for many processes, and that it was difficult to provide incentives for special competence because the director's freedom to allocate the wages fund did not extend to administrative and technical personnel, because the maximum and minimum rates for other posts had often not been fixed and especially because the maximum for foremen had been fixed at a lower point than that for the best workers. The director was free to acquire a new item of equipment only up to the value of 300 roubles, and above that had to involve himself in the complexities of an application to the Industrial Bank. The agencies of the Ministry of Finance regulated minutely the sums which might be spent, even from the firm's own amortisation fund, for purposes of capital repairs. A business journey by a member of the staff required the approval of the chief administration, and a transfer of raw materials required that of the minister. These criticisms, like most appearing in the Soviet press, had obvious official endorsement. Mr. Bulganin, at the plenary session of the party Central Committee in July 1955, substantially repeated them and denounced procedural limitations on use of spare plant capacity. The resulting resolution demanded extension of directors' powers and the Council of Ministers duly produced a decree of the 9th August 1955. In the middle of 1957, however, the same grievances were still there; the measure, it was said, did not go far enough, the ministries failed to observe it, and the Bank interpreted it very restrictively. An enterprise could not obtain a supply of metal outside its allocation to meet a rush order, even where it could find a supplier with a stock of it. Not even a ministry could release additional stocks of cement. Yet the enterprise's own allocation might not be fully met.[1] Moreover directors hesitated to take on casual orders, lest in future years they find them added to their plans. Powers to pay bonuses or to spend money out of the enterprise's amortisation fund were still very restricted—the decree of August 1955 allowed expenditure on new equipment only up to 500 roubles—and plans were still made for unrealistically short periods and subject to arbitrary amendment during the year. If, however, the director was often set an impossible task, the inducements to find a way out might be considerable. Bonuses payable only if all obligations in the plan had been fulfilled, and increased greatly for any over-fulfilment, might amount to a substantial proportion of his salary. But, on the other hand, impossibility of performance because of conditions created by higher authority or external circumstances was considered no excuse for non-fulfilment of the assignment. Subsequent increased attention to profits and a resulting new motivational structure based on them rather than on plan over-fulfilment—though fulfilment is still required—has not liberated him from commands, materials allocations or inspectorates.

In this situation industry has to find unofficial methods, ranging from the semi-legal to the plainly illegal, of regulating its affairs.

[1] A. Krylov (a factory director) in *Kommunist*, No. 6 of 1957, pp. 44–9.

'The Soviet industrial executive should never behave cunningly towards the state and put narrow interests before those of the state. Nevertheless, it is known that certain executives intentionally submit incorrect plan fulfilment figures in order to win bonuses or conceal defects.'[1] Apart from plain cooking of the record there are such methods as concentration on the more easily produced lines, so as to give a good overall result, and this is done on such a scale as to show up markedly in the figures for whole industries.[2] Influence again plays a part here. Many, or perhaps even most, enterprises maintain under various titles their purchasing agents and contact men to discover supplies, circumvent the usual channels and avoid unpleasantnesses. Some are virtually in private practice of their irregular profession. Satirical articles in the press mention the known pluralist obtaining from his various employers 5 per cent of the value of the supplies which he procures, plus expenses, and other agents, dealing in agricultural produce, monopolising the telephones at a town's post office. Probably the regime finds it advantageous to have the unorthodox ways of making the system work explored at the peril of individuals. Illegal practices which work can subsequently be legalised and generalised; those which do not can be denounced and punished. Apparently, however, the managers' propensity to the discovery of irregular but effective methods is not limited to ways of achieving regular ends, of making their business work, but extends to providing additional perquisites for themselves. On these the regime looks less tolerantly. A particularly frequent subject of denunciation in the press is the ingenuity of leading officials in contriving for themselves the additional prestige and comfort of a private motor car at the expense of their factory or department, and so of the state.

Agriculture

The nature of the processes of agriculture, the mingling of different crops on the same farms, has left less scope for the minute and shifting division of ministerial responsibility than in industry. Ministries for technical crops and for cotton-growing have made their appearance, but have proved short-lived. On the other hand, attempts to concentrate the whole of agriculture in one ministry have fared no better, lasting, in the period of the present constitution, only from March 1946 to February 1947, and from March 1953—the death of Stalin—to September of the same year. There have usually been three ministries. Two, amalgamated on the 30th May

[1] L. Slepov in *Pravda*, 4th September 1955.
[2] See p. 241.

1957, ran the farming. They were the Ministries of Agriculture—reponsible for the collective farm system—and of State Farms. The division is fairly obvious; the state farm is in effect a rural factory with a management and paid workers, while the collective farm is technically a co-operative association, though its land belongs to the state, which grants it the perpetual use of it. It was not, however, quite clearcut. The Ministry of State Farms had in fact control of only about three-quarters of the state farms. Specialised ministries, including the Ministry of Agriculture with, mostly fruit nurseries, ran the rest. Under the Khrushchov order state farms answered to councils of the economy, collective farms to district authorities before being both brought under district production administrations. The third traditional agency was the ministry concerned with the surrender of agricultural produce to the state and its marketing—a Ministry of Agricultural Procurements (*zagotovki*) or, from May 1956, of Grain Products. From 1961 a new tripartite structure was tried, with the Ministry of Agriculture reduced to concern with farming methods, a new Ministry of Production and Procurement of Agricultural Products, and *Seljhoztehnika*. The last survived the post-Khrushchov reordering; the second was absorbed into Agriculture, with Procurements, under its old name, as a State Committee.

The early years of the Soviet state produced several types of collective farms differing in the extent to which members retained control of the land and equipment. The favour of the state came to be given to what was in form an intermediate type, the *artelj*, in which cultivation is collectivised but consumption is not. In fact the differences between the system of management in such farms and those in enterprises in other parts of the economy are few and the differences between the position of the collective-farm member and that of the worker in an enterprise have not, in general, been to the former's advantage. Unlike the state-farm worker, he was not until 1966 entitled to a fixed wage, but only to his share, according to a formula set by the state, of such portion of the produce as the state thought fit to leave free for distribution. A model charter for agricultural *arteljs* was adopted by a congress of collective-farm shock workers—that is, exceptionally productive workers in agriculture—held in February 1935 and immediately confirmed by the government and the Central Committee of the party. Thereby it was held to have acquired the force of law, and the charters of the several farms could depart from its wording only at the points envisaged in the model itself—which were insignificant—or in subsequent state or party ordinances. These do not appear to have relaxed the rules before in March 1956 farms were given the right to depart in their charters from the model—subject to higher authority's approval. In January 1966 provision was at last made for regular monthly wages for members.

The chairman, who by reason of the theoretically co-operative character of the farm is not called a director, is closely comparable with one in function. The vice-chairman's post is apparently a full-time one only in the largest farms and otherwise combined with other duties. The other organs of management of a collective farm are the general assembly of the members, which meets only occasionally, and the management board (*pravlenie*) of five to nine members, which is required to meet not less than twice a month. The members of the latter body are drawn mainly from among the leaders of work gangs ('brigades'), the managers of livestock farms within the collective farm, the party secretary—who is usually free of other duties—and other specialists. The vice-chairman is always a member, being elected to that office by, and from among, the members of the board. The chairman, though elected to office by the general assembly, presides *ex officio* over meetings of the board. As we have seen, the appointment of chairmen and experts is not in fact freely made at the discretion of the members. Official Soviet sources admit of cases where the official nomination to such posts in a backward collective farm has been received with indifference and even hostility, but refusal to elect is apparently rare, and probably allowed to succeed only in cases where the authorities themselves know that they have a weak candidate.

As usual in the Soviet Union everything is checked and rechecked. Thus in addition to the management board there is a checking commission of three to five members, which is also elected by the general assembly, though subject to confirmation by the district soviet executive committee, and to which the officials of the farm are not eligible. This is to check the work of the management four times a year, to keep a general watch and report to the general assembly on the board's financial management, and to keep in touch with the local agencies of the ministry. The procurators are required to develop it and help it to stand up to the management board which it has often been reluctant to do. Certain personal responsibility for the accuracy of information given to higher authorities is placed upon a book-keeper who is appointed by the management board subject to confirmation by the general assembly and may be dismissed only by the general assembly upon the motion of the management board. Care is taken to avoid any victimisation of him by the members. He is under obligation to draw the attention of the chairman to any irregular order, and if it is confirmed in writing he should appeal to the checking commission and, if necessary, to supervising authority and the district procurator. If by performing it he would be committing a criminal offence he must go to the procurator. One of the many sinister alliances for which the authorities show themselves constantly on the watch is that between him and the chairman. Here as elsewhere, however, vigilance is probably only as constant as authority is vigilant to make it. Colleagues and neighbours have to be lived with.

On the respective merits of state farms and collective farms there was early a shift in official policy. The state farm was the obvious course of development for a regime of communist political opinion, and the regime in fact attached itself particularly to this form in its earlier days, and in constant minor or local reforms—not at present in broad Khrushchovian 'agro-town' projects—still pursues assimilation of conditions in agriculture to those of the factory. Interim reliance on collective farm proceeded mainly, it has been suggested, from a realisation that collective farmers did not have to be paid whilst state-farm workers did, and that it was not in fact within the regime's power to ensure the means of paying them in bad years.[1] State farms, all specialised in particular crops, unlike many of the collective farms, were retained as supplementary to the collective-farm system and as models of progressive methods, though in fact in this respect many state farms early showed themselves inferior to the best collective farms as marshalled by the machine-tractor stations. A powerful boost for the renewed trend in their direction was imparted by their choice for the development of the virgin lands of Kazakhstan, upon which Mr. Khrushchov set his heart as one of his sweeping solutions for Russian agricultural problems. In that case it could hardly have been otherwise, since there were there virtually no peasants to collectivise. At the end of 1955 the number of state farms stood at 5,134, an increase of 260 over the previous year—247 of the increase being in Kazakhstan—as against the total of 87,500 collective farms. As, in general, considerably larger units they already had about a fifth as much of the sown land as the collective farms and by the end of 1966 their continued advance—now independent of the unpromising fate of the virgin lands—had brought them close to equality in that respect. Seemingly the distinction of form is not now serious. The members of collective farms have proved as easy to manipulate as the workers of the state farms, 'completely removed from control in the organisation of production' and playing 'merely the passive role of a labour unit'.[2] The manner in which collective farms shall recompense their members for their

[1] Bienstock et al., op. cit., 177–8.
[2] *Pravda*, 8th April 1930, and *Izvestia*, 6th May 1930, quoted in Bienstock et al., op. cit., p. 155.

services has throughout been regulated according to the ideas of the central authorities—on the realism of which the course of events has provided no very flattering commentary—as to how best to induce them to work collectively rather than attend to their own personal plots, and the central authorities of the party have decided uniformly for the country as a whole, though with repeated changes of mind from time to time, on the best size for the working team in the collective farm, just as they decide the size of the farm itself.

Perhaps the principal distinction of the collective farmer at the moment is the possession of his personal plot guaranteed in the constitution, but it is an insecure right, exposed to shifts of policy, since though very small—usually only a quarter of a hectare (half an acre), sometimes twice as much—they are a constant temptation to the peasant to neglect his obligations in respect of collective-farm work, at the cost of sacrificing the very small earnings which the system allows him from such work, to grow something of his own of which he can at least be certain. This does not represent pure loss to the food supply of the non-farming population; in the provision of meat, dairy products, eggs, market-gardening produce and fruit, in particular, where the official system has shown least interest and adequacy, the private plots have been major contributors, but this has not won them official approval. In March 1956 a joint decree (*postanovlenie*) of the party Central Committee and the Council of Ministers advised farms to reduce the plots of families with members who did not contribute adequately to the collective works. The attitude to the plots continued to vary thereafter, and the decree was 'recognised as having lost force'. In compensation, the same decree sought to provide additional incentives for collective work by requiring the farms to make part of the payment to members for their collective work monthly, instead of annually upon completion of the harvest.[1]

Under the Stalin arrangements, elements of which lingered to 1965–66, the collective farm was required to deliver to the state at an artificially low price a quota of produce determined in the plan. There was also a tax element in the payment in kind to the machine-tractor stations for their services. Where there was no machine-tractor station farms paid an additional tax instead. Further sales to the state could be made by contract, and with the elimination in the Khrushchov period of both stations and compulsory deliveries this has become the basic means of procurement. Members' remuneration before 1966 came from shares—according to 'labour-days' (time worked heavily weighted by state rating of the job held)—in what remained.

[1] *Izvestia*, 10th March 1956.

In the early days of the regime there was some discussion whether collective farms might, as do state farms, own agricultural machinery. The decision was, and until 1958 remained, against this, and for the concentration of such machinery serving collective farms in the machine-tractor stations (M.T.S.). These came into being in 1927, originally as co-operative enterprises to which the peasant contributed part of the cost, receiving in exchange shares in the capital. This form was originally favoured as against ownership of the machinery by the individual farms, mainly, it seems, on the ground that it was unsafe to entrust valuable equipment to the mechanically incompetent peasants. But another motive was soon discovered for the establishment of M.T.S.s, in that they provided a very effective means of state control and party influence over the farm, and it was as such that they came to be principally developed. The practice was early evolved of sending selected bolsheviks to work there, which fitted in well with the requirement for technical skills, and this continued. The joint-stock organisation of the stations was not in any case readily acceptable to the communist mind, and by a resolution of the party Central Committee of the 11th January 1933 the stations were made state organisations upon the budget of the Ministry of Agriculture, and the collective farms were required to sell to them all complex equipment. A further resolution of the same date set up in each M.T.S. a political section under a deputy director to deal with opposition to the government's agricultural plans. It gave place after September 1953 to resident party secretaries and instructors.

The concentration of machinery in the hands of the M.T.S.s went on until the sudden decision early in 1958 to sell it to the now enlarged farms and dissolve the M.T.S.s. Stalin's last published work firmly refused to countenance such a concession to the collective farms; their growing resemblance in discipline and efficiency to state farms was not held decisive. The annual contract which the farm concluded with the M.T.S., and which was almost uniform in all cases and based upon the obligations defined in the plan, was the main regulating instrument determining the farm's production. By 1952, it was claimed, 99 per cent of collective-farm land in production was being served—and consequently supervised—by M.T.S.s. It was stated in 1955 that the average administrative district contained two M.T.S.s, twenty-one collective farms and about 30,000 hectares of land in cultivation. Local conditions, however, varied widely from the average. At the end of 1955, 5.3 per cent of the country's 9,009 M.T.S.s had over twenty collective farms in their zones, but 8.3 per cent had three or fewer. The official policy was to bring the average number down, both by establishment of new

M.T.S.s and by consolidation of farms. By the time of the decision to start the dissolution of M.T.S.s it was being revealed that many in the most developed areas had only one farm, and sometimes a common management with it. Some tractor teams had been permanently attached to particular work brigades.

The M.T.S. management was similar to that of an industrial enterprise, but the director was assisted by a council which included not only the leading officials of the station itself but also the chairmen and other leading workers of the collective farms which it served. Official writings on the subject indicated that discussion in their meetings ought not to be narrowly managerial but rather generally educative in progressive agricultural methods. By a decision of the party Congress of 1956 the stations were further to conform to the practice of industrial enterprises in their financing; they would cease to be borne on the ministry budget and become self-accounting and self-financing. The feasibility of this was hardly put to the test before their dissolution.

The quest for an alternative, and more effective, means of control —to which frequent crop failures seemed to impart urgency—has been continuing ever since. The productive administrations of the spring of 1962 were part of this process, and the inducement to splitting of the party and the local state administration seems to have come from the agricultural rather than the industrial side. Another new, and still surviving, institution was *seljhoztehnika*, the agency, of union-republican type and Council of Ministers status for its chairman, created in March 1963 to supply agricultural machinery, fertilisers, etc., to farms of both types. There seems to be no suggestion that this was intended to be a means of pressure or anything other than what it purports to be. Authority apparently now appreciates that for efficient agriculture enforced compliance is not enough; the producers must be appropriately equipped and motivated. As yet the equipment is clearly often inappropriate, and therefore ineffectively employed; and the policy of incentives has yet to prevail against a tradition, operative under the Tsars as under Stalin, by which the weight of stringencies in the economy could always be shifted on to the peasantry. It is not surprising that the latter tends not to be spontaneously co-operative.

Similarly the managerial corps of Soviet agriculture has about it little of the self-assurance and autonomy (within limits) which makes the heads of manufacturing enterprises recognisably in some respects a separate order in the state. Keeping up to the productive mark a labour force (before 1965–66) underpaid—or unpaid— underprivileged, overcharged—by differential pricing of goods— and of hostility to the regime has not been a very attractive task, and it has not been rendered any easier by the exceptional degree of involvement of territorial party officials in day-to-day management in this sector of business activity. To a greater degree than in other industries collective farm chairmen seem to have been drawn from the intertwined career structures of party and soviet executive committee officials and, if successful to have returned there. Assimilation of state and collective farms to one another, and of both to the style of other enterprises—in the current self-financing manner—may tend to diminish this difference of career pattern and administrative structure. Local soviet influence is already diminished; the party may be more resistant.

Organs of Detection and Regulation

The ministries and the industries or other services which they operate are only parts of a whole, and there exists elaborate machinery to ensure that they and their agents do not lose sight of this fact. Apart from the duality of state and party and the dual subordination of most organs in each, the state system itself, like that of the party, is well provided with organs of general oversight. In a state which is also, and primarily, a business concern this category brings together in a way foreign to liberal states such familiar mechanisms as audit, banking and police as well as others belonging more peculiarly to the Russian tradition, old or new. That we consider them together does not mean that each has not functions in which it diverges from the rest. Banking is a providing, as well as a regulating, service, and the police are concerned with the private citizen's propensity to larceny or homicide no less than in other countries. But we draw attention to the similarity of function which might the more easily be overlooked.

Annual audit by the several ministries of the accounts of all enterprises and services under their direction was instituted in 1936. In the following year the Ministry of Finance was charged to duplicate these services through its audit administration (*kontroljno-revizionnoe upravelenie*).It has the right of access to all financial records throughout the system. All approved establishments and salary scales are registered with the same ministry or with its subordinate branches in the soviet executive committees, and regular returns of expenditure are made by budgetary institutions for all, and by self-accounting enterprises for most, of their funds. Recurrent letters and other references in the press over recent years complain that such supervision is so minute as to discourage local initiative and progress.

For general supervision there were stated to be, in early 1964, twenty-two state inspectorates—sixteen in the field of industry, transport, agriculture and commerce, and two each in health, public order and finance and credit. In a system making such extensive use of general supervision, both within and between the several administrative services, and when the authorities were giving great publicity and encouragement to the enquiries of a variety of ostensibly voluntary investigating bodies of citizens, it could hardly have been clear to them where their responsibilities began and ended. In practice a principal centre of co-ordination was the Party-State Control Committee of the Central Committee of the C.P.S.U. and of the U.S.S.R. Council of Ministers, though there were complaints that it was not its proper function to give orders to other bodies.

This cumbrously dual-titled body, heading a system of similarly styled bodies throughout the administrative structure, had inherited its work and probably in large part its specialised corps of inspectors from a succession of previous 'control' bodies of various names (e.g. a Ministry of State Control, 1940–57), and its conversion after the fall of Khrushchov into a Committee of People's Control seems to have had chiefly the effect that its head at each level lost his status, and probably additional influence, as an *ex officio* party secretary. He remained a powerful figure in the state administration. Even apart from the peculiar temptations to interference offered to still centralised services by the prescription of decentralised decision-making to an administration ill-equipped, in resources or inclinations to operate it, Control has been given to duplicating the audit and other work of other agencies, including Finance. In this manifestation of the recurrent Soviet recognition of the inadequacy of machinery to tasks assigned, Control can wield against rival agencies the historic appeal of its home-grown character, its derivation from the revolutionary worker—peasant inspection. The desire of post-Stalin authority to make manifest the support for its purposes has been shown in wide publicity for Control's work and its extensive use of mass collective action and part-time work. As with previous control bodies, the powers of the control committees extend beyond inspection to the giving of obligatory directions and, with the government's permission, to the infliction of penalties for irregularities detected.

All enterprises, co-operative organisations and permitted associations are required to keep accounts with the State Bank, and to settle their accounts with one another only through its books. The Bank collects and transfers their tax obligations to the state, meets demands on their funds in accordance with a prescribed order of priorities in which obligations for wages and salaries and liabilities to the state budget have first place,[1] and gives short-term credits to

---

[1] See list of categories in M. H. Zhebrak, *Kurs promyshlennogo uchjota* (1955), p. 267.

cover deficiencies in their circulating capital, since this is not intended to cover all contingencies. In this it works upon a monthly
credit plan fixed by the federal Council of Ministers. The terms on
which the Bank grants credits are intended to promote adherence to
the requirements of the state economic plan, by varying the period
of loan according to the planned rate of turnover in the industry
concerned and similar considerations, and since August 1954 the
Bank has had power to impose special conditions on enterprises
which do less than they could to get their costs of production down,
or which hold excessive stocks or otherwise offend. In this it is considered to act not as a person in civil law—an enterprise dealing with
other enterprises and settling disputes with them through the courts
—but as a part of the state's administrative machine. The result is
claimed to be 'a system of bank control on the use not only of loans
but also of the economic organisations' own means'. In giving credit
to cover a relatively small part of the firm's operations, the Bank
establishes a check on the rest. 'Thus the Bank places under supervision the whole course of economic-financial activity of the organisation and the fulfilment of its plan as a whole.'[1] For the granting of
longer-term credits there is Stroibank, under the federal Council of
Ministers[2] replacing a number of specialised banks for the several
fields of economic activity, formerly organised under the Ministry
of Finance. Like the State Bank, they act as agents of the government, and their own function, it is asserted, is only to ensure that
the conditions prescribed in the credit plan have been complied
with by the borrower. It seems that the banks generally are not
always as strict as they should be about such requirements. It has
been suggested that the existence of a variety of long-term credit
banks leads to difficulties of co-ordination in such fields as the
building of housing in which enterprises of all branches and also
local soviets engage.

The designation of the ministries responsible for police work has
changed considerably over time but the function has throughout
been kept particularly under the control of the party. In the earlier
years consideration of the most important cases, regarded as
threatening the security of the state, was separated from the general
ministerial structure and placed in the hands of a body known as
the special commission or *Che-ka*, subsequently known as the State
Political Administration or G.P.U., which with the formation of the
federation became the Unified State Political Administration or
O.G.P.U. In 1934, when a federal People's Commissariat for Internal
Affairs was set up, it took over the functions of the O.G.P.U. in

[1] M. A. Gurvich, *Sovetskoe Finansovoe Pravo* (1954), p. 317.
[2] There is also a specialised bank for foreign trade.

addition to the general police work previously performed by the
republican People's Commissariats for Internal Affairs. In 1941 part
of its function was removed to a separate Commissariat for State
Security; and in 1946, like the other People's Commissariat, these
two bodies became ministries—the Ministry of Internal Affairs
(M.V.D.) and the Ministry of State Security (M.G.B.). In March
1953, upon the death of Stalin the two ministries were merged into
one under Beria, but upon his fall state security was again detached
from the ministry and placed under a commission responsible to
the Council of Ministers. A few months later, however, the chairman
of the commission was admitted to membership of the Council of
Ministers, so that in effect, although not in name, it became a
ministry again. Internal Affairs suffered the apparently worse fate
of both a change of name (Preservation of Public Order, 1962–68)
and reduction to the republican type of ministry organisation. Its
restoration in the post-Khrushchov period first to its old union-
republican organisation and later to its old name had the appearance of a general gesture of warning.

Apart from its judicial and correctional functions, the Ministry
of Internal Affairs directed another network for the checking of
performance generally, extending to the economic field as to the
armed forces, a distinct career service of which the representative
was locally a leading figure, at least equal to the chairman of the
executive committee and apparently to be treated with respect even
by the party first secretary. As restored it is still somewhat diminished, and its growth prospects are matter for conjecture. For
routine police work it has the Militia, an enforcement body without
most of the functions of maintenance of records and criminal investigation and prosecution included in the work of British police
forces. For such work the ministry maintained its own officials
separate from the Militia at local levels, attached to but independent
of the local soviets. An instrument (*polozhenie*) confirmed by edict
of the Praesidium of the Supreme Soviet of the 24th May 1955
declared the investigators to be in the procurator service and under
its orders. Appeal against their action was to lie to the procurator.
It is not clear what functions remain to the internal affairs administrations as now placed under regional soviet executive committees,
except to supervise the militia administrations similarly placed at
district level. The case has been officially made for changes in the
system by which any investigation done by the Militia was done
again by the ministry investigators.[1] But these investigators remain,
still out of local hands.

[1] M. V. Barsukov (Head of Chief Administration of Militia), *S.G. i P.*, No.
2 of 1957.

The procurator service, which in designation and function recalls the system of before the 1864 reforms, is another such distinct corps. The procurators are still today direct representatives of the centre without concession even to the form of federalism. The head of the service, the Procurator-General, as he has been designated since March 1946, is appointed (for a seven-year term) by the Supreme Soviet, as, upon his nomination are his deputies but the procurators of union republics and the Chief Military Procurators are appointed by him, and lower grades of the service similarly derive office from their hierarchic superiors without reference to the local soviet executive committee. Their rank titles—variants of 'counsellor of justice'—imply no dependence on the court system. They are mainly concerned with such forms of improper conduct as may involve judicial proceedings, and conduct many of the prosecutions coming before the courts as well, apparently, as participating in the judge's preliminary hearing of all criminal cases,[1] but they are not solely public prosecutors. They are charged to intervene in proceedings in order to protect the state's interests and empowered to 'protest' against decisions, without any limitation of time, up to the level of the federal Supreme Court or, if necessary, the Praesidium of the Supreme Soviet. They must apparently attend all hearings of certain classes of cases—such as those involving labour relations and employees' rights to compensation—in any court, and give a legal summing-up for the guidance of the bench.[2] If they think fit they may initiate or continue civil proceedings on behalf of other individual or corporate parties where these do not proceed. They are, however, not confined to the preparation and presentation of cases discovered by other agencies, but have a general right and duty of inspection of the work of all public bodies, and accounts are given in the press of appeals made to them by the public for redress of grievances. The constitution itself gives to them as to the courts the power of arrest, and they are also empowered to detain. They are mainly a control over the officialdom, but other citizens too may suffer from their activities. Accounts have been given in the press of citizens being detained by the procurator for such offences as 'slander of an official'; that is to say, for a complaint which the prosecutor chose to consider malicious. In one such case reported as having happened in Azerbaidjan in the spring of 1955, the parties—two brothers, one of them a collective-farm work brigade leader who had criticised the chairman of his farm—were kept in custody by the district procurator even after the republican Supreme Court

[1] A. Kiralfy, 'The Soviet People's Court—A comparative review', *Soviet Studies*, vol. iii, No. 4, pp. 396–7.
[2] See cases in Marshall MacDuffie, *The Red Carpet* (1955), pp. 51, 59.

had ordered their release on the ground that a new charge was being framed. It needed a letter to the national newspaper of the youth movement and action by the Assistant Procurator-General to get them released and a severe reprimand administered to the district procurator and a warning to the regional procurator who had supported him. An edict of the Praesidium of the Supreme Soviet of the 7th April 1956 provided for the establishment within the procurator's service of the following departments: General Oversight and Investigation Administration; Staff Administration; Department for Oversight of Investigation work in the State Security organs; Department for Oversight of the Consideration of Criminal Court Business; Department for Oversight of the Consideration of Civil Court Business; Department for Oversight of Places of Deprivation of Liberty (i.e. prisons); Department for Affairs of Juveniles; Control and Inspection Department; Section for Systematisation of Legislation; Statistical Department; Economic and Financial Administration and the General Office and Reception, both with the status of departments. It was also to include the services of the Chief Military Procurator and of the Chief Transport Procurator (since abolished). Attached to the Procurator-General personally were 'Investigators for specially important business', and a Methods Council. There were also to be attached to the service an institute for detection research and a journal to be published jointly with the Ministry of Justice and the Supreme Court. Previously, it seems, this service was remarkable for its complexity even by Soviet standards; in some branches its federal organisation duplicated its own republican organisation, so that investigational work in the R.S.F.S.R. was done entirely by a section of the Procuracy of the Union, which had no other functions, despite the existence of a procuracy for the R.S.F.S.R.

Organs of Adjudication

As in other fields of Soviet government, the economic theme is dominant in the work of the courts and other organs of adjudication. One of their principal functions is to complete the work of the administration of which they are, in fact, a part by determining the order of priority of the divergent instructions which enterprises and other economic agencies may have received through the multiple channels of management and general oversight to which they owe obedience, and sorting out the obligations in which they may find themselves involved.

Where the conflicts of obligations are between state-owned enterprises a special court system is involved, the arbitrations (*arbitrazh*) within the several ministries for their own enterprises and the State Arbitration (*Gosarbitrazh*) for disputes between enterprises of different ministries and, since 1959, between state enterprises and organisations (other than collective farms) held to be co-operatives. These bodies were established with their present names and something like their present tasks in 1931 and function now according to legislation of 1959 amplified by rules of the following year for the State Arbitration. The latter is established at federal, republican, territorial and regional levels, and in Moscow, Leningrad and possibly other major industrial cities under a Chief Arbitrator independent of any ministry and subordinate directly to the federal Council of Ministers. In each case a single arbitrator sits with a representative of each party to the dispute. Those bodies were originally conceived as administrative tribunals guided exclusively by considerations of public policy, especially as embodied in the economic plan, but the arbiters who, though not necessarily lawyers, are all full-time specialists in the work and have legal assistance, have come in time to function very much like courts, applying both the Civil Code and a considerable case law of their own devising. Their procedure is expeditious and reasonably informal, though there have been suggestions that their para-judicial character encourages the legalistic strain in Soviet management. The tribunals are prepared to give guidance before damage is done and liability incurred, and in particular to rule on the terms in which a contract should be made rather than have to hear disputes concerning breach of it.[1] Such advance ruling is possible because the contracting parties are not in fact free agents, but already bound by obligations which a tribunal can assess and reconcile. But in Soviet circumstances it is a useful service. It is suggested that they provide the most convenient means by which officials of state enterprises may obtain a reconciliation of the conflicting instructions which they are apt to receive from the various co-ordinate authorities placed over them by the complex Soviet administrative system.[2] The arbiters are appointed by the Councils of Ministers and executive committees at their several levels.

Courts of the general judicial system are established at all levels of the administrative structure from the district or town up to the federation. At the lowest level they are known as People's Courts, above that as Area, Regional, Territorial or City Courts, and in all units styled republics, whether autonomous or union, as Supreme Courts. There is a Supreme Court of the U.S.S.R. as a whole. Judges

[1] H. J. Berman, *Justice in Russia* (1950), pp. 248–9.
[2] See case in John N. Hazard, *Law and Social Change in the U.S.S.R.* (1953) p. 55.

of people's courts are directly elected for terms of three years,[1] and judges of all higher courts elected indirectly by the soviets or Supreme Soviets at their several levels for terms of five years.[2] In addition to the judges who are paid full-time officials there are also elected by the same procedures panels of assessors, of whom no individual is supposed to sit for more than ten days in the year. A court in most first-instance proceedings consists of one judge and two assessors; in cases involving technical knowledge one assessor may be a specialist,[3] but otherwise both are taken from a panel. Thus a people's court, which does only first-instance work, has a panel of between fifty and seventy-five assessors and only one full-time judge.[4] In the absence of the latter a substitute may be appointed by the republican Supreme Court from among other locally resident professional judges or one of the assessors may be deputed by the local soviet—presumably by its executive committee —to act. During such service the assessor is paid at not less than the rate of the regular judge's salary. Otherwise he gets the equivalent of his own usual salary for each day on which he sits.

Of recent years authority has shown concern to make provision by the publication of textbooks and by short courses for the legal training of assessors, and Soviet publications periodically insist that greater effort should be made in this direction. The professional judges of people's courts themselves seem not to be all legally trained; apart from the law faculties of the universities (in which probably only a bare majority of the judges even of the higher courts have been trained) such training is available in legal schools of middle grade, or for remoter areas by correspondence course, and official publications suggest anxiety to remedy defects in this respect. The status of the professional judge and the assessors is equal on the bench and the verdict is reached by majority vote of all three. No dissent is expressed in court, though the judge may note it on the record for use in the event of an appeal. It seems that in general the assessor defers readily to his professional colleague. He is apparently not always treated by him with much respect. It is complained that assessors are regularly summoned only on the day before they are required, and rarely sent the papers in advance. Certain classes of cases are heard by benches composed entirely of professional judges without assessors. These include all appeals, which come before the same system of courts, but mainly in the

---

[1] Article 109 of federal constitution.
[2] Articles 105–8.
[3] Case in Berman, op. cit., p. 89. He notes, however, that this provision is little known.
[4] Kiralfy, op. cit., p. 388.

upper ranges. Labour discipline cases—though not other cases involving labour relations—were also tried entirely by professional judges, but this class of business seems to have been entirely abolished by the legislation of April 1956. Thus the superior courts have much smaller assessor panels than the people's courts, even though their proportion to the professionals is now much increased since Stalin's time; the federal Supreme Court elected in 1967 had forty-five as against a chairman, three vice-chairmen and sixteen members. All courts above the people's court have more than one judge.

Union-republic supreme courts are divided into collegia (divisions) on civil and on criminal cases. The federal court has, in addition, a military collegium, a special collegium for consultation and other duties and a statistical office. Until February 1957 it had also collegia to deal with appeals from the former rail transport and water transport courts (dealing mainly with breaches of labour discipline and other acts tending to disorganise the transport system). All supreme courts can meet in plenary session of their professional membership for such business as the prescribing of rules of interpretation. Chairmen of union-republic supreme courts are *ex officio* members of such plenary sessions of the federal court. The function of the federal collegium for consultation appears to be to meet requests from other courts for advice on points of law.

By an edict of the Praesidium of the Supreme Soviet of the 14th August 1954 a further level of appeals was provided 'in order to increase the role of local judicial agencies in the matter of court review'. These are the praesidia of union- and autonomous-republic supreme courts and of the courts of territories, regions and autonomous regions. They are to be formed of the chairman of the court, the vice-chairman and two members of the court, and the selection of people to them is to be confirmed by the Praesidium of the Supreme Soviet or the soviet executive committee at the appropriate levels. As the procedure has been defined by a subsequent edict of 25th April 1955, protests against entry into force of sentences and decisions may be made by the federal Procurator-General or the chairman of the federal Supreme Court and their deputies to the praesidia of all courts, and by the corresponding officials at lower levels to the praesidia of courts at or below their own level. The protests may be made against a judgment on appeal regardless of the motives for which it is given. A member of the court who has sat upon the case at an earlier instance is disqualified from hearing the protest as a member of the praesidium. If in consequence there is no quorum the matter goes to a higher court. The decisions of a praesidium may themselves be protested up to the level of a collegium of the federal Supreme Court. This has no praesidium. The Supreme Court, like all other courts, hears cases on ordinary appeal from the level of courts immediately below, in addition to those brought to it by the Procurator-General (or Chief Military Procurator). With assessors it may even take cases of special importance at first instance, but it is unlikely that it gets much such business.

The number of levels of appeal available varies with the complexity of the administrative structure of the republic of origin. In small republics the level between people's court and supreme court is missing.

The civil proceedings before these courts are largely concerned with much the same sort of disputes on economic matters as engage the State Arbitration, but where one of the parties is a collective farm or perhaps a para-economic body in a type of dispute not expressly excluded. Disputes among private individuals or between such individuals and organisations including state enterprises remain within their jurisdiction and seem to provide them with no lack of business, even though the omnipresence of the state—as landlord among its other roles—removes to administrative channels much that in other countries would come before the courts of civil jurisdiction as disputes between individuals. Minor property cases, including those arising from wills, and family matters, including contested divorces—have been prominent categories of business, though under new basic rules of family law coming into force in October 1968 divorces at least should be markedly less demanding of court time; previously a complex conciliation procedure was mandatory but in future divorce by consent will be allowed in uncontested cases where there are no children, and in other cases the people's court is now given full jurisdiction. Citizens may sue enterprises, ministries or other public agencies, or co-operatives (including collective farms) for damages for wrongs done to them, for reinstatement in case of wrongful dismissal or transfer and for the recovery of wages or share of collective-farm produce due to them. They can be sued for failure to fulfil their production norms, though it seems that they rarely are. The first recourse for the settlement of disputes and complaints between management and workers has been to the norms and conflict commissions (R.K.K.) representing equally management and the (official) trade unions. A director who prevented the establishment of such a commission on the ground that there were no disputes in his factory was held to be at fault.[1] Recourse to the people's court, it seems, was by leave, or action, of the trade union. An edict of January 1957 established an

[1] *Trud*, 29th December 1955.

intermediate appeal to the full factory or local trade-union committee, if any, made both appeals matters of right, and stated the periods for application and defined the considerable limitations on the powers of the R.K.K.—which it renamed 'commissions on labour disputes'. Holders of a very wide range of responsible posts are excluded from recourse to the commissions and courts and can look only to higher authority in their branches.

All cases heard in the courts may be appealed to the next higher court within a set limit of time. There they end unless taken higher by the procurator or the higher courts themselves.

Criminal cases come before the same courts. The procedures seem to differ only at the preparatory stage; the judge, in ascertaining whether there is a case to answer and what witnesses should be called, acts on his own in civil cases but should call in his assessors in criminal matters.[1] The criminal code is distinguished from those of most systems by extreme vagueness both in its definition of offences and in the sentences which it prescribes for them, and there is a similar failure to prescribe which levels of the system shall be competent to deal with which offences. Even the most serious offences by Soviet standards are all placed within the competence of the regional and equivalent courts. It seems that the procurators have among their tasks that of deciding at which level it is convenient to bring any particular case, though it rests with the court to accept or refuse it. The vagueness in the other respects, gives the courts wide discretion in which they have until recently been expected to be guided by analogy from similar offences more specifically provided for, by regard for the whole motivation and record of the accused rather than the mere fact of commission, and by considerations of public educative effect in view of the administration's concern, for the time being, to suppress particular forms of conduct and inculcate particular attitudes. The new Criminal Code of 1961 (preceded by basic rules for the same area of 1958) is supposed to have removed the need for the doctrine of analogy, which ill accorded with recent official emphasis on respect for legality, but the survival of considerable vagueness and the attitudes to crime which continue to be expressed in the Soviet press and in Soviet action suggest that something of the sort will continue to be applied in the courts' decisions. The educative and exemplary purpose of court proceedings—to make policy clear to the citizens—is evidenced in the reporting of them in the press. The reports are brief and make few concessions to professional interest in legal complexities or to general public interest in the personalities involved. They are exemplary and concentrate on the offence and the

[1] Kiralfy, op. cit., p. 396.

penalty imposed. Thus since the war, when the authorities have been particularly concerned with acts of violence, and at all times when they have been troubled by official malpractices, cases of prosecution for such offences have become prominent in the daily press. Civil proceedings, having no exemplary quality, are not reported. For the same reasons trials of especial relevance to some message which the authorities wish to drive home may be held in a public hall or in the factory or farm where the offence was committed, rather than in the regular courtroom. The great show trials of the late 'thirties and, less spectacularly, since then, with their public confessions of the improbable, can be explained only by similar considerations. Such events as these, and the record of readiness by prosecuting and judicial authorities to impute to an accused person the logical consequences, by Marxian analysis, of his actions, even if he had himself never envisaged them, may cast some doubt on the statement that Soviet criminal law is exceptionally concerned, or concerned at all, with motivation. But in fact the motives which engage its attention are those which have made the accused the person which he is rather than those which have impelled him to the act with which he is charged. The belief is probably genuinely held by many in authority that a propensity towards acts disruptive of the socialist order of Soviet society can be revealed by acts not themselves amounting to definable offences, though they may need to be represented as such for public edification, and that it is important that such a propensity should be eradicated. Certainly the courts go to great length to enquire into the circumstances, attitude and character of those who come before them and seek to adjust the sentence to what they think they find.

Cases of a criminal nature—though not so described in Soviet terminology—may, like much civil business, be settled administratively without reference to the courts. In addition to the punitive powers of the Commission of Soviet Control and the power of factory directors to deprive some unsatisfactory workers of certain social welfare benefits, there are the village soviet powers and various minor departmental powers to inflict small fines. But the most important of such powers has hitherto been that of the Ministry of Internal Affairs to hear political cases, in a very wide sense of the term, in private, without the presence of the accused or any of the safeguards of the general judicial system such as the right to legal representation or the right of appeal. The decree of the Central Executive Committee and the Council of People's Commissars of 10th July 1934 setting up the federal People's Commissariat for Internal Affairs created a 'special consultation' (*osoboe soveshchanie*), consisting, as subsequently defined, of the minister, his deputies, the head of the police service, and the minister of the appropriate republic, which 'shall be granted the right to apply in an administrative procedure banishment from certain localities, banishment with settlement in a locality, confinement in a correctional labour camp up to five years and deportation abroad'.[1] Despite the limitation of sentence to five years the lack of any public proceedings meant that further sentences might be imposed as soon as the original one had expired. In practice similar powers were exercised both by local tribunals of the ministry and by special tripartite commissions (*troika*) composed of a representative of the state authorities, one of the party and one of the Internal Affairs Ministry. In February 1956 it was announced that the special consultation had been abolished in 1953, and its business transferred to the regular courts.[2]

Curiously at variance with the repeated emphasis of recent years on the right of citizens to a fair trial, and indicative that authority finds it hard to understand the implications of the rule of law or, at least, to accept the slackening of the powers of control which would result from such a development were the procedures adopted in the various republics over the period 1957–61 for trial of persons held to be avoiding work or otherwise parasitic upon society—judgment by fellow workers with confirmation of sentence by the executive committee of a local soviet. An alternative procedure, trial by people's court was available at discretion of the local procurator; in the case of an alleged offender with no employment—and so no fellow workers—it alone was applicable. Sentence seems always to have been exile to the remoter parts of the Union, with forced labour. Abolition of this anomaly started before all republics had adopted it. The former procedure disappeared; the latter—and the exile sentence—was confined to Moscow and Leningrad. Elsewhere the soviet executive committee became the court and the forced labour sentence was to be served locally.

Soviet writings allow that the constitutional guarantee of judicial independence (Act 112) does not mean freedom from the policy of the Party. Apart from the manner of the judge's election and the short term of his office, and also the possibility of his being recalled at any time during that term (as six judges of the federal Supreme Court were by decree of the Supreme Soviet at its meeting of February 1955), he is subject to constant pressures in his work

---

[1] V. Gsovski, *Soviet Civil Law* (1948), vol. ii, p. 23, gives in English the relevant article from this measure; W. W. Kulski, *The Soviet Regime* (1954), pp. 233–4, gives *in extenso* an English text of the consequent decree of the same authorities concerning the organisation and jurisdiction of this body.

[2] *S.G. i P.*, No. 1 of 1956, p. 3.

which are opposed to the ideas of judicial independence held in other countries. Thus the press repeatedly comments on unsatisfactory verdicts and carries threats of disciplinary penalties upon judges for excessive leniency in the treatment of offences which the authorities are, for the time being, particularly anxious to suppress. Judges have at times been specifically instructed by the Ministry of Justice to take account of comment in the press and to meet periodically with its representatives to discuss the investigation of complaints. Any greater concessions to judicial independence would, in fact, be surprising in the Soviet setting, where government policy, which means the policy of the Communist Party, is not the purpose of a transient administration but, in principle at least, the spirit underlying the laws themselves.

Within their limits the ordinary courts seem to be consistent in their practices, to take their tasks seriously and to seek to give effective protection to the citizen from these forces in society against which he may need it. By the definition of its functions as supreme protector, the state as a whole, always correctly interpreting the instructions of the party, cannot be one of these forces. It is said that opening of criminal proceedings before the courts generally stays any further administrative action, and that this is a fact known to, and counted upon by, the comparatively large section of the Soviet population, whose daily activities are apt to bring it sometimes into conflict with the law.

Other Lines of Control

The English term 'trade union' has always had a contemptuous implication in Russian communist usage, suggesting the 'economists' of pre-revolutionary days with their readiness to negotiate with capitalism for material benefits. Nevertheless, trade unions—professional league (*profsojuz*) in good Russian and without any pejorative sense—are a useful, if subordinate, means of enlisting aid for the state's purposes and keeping a check on industry. They became important allies of the Bolsheviks in the latter part of 1917, once they had been captured from their earlier Menshevik allegiance, and gave promise of being a powerful influence in the new society. The 1919 programme of the party went so far as to envisage the eventual concentration in their hands of the whole administration of the economy, but in fact they had then already lost much of the administrative power which they had briefly held—particularly the management of the social-insurance scheme. The concern of the leaders of the movement to secure for the workers an adequate participation, by way of wage increases, in the country's growing industrial production brought them increasingly into conflict with the party leadership which was convinced of the need for absolute priority for investment and of its own superior competence to speak the real will of the workers, as against their transient inclinations. The adoption, from 1928, of comprehensive economic planning exacerbated relations. By fixing in advance the unalterable share of labour it rendered vain and obstructive any union representations; for its fulfilment it demanded a return to direction of labour and the identification of party and state with the new order of managers which they were building up, rather than with the workers. The party's technique of use of the party group for disruption was brought into play early and effectively, and in 1929 the trade-union leaders were drastically purged by Stalin for resistance. Mr. Shvernik was installed as chairman of the Central Council of the Trade Unions, which office he held until 1944 and again from March 1953 to March 1956. In the interval between his two periods of office the post was occupied by Mr. V. V. Kuznetsov, a professional engineer previously employed in a management capacity in the steel industry, and from March 1956 it was held by Mr. V. V. Grishin, formerly a party official, who in turn was replaced in July 1967 by Mr. A. N. Shelepin, whose career had led from the youth movement leadership, through State Security and Control to a party Central Committee secretaryship. This appeared to be an upgrading of the trade unions rather than a down-grading of the new incumbent of their leading office. At all levels the leaders have been appointed by the party, commonly from among its own subordinate officials.

The current functions of the movement are still largely those transferred to it from the People's Commissariat for Labour on the latter's abolition in 1933—social insurance, safety and conditions of work, welfare of new workers (recruitment being left to the several industries). In 1947 unions had restored to them power to make local collective labour norms, conditions and wages agreements, lost in 1933, though such agreements were to conform to collective agreements made for the whole industry at ministry level—which in fact left very little room for local manoeuvre. Revision, in 1958, of the rules under which they operate confirmed the right of the factory committee of the union to be consulted on management proposals for overtime working, on proposed dismissals and other matters, to express itself on any disputes and to be represented on the standing production conferences which are supposed to be consulted on the firm's planning assignment and to exercise a continuous watch over production methods. From subsequent press articles it seems doubtful whether the increase in union influence amounts to much.

Even thus subordinate, union functions are held to warrant an elaborate organisational structure. The several unions provide for all workers, regardless of craft or standing, in an industry as defined by the existence of a responsible ministry—which has involved the trade-union structure in the fluidity of the state organisation—with committees elected by secret ballot at all levels down to the town and the factory, the last having under it separate committees for the several sections, where these have at least a hundred workers each, and below those groups of twenty members. The quality of elections appears to be very much as in others in the Soviet Union, though factory directors are cautioned that they should not seek to get their own men elected, or not in such a manner as to arouse objection.[1] At federal level all unions come together in an occasional congress—the latest, the fourteenth, being held in March 1968, the thirteenth in October 1963 and three others since World War II—an All Union Central Council, which as elected in 1968 had 304 members and 105 candidates; its praesidium (chairman, seven secretaries and nineteen members), and a central checking commission of 55. All show even more than the usual Soviet tendency to expand. Since 1948 there have also been links at lower levels in the form of territorial, regional and town councils of trade unions elected for two-year terms by local inter-union conferences of delegates from general union meetings in the several enterprises. The central organisations both of the several unions and of the movement as a whole maintain their own publications, research institutions and staffs for the running of the various services which they administer including the social-insurance service and welfare institutions such as hospitals and holiday homes, and a force of labour inspectors. Voluntary service is said to limit the resulting bureaucracy; there were 12,000,000 activists declared in 1968, and the range of activities of the commissions and other bodies on which they served as wide as ever and apparently as much social as narrowly industrial. It is probably for its services in thus mobilising a large proportion of the working population to commitment to the system by personal activity in matters of relatively safe detail, rather than for any positive result achieved by such activity, that the movement is valued and retained by the authorities. Probably also an additional, interested eye on the behaviour of managers is thought useful, but it does not seem that in those of their ostensible purposes which are most relevant to the work of management the union bodies are very effective. The 1968 membership of the movement (86,130,000) looks very like total mobilisation of the employed population, after decades around the 90 per cent mark.

[1] Case in *Trud*, 29th December 1955.

The press—in common with all other media of communication under a totality of control which other systems of government can hardly hope to emulate—provides more than a pulpit for the party, and with the party's sanction for such other systems as the *komsomol* or the trade unions. It is itself a channel of control of performance. The visit of a correspondent from *Pravda*, or even from some less authoritative organ, can hardly fail to arouse misgivings in managers, chairmen or other holders of such precarious authority as the Soviet system offers. He may be looking for an inspiring story of achievement, but it is virtually certain that his article will contain, if only incidentally, slashing criticisms, and the matter may well not end there. Feuilltons (satirical articles in semifictional form) and reports in *Pravda* and *Izvestia*—covering principally party and soviet systems respectively—and more specialised papers regularly uncover some scandal of more than usual gravity—followed by assurance that the appropriate higher authority has investigated the charge, found it fully justified and taken the necessary action, including reprimands and sometimes more severe penalties upon the culprits. Such cases have certainly been cleared by authority in advance of publication, since every word printed—except in *Pravda* which is above suspicion—must come under the eyes of an official of the Chief Administration for Literature and Publishing Matters (*Glavlit*) of the Ministry of Culture—who in the case of a newspaper or publishing house is resident in its own office —operating in knowledge of the policy of the party's propaganda and agitation department and the police authorities and backed by an elaborate web of personal editorial responsibilities. It may be that the correspondent sets out on his travels only when the organs of the party or state have found a case and some moral which can usefully be pointed by it. But it seems probable that the press, in knowledge of what dirt is required and the screening to which it will be subjected, is left some discretion to plan the dig. Much the same probably applies to letters from the public. Very few are published, and those often, it seems, inspired, and always so chosen as to fit into the paper's current campaign or perhaps to inaugurate a new one, but it may well be that many more are received and taken into account in the paper's own investigations. Certainly official insistence on the importance of the organisation in newspaper offices, as in party and soviet organs, for dealing with such business, suggests that it is of more value than the published matter proves. Such of this correspondence as appears is always of weight and usually informed by burning indignation without any of the amiable trivialities which appear in the correspondence columns of even the most august British newspapers.

No association, from the centre down to the local co-operative, sports club or cultural society, may be formed, and no meeting of any sort may be held, without license from the organ of the state authority for the area from which the participants are to be drawn. Where a model charter has been approved for the type of association, as for the collective farms before 1956, it must be followed; if there is none, the law requires the authority of the Praesidium of the republican Supreme Soviet for each foundation. Thus all legal organisational systems in Soviet society can be, and are, in some way made to serve the purposes of the Soviet state in organising the masses, the people at large, and so both redeeming them from uncommitted and unsupervised apathy and establishing a potential claim to their services against the other established hierarchies in case the need should arise so to use them. In general the authorities of the Soviet Union seem to distrust the unorganised as potentially dangerous. Most of their safeguards are to be found among the social, cultural and sporting societies which share with the party the honours of an appearance in Article 126 of the constitution. Even the Orthodox Church, however, has had its moments of mild approval, notably during the war, when it helped the authorities to tap springs of traditional patriotism not otherwise so readily available to them, and in the early Khrushchov period. An order of the party Central Committee of 10th November 1954 forbade actions offensive to religious believers and administrative action against the Church. Though it was always made clear that the Church was not for communists or members of the *Komsomol*, and though it was throughout denied permission to teach, it had most of the badges of a permitted organisation, including its own journal. Latterly, however, the inability of the regime to work with organisations which by their nature cannot fully accept its ideology seems to have reasserted itself, and administrative action has again been turned against the believers. Other religious communities, particularly those connected with stronger communities abroad, have in general been viewed with more suspicion, and for Jews and the less compliant sects of Baptists in particular official approval is at best brittle and apt for individuals and whole communities to deteriorate into very positive persecution.

The Men in the Machine

The ministry, as evolved under Stalin, was very largely a self-contained world, recruiting and training staff for its service at all levels down to the manufacturing enterprises subordinate to it and, subject to the very limited rights of the soviet executive committees, the other participants in the system of dual subordination, and the much more real power of the party leadership, presiding over their whole careers. Establishments required confirmation by higher authority throughout the system, with presumably the advice of the State Establishments Administration of the Ministry of Finance, and general proportions of pay for each grade were fixed by the federal Council of Ministers.

Specialists were generally trained by ministries in their own schools or occasionally by courses provided to their requirements in schools of the general educational system. In general the best pupils of the schools of that system, as tested in the state's examinations, were admitted to ministry schools of higher educational standing without further tests, and others on the result of a special examination, as was then the practice for university admissions. At a lower level, the system of Labour Reserves, begun mainly as a drive to get surplus young people away from the farms, trained and posted skilled workers.

The 1957 reforms, instituting a regional structure of industry necessarily changed all this, and the ministries as now reformed seem likely to remain deprived at least of their training powers. The ministry technical schools were at the time of decentralisation brought within the system of the Ministry of Higher Education, which added the words 'and Middle Technical' (now, 'and Specialised Middle') to its title to accommodate them. The Labour Reserves, which under Stalin had been directed by a separate ministry and after his death had passed under the Ministry of Culture, are now run by a chief administration directly under the federal Council of Ministers; conscription seems no longer to be required since voluntary recruitment has proved adequate. The Reserves' original purpose, however, still goes on; soviet executive committees in rural parts still maintain departments for the recruitment and transfer of labour. Nor does the transfer of most technical education to the general educational ministries mean that students are no longer trained for more or less specifically envisaged posts; that is a characteristic of all Soviet education.

To minor posts as clerks or manual workers the head of the unit has apparently a substantially free power of appointment, and there have been frequent allegations in the Soviet press of lack of discretion in the exercise of this power, particularly failure to consult the labour books and other records concerning persons who subsequently proved to be dishonest or particularly unreliable. The labour book, instituted by decree of the Council of People's Commissars in December 1938, is a personal career record maintained for every Soviet citizen in employment and containing, among other details, records of posts held, reasons for leaving them and rates of pay received. It moves with the employee from post to post. In addition, since 1940 all residents in urban areas and within a wide radius of Moscow, Leningrad and Kiev are required to have internal passports, issued by town or district militia (police) headquarters upon application certificated by the soviet executive committee, which have to be registered with the police before they are allowed to take up residence, and these also record changes of employment. Cases are reported where with the aid of gullible officials wrong-minded citizens can get round even this obstacle to mobility. But if the system works properly the Soviet citizen should be well documented, and officials engaging staff are expected to take account of the fact.

The problem posed by the admission of trainees is less one of selection than of finding people of something like adequate quality, and training, posting and retaining them. A particular difficulty in respect of posting obviously arises from reluctance to serve on remote stations. Accounts are commonly given of intrigue among students completing their courses in ministry training schools and among officials already in state service to secure town posts or posts in the more advanced parts of the country. Personal contacts play a large part in this process of intrigue, and leading officials intervene to obtain satisfactory postings for their children. It is complained that excessive lenience is shown with the insubordinate and unreliable at all levels, such as the graduates who flatly refuse the postings offered. This is probably in consequence of the shortage of manpower, and especially educated and skilled manpower, in the Soviet economy. Where a course of training leads to a formal qualification refusal of appointment may apparently lead to its forfeiture, but trainees presumably understand the protective value of their indispensability. Once appointed, moreover, officials seem to have a tendency to drift back to the principal urban centres, or, with less obvious illegality but still contrary to approved policy, to continue to live in town while holding a rural post. Collective-farm chairmen and technical specialists and soviet executive committee chairmen seem particularly to offend in this respect. This results partly from habituation of leading officials to the middle-class comforts which their position enables them to enjoy in the towns, but it is akin to a similar problem of scarcity and instability of labour generally. An edict of the Praesidium of the Supreme Soviet of 26th June 1940 made the wilful abandonment of employment or absenteeism by any worker or official a criminal offence, but by an edict of the 25th April 1956 the criminal penalty for those offences was abolished, allegedly on the ground that the conscientiousness of labour had improved. Sanctions of a less drastic sort were still retained to induce labour to remain at its post. Persons changing their places of employment at their own request, with certain exceptions, and those dismissed for persistent absenteeism were to lose for a period of six months all service bonuses and the right to benefit for temporary incapacitation for work, and for the latter offence an entry was to be made in their labour books. Incapacitation benefit was restored to them in cases of industrial injury or occupational disease by edict of 31st January 1957, and in all other cases by one of 25th January 1960.

In general, the picture of the men in the machine presented by Soviet sources—very well trained organisation men at the top, though with considerable hard-won skill in spying out in advance the organisation's darker purposes and contriving ways round them, and foot-loose unenthusiasts at the bottom—does not seem to change much. It is one of the more important tasks of party members to frustrate unofficial purposes at all levels; less pressure and more consideration from the top might be more effective.

Education and the Educated

The state-party structure is the sole provider of education, and the power which this gives for shaping the dispositions of the participants in the system has been jealously safeguarded. Resources, especially of teaching manpower, have throughout been very limited; and the revolution, with its early distrust of formal schooling and of a teaching profession, which, though largely socialist, was often not Bolshevik, did not help. Since the beginning of the Stalin-Zhdanov period there has been a drive of increasing intensity to improve facilities, but compulsory seven-year education (normally for ages seven to fourteen) was declared achieved only in 1949 and written into the constitution as a citizen's right in 1956. Two years later, as part of a general reform of education, the constitutional guarantee was extended to eight years. At that time it appeared that some children in undeveloped areas were receiving only the first four years provided by the elementary (*nachalnaja*) school, into which category 112,400 of the country's 199,700 schools then fell. The sixth Five-Year Plan (1956) had envisaged compulsory ten-year schooling by 1961, but this was dropped as being too ambitious.

It is highly probable that there is still in the country a considerable preponderance of elementary schools. This does not mean that a majority of Soviet children are condemned to have only a partial education. The 'eight-year schools' covering these same four years and also the other four of compulsory education, and the complete 'middle polytechnical schools' which, despite their name, cover the whole of this period as well as an additional two years, are supposed to teach to exactly the same syllabus in all subjects, so that pupils can be freely transferred from one to another. Also the elementary schools, though numerous, contain only a minority of the pupils—in 1958–9 some 4.5 million out of 29.6 million. Where, as in the larger towns, facilities exist complete 'middle' (i.e. ten-year) schooling is probably already the rule; in some rural areas distance and the demands of farm work may severely restrict education.

The return, under the Khrushchov legislation of 1958, to the principle of 'polytechnical' education, by which the last three years of 'middle' schooling were to contain a high proportion of practical industrial work, was apparently intended to induce acceptance by the many young people who must work on the less inviting side of the gulf which a successful policy of academic education had opened in industrial life, and understanding among those who reached the other side. The policy's failure swept away also the partially applied requirement of a period of full-time work in industry (usually, of two years) before higher education.

Given middle schooling and the basic work and general character qualifications, admission is by competitive examination to universities and other institutes of higher education providing a four- or five-year course or to the lowest form of teacher training which provides a two-year course. As an alternative to the last two (post-compulsory) years of middle school students may be admitted either to rather more practically oriented special middle schools or to fully specialised institutions, generally known as 'technikums', providing a vocational, though not necessarily technical, education. On completion any student at university or technicum level must work for three years in the appropriate branch of the economy. The university student may proceed directly to post-graduate work, but for the technicum student further full-time education is excluded for the three-year period of compulsory service.

The system provides also for the continuation of education on a part-time basis by those already at work. 'Schools of working youth', 'schools of rural youth' and adult schools make up the deficiencies of the general educational system, though a marked swing away from the more elementary classes of the rural schools of recent years suggests some improvement. External students, studying by correspondence, have latterly outnumbered full-time students of institutes of higher education and have been over half as numerous as full-timers on the rolls of specialised middle educational institutions.

Traditionally the Soviet school has been a day school, but boarding establishments (*internat*) are attached to many of them, principally as the only answer to natural conditions which make for very bad school attendance in some areas—long a cause of concern to the authorities. Village soviets are often blamed for failure to get their children to school, but as often the imputation of fault probably covers an objective impossibility. Pupils living in remote districts must sometimes travel as much as ten miles to attend a seven-year school, over very bad roads and with a great shortage of means of transport. The *shkola-internat*, promoted by Mr. Khrushchov at the Twentieth Party Congress and embodied in republican legislation in the following year (1957) seemed more ambitiously planned, providing in addition to accommodation and instruction a full range of physical and other out-of-school activities. Despite the innovator's expressed emulation of such pre-revolutionary institutions as the pages' corps and the launch of the idea in the Soviet press with approving references to the British public school, it seems doubtful whether authority intended a special form of education for an élite. A tighter ideological and disciplinary hold on the new generation probably was desired; at first it seemed that children were only to be released once in the year, for their parents' summer holiday, but practice has been more liberal—based in most areas on weekly boarding. Although initially growth was rapid, the suggestion of the early days of the development that it would ultimately become the normal form of education never showed much prospect of fulfilment, since it was evident that there were not nearly enough buildings and other resources even for boarding establishments of the older type and since the closer supervision envisaged would make further heavy demands on resources of manpower already long stretched beyond their efficient limits. In practice these factors have been operative to confine this form of education to a limited role for special cases, mainly in difficult family circumstances. There is a small element of selection of the specially gifted, mainly in mathematics or music. Otherwise the curriculum is that of a normal eight- or ten-year school with additional activities. Pupils are supposed to participate in the running of the school—and presumably to learn the Soviet system of government—through their own elected councils, with the *Komsomol* branch playing guiding and organising role of the party in the organs of the state outside.[1]

Tuition fees introduced in 1940 for the last three years of middle school and all higher education were abolished in June 1956. Boarding fees are charged, with relief for the poorer parents.[2]

[1] G. Arnautov (sector head in the Academy of Pedagogical Sciences of the R.S.F.S.R.) in *Narodnoe Obrazovanie*, No. 8 of 1956.
[2] Mr. Khrushchov's speech, *Izvestia*, 15th February 1956.

All courses at university level require the ministry's approval, the allocation of students is apparently within its discretion and the maintenance of standards in the award of academic degrees and titles rests with it. Possibly, as in other fields, the rigidity of the system is not as absolute in practice as on paper. There is evidently some room left to local initiative even in the planning of courses, which may lead to conflict with the plans of other levels. Thus it was reported in 1953 that the University of Lvov had established, in the face of indifference from the Ministry of Culture which was then responsible for the universities, a course in State Law designed especially for future administrators in soviets or other agencies, but found that on completion its students were commonly assigned to the courts or procurators' offices for which their concentration on administrative matters and their lack of experience of criminal law and procedure unfitted them. Even where the subjects, hours and forms of teaching are prescribed, some scope has to be left to the teaching staff to vary the manner in which it is given, and advantage is taken of this.[1] Moreover, the ministry can be subjected to argument; we hear of regular annual encounters by correspondence on such issues as a ministerial attempt to force a university to take its quota of research students (*aspirant*) in subjects in which it has no qualified staff, to the neglect of the subjects in which it specialises, though the outcome is not clearly indicated. Nevertheless the assignment in courses common to a number of universities is uniform in all essentials and very heavy. Compulsory lectures should take up some thirty-six hours a week of the students' time, and some universities irregularly impose up to twelve more. The demand which this makes on the time of the staff has latterly led to complaint at the sharp division which has appeared in some subjects between teachers and researchers. Beyond the first course, which though constituting a recognised qualification does not lead to any degree, most universities and institutes of comparable status, including, as we have seen, the federal party school, provide courses of research study, normally of three years, leading to the degree of 'candidate', and beyond that to the doctorate. Rather under three-quarters of the research students are studying 'with break from production' (that is, full time),[2] and are paid a state stipend. The award of the higher degrees, upon assessment of the dissertation or other work by the university council, is subject to the approval of a Higher Certificating Commission (V.A.K.), in the ministry, the

[1] See S. V. Utechin, 'Moscow University—Reflections of a Former Student', *Universities Quarterly*, August 1955.
[1] Details in *Narodnoe Hozjajstvo SSSR*, p. 235.

powers of which are clearly no formality.[1] Cases have been observed
of refusal of higher degrees even in scientific subjects for alleged
servility to foreign achievements, though studies in the humanities
are more subject to this political force. Understandably, political
limitations are particularly severe in the social sciences including
history, where research seems to be possible only on topics approved
in advance by the ministry. The results may be seen in complaints in
the Soviet press of the dogmatic scholastic approach of researches
in this field, and also in the titles of the dissertations and published
works which suggest almost exclusive concentration on subjects
likely to produce conclusions of obvious utility for propaganda
purposes. In the natural sciences, however, the results of the Soviet
educational system are impressive. The regime's traditional attachment to science (though it has not always withstood the stress of
practice), its concern with practical economic needs and its ability
both to direct and richly to reward those whom it trains enable it to
produce scientists and technologists as few free educational systems
can do. The problem seems to be how to support them with an
adequate supply of technicians of a middle-school standard of
education,[2] and to this the 'polytechnicisation' of the middle schools
in 1958 was apparently intended to provide the solution.

A marked preponderance of scientific subjects in the curriculum
at all stages reflects the regime's concern with the useful. Even in the
non-scientific subjects Soviet education is markedly and explicitly
directed towards the provision of trained staff (cadres) for the
operation of the system, and for this and other reasons it is closely
tied to the economic plan. In a revision of university courses towards the end of 1955, apparently designed primarily to eliminate
over-specialisation which had occurred in both arts and sciences,
the occasion was taken to include in all courses in the philological,
historical, geographical, biological, physical, mathematical and
chemical faculties compulsory lectures on teaching method and
teaching practice. It was stated that from 1956 not less than 80 per
cent of graduates in the first four of these faculties and not less than

[1] V. N. Sementovski (in *Vestnik Vyshej Shkoly*, No. 9 of 1955, p. 17) complains of the capricious standards of this body. It has proved particularly
obstructive to nominations to doctorates on the basis of the candidates' work
in general without defence of a dissertation. He suggests that the report made
by the commission's referee on the dissertation should not, as at present, be
secret, as it would be of use to teachers.

[2] *Izvestia* (17th September 1954) complained that in some branches of
industry there were almost as many engineers as technicians. Mr. Bulganin,
in his report to the plenary session of the party Central Committee in July
1955, stated that in industry as a whole there were less than two technicians
to one engineer (*Pravda*, 17th July 1955).

60 per cent of those of the other two were to be directed to middle-school teaching,[1] which has always been a weak spot in the system.

Systematic Marxist indoctrination at the school stage has been given a minor place, as of less importance than such equipment for economic function and less easily imparted to the young mind. However; even as early as the fourth class the study of history, introduced at that level, is required to explain the rightness of the party and its leaders in the move towards communism and to 'arouse in the children a feeling of supreme love for the socialist homeland and an ardent hatred for all enemies and oppressors of the working class'.[2] In the top years of the full middle school a basic course on Marxism-Leninism, with recent history, is now given, and group tutors in the boarding schools have been charged to organise regular political and informational talks for their charges. All university and technicum courses include compulsory and specified instruction in party history, political economy and dialectical and historical materialism. The importance of politcal soundness and awareness in teachers at all levels is constantly emphasised.

Closely related are the country's central learned institutions. Of these by far the most important is the Academy of Sciences, an eighteenth-century foundation which has gradually been made into the principal channel for the considerable sums provided for projects of research in fields of learning likely to serve the authorities' purposes. It is a co-ordinating body directing through its eight departments some hundred institutes concerned not only with the several branches of the natural sciences but also with such fields as geography, economics, history, law and linguistics. All the research in history done in 1955 is said to have been done in the Academy's Institute of History, and not in the universities. The Academy has fourteen branches throughout the R.S.F.S.R. and one in the union republic of Moldavia. The other union republics except the R.S.F.S.R. have their own academies of sciences watched and marshalled by it.[3] It answers directly to the federal Council of Ministers for its work, and of recent years has been under close control. Other Academies—Agricultural Sciences, Medical Sciences, Juridical

[1] M. G. Uroev (Head of the Chief Administration for Universities and Higher Education Institutes of Law and Economics in the Ministry of Higher Education) in *Vestnik Vyshej Shkoly*, No. 11 of 1955, pp. 28, 32.

[2] E. N. Medinski, *Narodnoe Obrazovanie v SSSR* (Moscow, 1952), p. 63, quoted in I. & N. Kazarevich, *Narodnoe Obrazovanie v SSSR*. Institut po Izucheniju SSSR (Munich) 1956, p. 38.

[3] A. V. Topchiev, Chief Academic Secretary of the Academy (*Vestnik Akademii Nauk SSSR*, No. 3 of 1955, translated in *Current Digest of the Soviet Press*, No. 29 of 1955), defines the nature of this relationship and also gives examples of the projects being undertaken in the various fields of the Academy's work.

Sciences, Pedagogical Sciences—answer either similarly to the Council or to individual ministries. Another eighteenth-century foundation, the Academy of Arts, is of little importance and mainly a teaching body. The main channels of control over practitioners of the arts are the Unions of Soviet Artists, of Soviet Composers and of Soviet Writers, all established in 1932, with power to give directives, demand results and administer rebukes for non-performance, which usually (though less certainly in the present period of heightened professional self-respect) are sufficient to induce public repentance or lasting silence by the offender. In the last resort authority has control of the media and the sanctions of law.

The nature of the assignments which through these channels the authorities instruct the educated to perform is fairly clear. For creative artists and workers in the humanities generally the task is to maintain contentment, promote a proper attitude and enhance national prestige; whether their activities bring them personal gratification and comfort is a minor consideration. For the scientist the task is to contribute to such purposes as productivity, national defence, health and well-being. Not all of this stress on obvious utility, it is clear, is stultifying to the scientist; he is restrained from the temptations which beset many of his fellows in other countries to follow mere fashion, to become a literary man or popular personality, or to withdraw from the world. The temptation which the Soviet system does offer him is to become, as for a time did Mr. Lysenko, a court magician, to offer more than he could reasonably be confident of being able to fulfil. For a time Lysenko established himself as dictator of all scientific activity, with the power, which he too frequently exercised, to blast the careers of others of whom he disapproved. This is obviously a fault in the circumstances of Soviet intellectual life, but the effect of the system in corrupting the scientist is probably not so serious as it looks; the sensible man probably considers well how firmly he may hold on to the regime's current line without burning his fingers. Party control is more likely to be stultifying for scholars in the field of human studies and for creative artists, concerned as they must be with understanding and epitomising the motivation of men—including their own—or evoking or expressing a mood. Not the utility of the results but the honesty of the pursuit is the excellence of practitioners in these fields, and in this the Soviet regime is not interested. This is more than just discouraging. The regime has a monopoly of the principal means of artistic expression. As we have suggested, only approved organisations may have newspapers, and the party keeps a particularly close control of their editorial personnel. All other publications, lectures, broadcasts and exhibitions require the approval of the Chief Administration for Literature of the Ministry of Culture, and may subsequently be banned by it. Private printing is impossible since sale, loan or the extension of use of printing, or even duplicating, equipment to private persons is forbidden, and its possession by organisations, themselves licensed and controlled, is registered and strictly supervised by the same chief administration and by the militia (police). Theatrical and concert repertoires are controlled on a federation-wide scale by a committee answerable to the federal Council of Ministers.[1] If the regime sees no utility in an artistic creation—and it usually looks for utility of a fairly tangible kind—that creation will travel no further into the world than the private conversation or the typed copy can carry it. The regime means the official on the spot, and he may well have some odd ideas of what may fittingly go into the local newspaper or review. But with the threat of denunciation, in *Pravda* or otherwise, hanging over him he is unlikely to err far on the side of daring.

We cannot say what is the political influence of the scholar; though his power, of his own motion, to influence public opinion at large is negligible, he may often have access to the greater or lesser makers of policy. Scientists at least must have the power to pronounce an idea unfeasible. It may be perilous to do so—under Stalin it evidently often was—but it is probable that despite a few obvious and immense errors the leaders have developed a fair eye for the sycophant and willingness to take honest advice tactfully expressed. If the Russian academic is at times and in some places remote from the world of practical action it is not by official design; the universities, it is insisted, must be fully integrated as regular consultants in the economic life of their several regions.[2] It is from the ranks of the holders of formal educational qualifications, and especially technical qualifications, that the administrative leadership is largely and increasingly recruited. Even many of the top leaders of the revolutionary generation had engineering qualifications of a

---

[1] On the processes see Kulski, op. cit., pp. 251–3.

[2] Mr. Bulganin, in his report to the plenary session of the party Central Committee, 4th July 1955, deplored the fact that, although much important research work for the national economy was being carried out by members of teaching staffs of institutes of higher education, only a fifth of them were at that time so engaged. He added that the Ministry of Higher Education should organise such work, and the industrial ministries should be bolder in setting research tasks for the academics. He also deplored the lack of co-ordination: 'Scientific institutions, branch institutes and higher-educational institutions are out of contact with each other, which is absolutely intolerable in a socialist state where every possibility exists for co-ordinated activity' (*Pravda*, 17th July 1955). M. A. Prokofjev, Deputy Minister for Higher Education (in *Vestnik Vyshej Shkoly*, No. 5 of 1956, p. 10) stresses the importance of the integration of the universities in their regions as consultants.

somewhat irregular sort acquired on short courses. Such posts as leading party secretaryships, central or local, tend increasingly to fall to those similarly, but more orthodoxly qualified, and, as in the Khrushchov family, the son of the old bolshevik goes into technology. This tendency does not mean that the expert will take over from the hustler and organiser, but it suggests that, like the military commander and the political officer, they will come to have a large common element of training.

The Armed Forces

The regular armed forces, formerly known as the Red Army and Red Fleet, but since 1946 as the Soviet Army and Naval Forces, do not appear to be a regular means of supervision and manipulation in Soviet internal politics. For any such purposes the Ministry of Internal Affairs had its own troops, including Air Force—which as reconstituted it now seems to lack. Nevertheless, from the concern of the regime from its earliest days with consideration of external security, the regular forces are a presence which the citizens can hardly ignore, with a network of garrisons covering the whole country and represented by senior serving officers on the local and central elected bodies of the state and party in a way which contrasts markedly with the practices of most other countries. Moreover, as in most other countries at present, it is a system through which most of the younger citizens have themselves at some time passed. Military service, originally restricted to the approved social classes, has since 1939 been compulsory for all for terms varying with the arm of the service from two years up to five in the navy, with periods of reserve service of diminishing frequency and duration up to the age of 50. Leave is rare, free time limited and the amenities provided in the service superior to those outside; control over the men is therefore far-reaching. The party through its political administration makes full use of its opportunity for the indoctrination of the citizen thus brought within its reach. Political studies according to a centrally prescribed syllabus are required of all, apart from the special obligations of members of party primary organisations as such. Hours of instruction on political matters and state and party history seem to have amounted to about five a week immediately before the war—or perhaps more if general informative talks be included—and to continue on much the same scale. All commanders are charged with political work in their units as a regular part of their military duties, and are responsible to the *zampolit*[1] at the next higher level for it. Usually, it seems, the *zampolit* conducts the political education of the higher ranks under his charge,

[1] See p. 156.

leaving to his subordinates and to the regimental officers the education of the lower. In addition he is required to report every few days on the state of morale of his charges. Recreational facilities, clubs and reading-rooms are all within the responsibility of the *zampolit*, and down to regimental level he is provided with subordinate staff to manage such activities.[1] On the whole the army is probably popular, and serves to win some support for the regime. It seems that it is still one of the party's best recruiting grounds, and though many of its recruits are among the officers for whom membership is a professional requirement, it is likely that many conscripts are caught in the net, if not of the party at least of the *Komsomol*.

Apart from the opportunities for shaping minds the service offers —as do other approved organisations to a lesser extent—a chance to build up detailed information on the character of individuals. This can be done both through the party network and through the counter-intelligence sections (or Special Sections), the agents of the Chief Administration for Counter-Intelligence in the Armed Forces (linked with the Committee of State Security) attached to formations down to division and independent brigade, and with individual officers in all units down to battalion and an extensive staff of informers of all ranks at all levels,[2] and exercising surveillance over all, including the party.

The Soviet Union is more generous than most countries in its granting of exemption from military service to those whose services are valuable to the state in other ways, including, it seems, all those with higher-educational qualifications. This is hardly surprising where all occupations are forms of disciplined state service. The political indoctrination which people so exempted thus miss is made up in other forms, as for instance in the compulsory political instruction at universities and other institutions of higher education. No provision is made for exemption on grounds of conscience.

The officers of the armed forces seem all to serve on longer engagements than that of normal compulsory service, and a great preponderance are professionals. In theory rank designations were abolished at the time of the revolution, and they did not begin to be introduced again until 1935, after which they gradually penetrated through the system until by the time of the war the complete con-

[1] Summarised from Zbigniew Brzezinski (ed.), *Political Controls in the Soviet Army—a study based on reports by former Soviet officers* (who are named and severally contribute sections to the book), Research Programme on the U.S.S.R. (1954), and comments of Raymond L. Garthoff on it in *Problems of Communism*, No. 1 of 1955; see also Fainsod, op. cit., pp. 408–13.

[2] Brzezinski, op. cit.

ventional structure of ranks had been reintroduced. In practice, however, clearly recognised graduations of rank, and the distinction between officers and others in status, authority and living conditions had existed throughout. The distinction is now considerably more rigid than in most armies. Entry into officer rank, as into the higher grades of the state and party bureaucracy generally, is apparently now based very largely on educational qualifications and completion of exceptionally thorough courses of training. Political soundness, as judged by the party, is a condition, but not a sufficient condition, of advancement. Political leaders without military attainments were given high rank during the war of 1941–5, but this is not typical of the system. The military career still seems to be open to ability; there is no clear evidence of the establishment of any form of hereditary military caste, although in 1943 schools were established to train boys—originally war orphans, the sons of men with distinguished military careers—for entry to the services in officer rank, and these may offer the higher ranks the means of perpetuating themselves.

However, as the officers of revolutionary and civil war background die out a new professionalism has begun to appear in the higher command of the forces, somewhat resistant to domination by the party. Hitherto political connections and the divisions of the military profession itself have kept it under control.

We have seen that military representation in the Supreme Soviet is high by the standards of most other countries, and it seems that much the same applies to elected bodies lower down the Soviet system. Until recently the same has not been true of the party structure, though in this respect there seems to have been some change of late. The senior ranks of the army are now represented, rather more fully than hitherto, on the Central Committee and the Central Checking Commission, and in the person of Marshal Zhukov one briefly appeared for the first time as a member of the party Praesidium. This, however, probably does not represent any current danger of military dictatorship. The well-read Marxist is aware of the danger of a Bonaparte, and the powerful apparatus of party and police control permeating the army is the answer to it. The military figures who achieved prominence and personal popularity during the war, including Marshal Zhukov himself, were reduced to obscurity and unimportance in Stalin's last years. After his death they achieved a new prominence as an element in the ruling junta's appeal to the people, and perhaps increasingly in its internal balance of power. But they are probably still not a much more considerable factor than the factory managers, the scientists, or the administrative officials, and as fully integrated into the party.

CHAPTER VI

Decision and Performance

The Soviet style in public political discourse is impersonal, hortatory or polemical, unsystematic and imprecise. The things people say in public rarely contain any expression of motivation such as would square with the record of shifting personal balance in an oligarchic directing group, and the quality both of legal draughtsmanship—with its almost total lack of interpretative clauses and extreme vagueness as to dates and responsibilities—and of quantitative economic information and instructions is not such as to be of much assistance to the official conscientiously seeking to follow instruction. The moment, and commonly the exact nature, of decision is here occluded to a degree obviously inconvenient for any system and incredible in one purporting to be based on democratic centralism. Practice seems to have been consistently based on arrangements for the detection and punishing of non-performance more than on the facilitation of performance.

Top-level Decisions

The sovereign decision-taking body in the Soviet system of government cannot be identified for all purposes with any particular organ of the state or party structure. In this extreme complexity and fluidity nothing even so formally simple as Parliament addressing the courts can be distinguished; rather it is a permanent revolutionary situation in which each ostensible decision and decision-maker must be judged by results. Some apparent locations of power are more convincingly so than others; none is certain at all times. Any formally constituted body is liable to the necessity of sometimes taking in a person who cannot be eliminated from the scene altogether, because his advice may occasionally be needed, or because he has influential connections, and who would be troublesome if left just outside the circle, but whose opinions are not in general of much account. After Stalin Mr. Voroshilov might attend meetings of the party praesidium without the humiliation of having to ask for leave, as, we are told, he had to do previously, but it is unlikely that Mr. Khrushchov often telephoned him to try out a new idea, which was probably a more significant process in the making of

234

new policies than anything which then happened at a formal meeting.

There seemed to be in the early post-Stalin period, as also, apparently, there has been since the deposition of Mr. Khrushchov, a central directing group sufficiently near equality for such leader as there might be within it to feel unable to take the more difficult decisions without some consultation. In his last years in office, in contrast, Mr. Khrushchov seemed to go out of his way to emphasise that he had not consulted his colleagues before making public, virtually mandatory, statements on future lines of economic policy. Since they proved able to put him out this was probably unwise, though useful to them after the event.

Such a group is likely to have included at all times when it was operative most of the members of the inner body of the party Central Committee—praesidium or politburo—and perhaps a few others in regular personal interaction. Clearly it has never included the whole membership of the Central Committee, the rest being only informed, called to witness and occasionally consulted. The wider body seems to have recently been convoked to receive advance news of the intended invasion of a friendly country, and it will be interesting to see whether this comes to be the regular practice on such occasions; there is no reason to suppose that advice was, or will be, asked, but at least the Central Committee seems to have progressed somewhat beyond its role in the later Khrushchov period when, inflated by large numbers of invited non-members, it provided a public arena for proclamations. The Praesidium itself at that time seemed to consist of advisers, rather than deciders, but probably relatively expert opinions were not flouted without equally highly powered counter opinions in fields not for the time being in the leader's eye.

There can be little on which the sovereign body can reach decisions entirely without advice from the outside. Probably the group's internal relations fall most easily into this category; it probably needed no consultation of external opinion to decide that Mr. Malenkov should be relieved of the office of Chairman of the Council of Ministers, though in the case of Mr. Beria, where violence was involved, there must have been some soundings taken to find out who could be relied upon for support or, more important, who could not. In other fields, particularly the economic, the leaders have cause to realise the inadequacy of commands to change the order of things. The presence of the Head of the Central Statistical Administration in the Council of Ministers testifies to a new un-Stalinist respect for facts, and there are signs that hopes for deliverance by computer and information systems generally is certainly not less in the Soviet world than elsewhere. Expert advice is no doubt taken on most matters of policy even if, as seems probable, residues of revolutionary optimism lead to its being even more frequently disregarded than in other countries. One matter of such advice must sometimes be the state of the public mind, or at least the probable attitudes of those whose co-operation may be crucial for the success of a contemplated policy. For all that, it remains true that in Soviet government a quite exceptionally wide range of matters is decided exclusively at the top level in that there is no overt sounding of opinion by public announcement of the prevailing tendency of thought in advance of a final decision. Though Stalin himself invited nation-wide discussion, in the press and otherwise, of his proposals for the 1936 constitution, and his successors have proceeded similarly in ostensibly less momentous issues the direction of the required counsel has always been fairly clearly indicated in advance, and opinions falling wide of it are virtually certain to produce no action; they are doing well if they even find expression. Turns in foreign policy are no less dramatic, and for the Soviet citizen, one would suppose, disconcerting in the present than in earlier phases of the state's history; friends become enemies and enemies friends without any official comment, and unofficial attempts to fill the gap are visited with marked and forcible signs of disapproval. It is perhaps a development of some historic significance that now they are even occasionally made. Even in areas less sensitive by traditional political standards there is a similar lack of free dialogue. The Soviet citizen, like the observer abroad, must infer from the leaders' speeches the degree of priority to be given to capital development over the production of consumer goods or the degree of severity to be applied to the peasants in the succeeding months. He is not consulted; he is not even told, in many cases until after the event. In agricultural matters at least Mr. Khrushchov seems to have formed policies on the basis of a succession of peripatetic dialogues with practising farmers—in contrast to Stalin's seclusion from reality which he had denounced—but the successive divergent decisions seem all to have come from him; what he appeared to seek was factual information, not a lead. The major decisions, especially long-term planning—show no signs of prior consultation.

Planning and Budgeting

At the Fifteenth Party Congress at the beginning of the period of the Five Year Plans in December 1927 Stalin announced that 'Our plans are neither predictions nor conjectures; they are directives.'

Some element of prediction there must, of course, be—a reasonable guess of what is possible with the given resources of men and materials. But in general Stalin was right. The plan is primarily a general order to all enterprises and institutions in the system, a matter of law based upon sanctions rather than of science based upon an objective assessment of probability. It is in consequence of this that overfulfilment in any branch is always even more welcome to the authorities than exact fulfilment. The plan targets are indications of direction, or acceptable minima; the maxima are fixed not by them but by the resources made available, which in conditions of forced rapid industrialisation are always scarce. Decisions on such priorities of allocation, the real planning, are taken not in the formal planning procedure but by such 'top-level' decisions as we have mentioned in the previous paragraph. Fulfilment of the plan in its more formal aspects is evidently far from complete. 'In 1951,' said Mr. Bulganin, 'the proportion of enterprises which failed to fulfil their annual plans amounted to 31 per cent, in 1952 to 39 per cent, in 1953 to 40 per cent and in 1954 to 36 per cent.' Moreover, the Ministries of Ferrous Metallurgy, Heavy Machine Building, the Machine-Tool Industry and Electrical Engineering, which in 1954 had overfulfilled whole major sections of their plan, had nevertheless fallen short on some of the most important products within those sections.[1] Since Stalin ceased to be available as a plausible explanation of non-fulfilment the facile stunts of Mr. Khrushchov have usefully filled the gap. More permanently, failures can often be concealed by target shifting, neglect of variety and quality where they work against production in quantity, and by quoting only particulars of those branches of economic activity which have succeeded. Yet it seems certain that in general the branches of industry in which the authorities are interested do succeed because at need the necessary resources in material, in managerial or technical skill or in labour power are always diverted to them. In the spirit of the economic bias of Marxism such planning extends to the regulation of the whole life of the community. Schools are among the economic enterprises comprised in local plans, both as making demands on local resources and as potential suppliers of labour power.

The instruments of long-term planning are principally the Five Year (for 1959–1965 the Seven Year) Plans for the whole of the economy, though there are also plans for particular branches and areas of which the terms may be shorter, longer or merely equal but not coincident. Officially mentioned examples are the Three Year Plan for the improvement of animal husbandry on collective and

[1] Report to plenary session of the party Central Committee, 4th July 1955 (*Pravda*, 17th July 1955).

state farms to run from 1949 to 1951, the Ten Year Plan for the reconstruction of Moscow to run from 1951 to 1960, and the Five Year Plan for development of cotton-growing in Uzbekistan for a period 1954 to 1958.[1] Within these plans and breaking them down into greater detail on particular products and processes and often varying them to take account of unforeseen developments, there are short-term plans for periods ranging from a year to a month made for the various ministries, republics, administrative areas, and individual enterprises, all of which, it is officially stressed, form a single national plan. It is an elaborate pattern of inter-related instruments repeated and completed by budgets and plans for the allocation of materials, by the general contracts concluded between ministries for the supply by the enterprises of one of them of the equipment or material required by another, and by the local contracts concluded between the several enterprises and by the agricultural co-operatives with their suppliers and outlets. Planning of one sort or another is a continuous process accompanied by equally continuous collection of details of the performance and capacity which form the basis of further planning. In practice, it seems clear, these details are often incorrect, through oversight or through deliberate misrepresentation by subordinates, and the planning little more than a reasonable guess at what these might be persuaded or bullied to within acceptable reach of performing.

There can be very little scope for initiative in the making of the lowest instruments of this system, but at least they serve as a solemn pledging of those who have to take the operative action on the instructions, and they may well in particular situations do more, mainly by providing to the lower levels the opportunity, and with the aid of the accompanying machinery of supervision the obligation, to reveal unknown resources and promise greater achievement. Consequently planning in this sense, as distinct from the fixing of basic priorities, is effected with protracted and widespread discussion. For the long-term plans this is something of a formality. They come to the public eye in the form of 'directives' of the party generally issued in draft in preparation for a party congress and passed unanimously at it, so that the part of the public is confined to such reverential reading and organised expression of approval as is usual with such congress material. The directives for the first Five Year Plan and the fourth were exceptional; the former were passed by a party conference (the Sixteenth, held in April 1929) instead of a congress and, unlike all others, also by a state organ, the fifth All-Union Congress of Soviets; the latter, prepared hurriedly on the

[1] B. I. Braginski and N. S. Kovalj, *Organizatsija planirovanija narodnogo hozjajstva SSSR* (Moscow), 1954, p. 75.

conclusion of the Second World War, came before neither congress nor conference. All have so emerged only some time after they had already come into effect in the country's economic life; in this respect the month's delay of the sixth Five Year Plan of 1956 is quite exceptionally short. The first plan was the work of Gosplan (the state planning commission) which submitted a number of drafts to the party Central Committee before approval was at last secured, and when it appeared it was with the accompaniment of a mass of supporting material. Subsequently Gosplan does not seem to have taken the initiative, and the volume of published documentation has diminished markedly over the whole period of the plans, though with some revival in 1954.

In the annual plans the process of negotiation is more marked, though of distinctively Soviet character, and within very narrow limits of time. The first stage is the preparation by Gosplan of 'control figures', the general framework on which the plan is to be based. These figures vary greatly in the extent to which they go into detail according to the importance of the various ranges of activity; only for capital work is there a full specification by ministries and union republics, and detailed industrial targets are given only for the most essential branches of production. In preparing them the commission is supposed to work in consultation with the ministries, to proceed from the basis of the Five Year Plan and governmental instructions and to take account of balances of stocks. This work begins some six to seven months before the start of the new year. Meanwhile the federal ministries and other authorities and the republics and territorial areas are preparing the preliminary draft of their own annual plans. In this they consult all levels subordinate to them, down to the factory and collective farm, a process designed to reveal all internal reserves—presumably in so far as the managers are not careful to retain them as a cushion for themselves against future circumstances—and to induce attention to improved methods. When data have been collected through the ministry channels—and for agriculture formerly through the soviet structure, now eliminated —planning passes to the second stage, preparation of the final government instructions applying to them and their submission to the federal Council of Ministers with a copy to the commission by a prescribed date, which in 1952 was the 15th August and is always thereabouts, and the commission submits the complete version to the Council of Ministers—in 1952 by the 10th October. Since 1957 it has then been presented to the Supreme Soviet for enactment as a law.

Budgeting accompanies the making of the plan, of which it is the financial expression. All budgets come within the plans at their corresponding levels, though not the whole of the material for the budget is to be found in the terms of the plan. All budgets, including those of the local soviets, are comprised in a general state budget for the country as a whole. This, in addition to providing for the central authorities' own services, makes available to the lower levels of the system the necessary funds for their budgets from the common revenues, and this process is repeated down the line, each budget providing for those of the subordinate authorities. Over the years of the present regime the proportion of the funds expended through local soviet budgets has declined and the services to which these local funds were applied have come increasingly to be of social rather than economic character.

The process of financial budgeting is closely similar to—and in the requirement of soviet legislative action anticipated—that of economic planning. Four to five months in advance the Ministry of Finance warns all federal ministries and republican ministries of finance of the limits within which they must budget for the coming year,[1] and on the basis of their proposals and in accordance with the state plan draws up the general state budget, which it submits simultaneously to the Council of Ministers and to the State Planning Committee. The former, taking account of the report of the latter, approves the budget, which is then presented to the budget commissions of the two houses of the Supreme Soviet, referred by them to preparatory commissions composed jointly of deputies and officials, and thereafter, as we have seen,[2] approved by them unanimously with identical amendments for presentation to the Supreme Soviet. The process at the union-republican level is similar and simultaneous. At the lower levels of the soviet system the process is simpler, and does not in the first instance involve consideration of the plans of subordinate bodies, but the consideration by commissions follows the same pattern.

The budget law provides no very detailed information on the financing of the Soviet system. The several divisions on the expenditure side specify the allocation to the several ministries for economic purposes and to the principal social and cultural purposes, such as education, regardless of the ministries by which they are provided. The paragraphs of the law further provide for the subdivisions of these sums between the several chief administrations of the ministries, institutions and services. The difficulty for the observer outside the system is to know exactly what services are affected by provisions to any particular ministry or agency. The local and ministerial budgets, which are more specific on these matters, are not

[1] The Soviet financial year is the calendar year.
[2] See p. 103.

normally published. The budget report of the Minister of Finance to the federal Supreme Soviet commonly gives rather more information than is contained in the law itself, but is not fully satisfactory, and the contribution of deputies to the debate is never in the direction of asking for fuller information.

The revenue section of the budget contains two main categories: taxation from the economy—broadly, indirect taxes—which is the main resource; and taxation from the population—the direct payment made by individuals—with separate sections for state loans and other minor sources. The structure is unusual. Since 1930 the principal source of revenue has been the turnover tax, a general levy on the product of the state-owned economy according to quantity, differential as between one branch and another, and falling particularly heavily upon food—taxed at its passage through the hands of the state procurement agencies—and consumers' goods. It is hard to tell how much of the selling price of such products is in fact taxation, since almost all the marketing is done through state agencies, which can in consequence largely fix their own price. In addition to this, the industry pays into the budgetary revenues of the state a proportion of its profits calculated separately for each enterprise so as to absorb whatever is left over after provision has been made for all recognised necessary purposes such as maintenance, investment and a contribution to the principal incentive to higher production, the enterprise fund. In the budget these tax receipts are specified according to the several ministries from the enterprises of which they come. Collective farms pay an income tax, partly in kind and partly in cash, at differential rates on produce sold to the state, produce sold on the open market and produce distributed to members. Co-operative organisations and social organisations, such as trade unions and sports clubs, each pay a graduated income tax, and enterprises providing services including entertainment pay a proportion of the takings. In addition the state derives revenues from the sale of property and various services (among which the work done by the former machine-tractor stations was once a very significant item). The main tax from the population is an income tax charged at rates varying with the type of employment and designed in general to discriminate in favour of state employees as against co-operative craftsmen and others. Collective farm and independent peasants pay an agricultural tax, falling not on the individual but on the household and levied according to the area of their private plots on scales varying from one republic to another. All persons without children pay an additional tax, and those with one or two children also pay it but at reduced rates.

The main source of revenue of the local soviets is a proportion of the several state taxes calculated for each authority by its superior authority in accordance with its supposed needs. It is left to the State Bank to make the allocation of funds to the accounts of the various authorities as they are collected. Provision is made for a limited number of local taxes, on building works, means of transport, land and cattle and collective farm markets, from some of which local executive committees are empowered to grant whole or partial exemption. No unauthorised tax may be levied, and maximum rates and certain obligatory exemptions are prescribed. The market tax is to be applied, as to 60 per cent, to the improvement of market facilities.[1]

The financing of industry and of the economy in general is mainly a federal matter, though industry and commerce of local subordination appears on the regional or territorial budget and to a very limited extent on those of districts and towns. Municipal economy—local public works—'is almost entirely carried on the town budgets'.[2] In agriculture a number of research and veterinary treatment establishments are mentioned as falling on regional and territorial budgets, while districts have some minor veterinary centres and the plant-protection service. Local roads are also mainly on regional and district budgets. Local social and cultural expenditure, it is stated, is mainly a district or town matter, while certain larger institutions such as teachers' training colleges, children's homes, homes for the incapacitated and specialised hospitals fall upon regional budgets. The concerns of the village, as we have already seen, are very small.

Low-level Decisions

Most of the matters on which the authorities require the benefit of local knowledge, such as the building of roads, schools or hospitals, as well as more purely economic matters, fall within the system of economic planning. Other matters which might appear likely to benefit by wide consultation, such as the teaching programme of the schools, do not in fact appear to receive it. Education is conceived of as primarily a matter of the training of cadres for the economic system as a whole, rather than for the benefiting of local life, and consequently it is highly standardised throughout the system. The public is consulted in the big demonstrations such as the making of the 1936 constitution and in a number of minor campaigns, although its advice is apt to be disregarded if it diverges from the line which the authorities have already worked out in their

[1] V. Shavrin, *Gosudarstvenny Bjudzhet SSSR* (1953), pp. 37–65.
[2] Ibid., p. 21.

own minds. There can be little doubt that the central authorities feel strongly the need for detailed information from below and desire to carry the public with them rather than to enforce their will upon it. But their whole doctrine operates to persuade them that they know best and that those who are not enlightened by mastery of the Marxist analysis are apt to be led astray and must at times for their own good be disregarded.

It is reasonable to assume that much which is done in the Soviet Union is done on initiative from below, though we can only say in very general terms how this happens. To get something done, to get a particular local road repaired, for example, or to secure some improvement in the local restaurants and canteens, the range of goods in the shops or the services locally available, it is probably most effective to approach some person well established in the party hierarchy even for matters which are to be taken up in the soviet executive committee. Letters to the press, which stands, as we have suggested, very close to the party centres of influence, may do some good by indicating to higher authorities a factual need of which they were previously unaware, and perhaps some unnoticed obstruction in the channel to its fulfilment. It is improbable that such letters influence the authorities by persuading them of the existence of a body or opinion to which, if they think it objectively incorrect, they are likely to be substantially indifferent. Executive committee or soviet members are likely to be of sufficient influence, or to know people of sufficient influence, to be useful points of first contact, but a direct raising of the matter in an executive committee meeting without previous clearance with the party would probably be fruitless, and raising it in a meeting of the full soviet even more so and possibly rather dangerous. For the improvement of amenities in a rural area there may be more to be hoped from the management of a well-run collective farm or the director of an appropriate enterprise, who can gratify particular interest under the guise of general economic purpose. Even in a large town we find citizens desiring the improvement of the local cultural facilities approaching the ministries to which the principal local industrial enterprises are subordinated. At such a high level the approach was legitimate; the criticism intended was of the ministries for their neglect, not of the petitioners for overlooking the local organs of state authority.[1] At a lower level, however, such an approach is precarious both for those who solicit favours and for those who grant them, and the resources at the disposal of such persons are commonly too much committed to enable them to confer more than small favours, usually against an equivalent counter-concession.

[1] *Izvestia*, 5th May 1956.

There is still some field for private agreement even in the Soviet Union. The disposal of private income and property for the purpose of pleasure is virtually unrestricted after payment of tax, and the rates of personal taxation are low. The principal restriction is the very limited supply of many of the things upon which successful citizens are particularly anxious to spend their money—accommodation, motor cars and probably, even now, good clothes. Private-house building on plots with a limited lease is now possible but is out of the range of the great majority of citizens. There is no scope for private investment. Subscription to state lottery loans has been invited, and indeed enforced; redemption, however, is now suspended. Direct investment in particular state projects is not as yet invited, and investment in private projects would be capitalism and is therefore entirely excluded. Also, any form of 'speculation'— that is to say, buying for resale—is to be avoided on pain of criminal action, though it quite evidently is not avoided in practice. The press is frequently provided with material by the activities of shrewd citizens in buying up the available resources of scarce commodities in circumstances which suggest that they are not entirely for their own use. But discrimination between legitimate disposal of surplus property and such speculation is always difficult and must lead to many hard cases.

Securing Performance—Economic

Under Stalin the motivation system for managers and workers in enterprises was simple, if not entirely rational. For managers all emphasis was placed on plan fulfilment, as the sources of bonuses which might be well in excess of their salaries and almost the only way to promotion; for workers the 'enterprise fund', instituted in 1936—and until 1955 called the 'director's fund', though its application was never in fact entirely in the director's discretion—made a limited share of the profits of the enterprise available for distribution in money or in the form of various amenities, including housing, the chronic deficiency good in the U.S.S.R.; for both, deficiencies or indiscipline, including unauthorised change of employment, incurred criminal penalties. The managers had their scarcity to plead for them, resurgence of the dismissed or demoted seems to have been remarkably frequent. It was not, however, a readily defensible system for a major industrial society and the early erosion of the more coercive elements of industrial Stalinism was in line not only with the partial trend back to humanity but with the demands of economic rationality. The incentives side of the system also early came under criticism on the latter ground. The domination of management thinking by plan fulfilment often clashed with other government policies; a manager, reminded of his duty to provide employment for young workers, objects that he has a plan to fulfil, and that the restricted hours of work prescribed for young workers make it impracticable for him to employ them. More generally, the large additional bonuses given for overfulfilment of plan requirements, as against mere fulfilment—and the increased contributions to the enterprise fund in respect of additional profits as against the rather theoretical profits provided for in the plan itself—represented an incentive not only to extra effort but also to discreet concealment of resources at the time when the plan was being drafted. Further, this bias could be detrimental to quality and the authorities were constantly exercised by the problem of how to take account of this factor, in the plan and otherwise, in a way which would enable it to withstand the worst excesses of the incessant and obvious demand for quantity. One fault regularly denounced in the press was that of 'storming' (*shturmovshchina*)—rushing at the end of a planning period to make up for the consequences of previous slacking, resulting in variations of quality and a disruption of the even tenor of the production process. Sometimes the pressure of the party was found operating so as to encourage this fault; the regional committee, instead of finding out how methods can be improved, sends a telegram demanding fulfilment in a few days' time, and as a result all other tasks are dropped. Frequent revisions of the plan itself during the course of the year might have the same effect. As a result, many enterprises came to accept storming as a regular, monthly or quarterly, recurrent fact of business life.

Thus to speak of problems of motivation in the past tense is almost certainly unrealistic. This is a communal economy in which for a long time to come most commands will continue to be given out of ignorance; real time information flows and instant managerial responses are, if at all thinkable, at best a dream of the remote future. But perhaps the extreme unbalancing effect of the old bonus system may have been removed or at least modified by reforms of the latter part of 1965 which broke up the enterprise fund into separate funds, all related to profits, for the several diverse purposes which it had been required to serve—self-financing of investment, incentives and miscellaneous welfare services—brought the managers' incentives on to the same, apparently more rational basis, as those of their workers and eliminated the bias in favour of over-fulfilment of plans. A bias, in the determination of profits to be retained, in favour of industries which the regime is for the time being particularly concerned to promote, which in general means those concerned with the production of heavy producer goods, remains, along with sufficient complexity to counsel caution in assessment of the prospect of improved working.

Even relaxation of coercion may have its negative side. Removal of penal deterrents to movement in search of higher wages may promote the excessive mobility which has dogged the authorities' plans from the first, and which (apart from any peculiarities of national character) is the natural joint consequence of living in a land of opportunity where there are few normal trade unionist remedies for unsatisfactory conditions. Managers with little more to fear from failure in assignments than staying unpromoted in a hard-pressed, unprivileged and so probably discontented enterprise may be a drag on the dynamism of the system. But most of us sincere well-wishers would probably advise risking it.

Securing Performance—General

The regime's principal guarantee for the performance of the tasks which it sets the people for their own good as it sees it is the universal inspectability from above, the general absence of freedom from supervision. 'To verify performance', Mr. Bulganin explained, 'means to organise people for a specific matter, to provide for the practical implementation of party and government directives, to prevent and correct errors on the basis of detailed study and to take measures for the future improvement of the work',[1] though he conceded a tendency to degenerate into negative collecting of reports on shortcomings and administering of rebukes and other sanctions. Concern lest all channels of supervision and complaint be blocked at the same time has led to creation—or tolerance of the growth—of a system of extreme complexity so obscuring organisation and responsibility as to make it very hard for a citizen to know how the machine works, or how he is to play his own part in it without laying himself opening to trouble. It makes excessive demands for scarce staff, duplicating the state organisation by that of the party, and the operative agencies within each by further purely supervisory agencies, which, to be effective, must be sufficiently engaged to understand the techniques of the supervised. The system probably also undermines the trust which contentment—a sense of being free of, or attuned to, external forces—seems to require, although we should not underestimate the capacity of human beings for adapting themselves to what from outside may seem to be the most intolerable circumstances.

Apart from this system of regularly operating pressures, the Soviet

[1] Mr. Bulganin's report to the plenary session of the party Central Committee, 14th July 1955 (*Pravda*, 17th July 1955).

political system, like any other, has a special apparatus of retribution for the intractable cases. The Soviet penal system, like that of the Russia of the Tsars before it, has always made comparatively little use of prisons in major centres of population. The corrective labour camp has been the general form of detention, especially since the onset of Five-Year-Plan high-Stalinism in 1928, leaving the prison as a place of remand and transit and for the short sentence, which in Soviet practice is comparatively rare. Such camps have been widely distributed over the territory of the Soviet Union, though with a tendency to the less developed and less inviting parts of the country where free labour was least easy to obtain. A number of them was specialised in particular classes of work—mining, canal building, road building, lumbering, or cultivation—others in particular classes of prisoners such as women or children, and others in the isolation and punishment of difficult cases rather than by labour function. Release has commonly been subject to restrictions on place of residence and other civil rights, many prisoners being required to settle as exiles in the neighbourhood of their former place of detention instead of being allowed to return to their place of origin. This large element of semi-free citizens led to a wide divergence of opinion as to the number of the Soviet Union's prisoner population, but it has certainly been larger than most other states which require less of their citizens have found reasonable. Since the latter part of 1955 there have been indications of a tendency towards increased reliance on exile rather than on penal servitude—in the distinction of the pre-revolutionary days—with relative freedom of living conditions within a prescribed area. This, it appears, can be used as a convenient device for disposal of those found inconvenient rather than dangerous, but the distinction in sentencing policy does not yet seem to be very clear. The camps, or 'colonies', were supposed to have been briefly transferred to the management of the Ministry of Justice after the fall of Beria, but with the abolition of that ministry at federal level the Ministries of Internal Affairs again became responsible, and presumably have so continued through successive reorganisations. What the supervisory function of the procuracy now amounts to, or ever amounted to, is not clear. In addition to penalties involving displacement, regular use has been made of forced labour at the normal place of work, which in effect means a period on a drastically reduced rate of pay. For minor offences fines may be inflicted and, as in other countries, the courts have to be warned from time to time against excessive use of this form of punishment.

Capital punishment except in the form of the massacre, principally of political opponents—though the term has of late been very widely interpreted—has never had a large place in Russian penal practice. It was abolished in 1946, but restored in the following year for cases of treason, and in 1953 for murder resulting from the deliberate practice of violence; latterly the press has repeatedly reported cases of its infliction as part of campaigns to suppress not only crimes of violence but also various economic offences—not all of exceptional enormity by the standards of the outside world—such as misuse of state property and the wide range of unauthorised commercial activity described in communist terminology as speculation. This development detracts seriously from the general picture of increasing civilisation.

In view of the variety of prohibitions and the inhumanly high standard of social discipline which the system imposes upon its citizens much leniency seems to be shown, at least in small matters. The reprimand without further penalty is a common answer to minor offences, both in the formal judicial system and in the internal discipline of factory or farm. Soviet writings suggest from time to time that officials are too much given to this course, and that offenders have learned not to take much notice of it. Where, however, a form of conduct is considered in some way to undermine the system retribution can be very severe. Policy can change markedly, as it has done over offences against private property, once of little account but now guarded almost as jealously as the state's own property. It can also be openly discriminatory as between persons, in accordance with the exemplary purposes which we have noticed. It has been suggested, for instance, that in cases of misappropriation of state, or collective, property courts have commonly dealt appreciably more severely with peasants than with officials.[1] Possibly this is because officials are valuable in their posts and also subject to a degree of supervision such as cannot be applied to peasant pilferage. On the other hand, unreasonable delay and other offences by officials which in other systems would be likely to lead to nothing worse than dismissal, if that, may involve a criminal penalty in the Soviet Union; and if the offence is one which the authorities are for the moment particularly anxious to stamp out, possibly a severe one.[2] The same purposes explain the increased severity with labour offences in the legislation of 1940, lately repealed, or the present movement of repression against crimes of violence.

It is hard to say from outside how far all this makes up an effective penal system. Probably to most citizens it all seems too indiscriminate to have the desired deterrent or reformatory effect. The current attempt once again to achieve something recognisable

[1] Dinerstein, op. cit., p. 121.
[2] Berman, op. cit., p. 272.

as legality may make for greater efficiency, though it is hard to make any penal system fully effective in a society in which the law is largely unknown and most citizens must, to live and prosper, infringe it in some respect.

The system of the labour camps as it has existed hitherto has not been merely a penal system. The value of the work done by the prisoners, highly inefficient though it probably was, has been considerable in that the tasks were such in nature and location that it would have been hard to get them done at all without severe coercion. In 1941 the budget provision for capital construction to the Ministry for Internal Affairs which then managed the camps was larger than that to any ministry other than those for the oil industry and the aircraft industry.[1] There can be no doubt that in his latter years Mr. Beria had an industrial empire of his own which was unrivalled in the Soviet Union, and on which the regime was largely dependent for its capital works. This meant that, as in other fields, such considerations as sound administration were neglected in the pressing demand for results.

But retribution and contrived pressures are not the only motive forces in the Soviet system. Like any other system, it has its self-operating elements, though perhaps they are less prominent than in most. It is a system which offers considerable opportunity to the able and the ambitious, probably a less egalitarian society than ours, with larger differentials of net income—at least if tax-free perquisites on both sides be left out of account—and also high social mobility. Achievement is all, and for the capable there is the possibility of their rising by a conjuncture of their own efforts with official favour to considerable power and social distinction. There is as yet little evidence of the emergence of hereditary castes, though a citizen's position in life is largely determined by the standard of education which the representatives of the state with whom he chances to come into contact see fit to give him, and this in an influence-ridden society seems to offer highly-placed parents the means of averting in most cases any extreme fall in social status from one generation to the next. Yet they can hardly hope to endow their children with such a fortune as will be more than a supplement to income from employment. Once he is in employment the pressure of the drive for production and whatever forces still operate against mobility of labour would seem to limit the citizen's chance of bettering himself. In particular, the peasants remain, as they were under the Tsars, both before and after emancipation, a people apart, more restricted in their movements physically and socially than

[1] Moore, *Terror and Progress U.S.S.R.*, pp. 28, 235n.

other citizens by their lack of passports and by other limitations,[1] though not now economically downtrodden as they were; urbanisation—in the agrotown or otherwise—may in time wipe out this distinction.

The bright prospects are not only for the individual. The Soviet peoples have received some earnest of achievement in the extension of the common stock. The repeated promises of greater comfort have never been fully realised, ostensibly, and in part actually, by reason of external circumstances and notably as a result of the war, but largely because the authorities have been unreasonably ambitious in their planning and are determined that whatever else may suffer in consequence of their failure to realise all that they desire, the projects of industrialisation and national security on which they set their hearts shall not. But much of the product of the industry and abstinence which the regime has imposed has been distributed. If many of its decisions were wrong, many were right, and have aroused no opposition, and the conditions of the individual citizens, if not perhaps better than they might have been had there been no revolution, are at least better than they were before the revolution. Moreover, the prospect of still better remains, and the unmistakable achievements of the country are a promise of this which the Soviet citizen must, and apparently in fact does, often appreciate. The ignorance of contemporary advances in the outside world, the suggestion, which seems somewhat ridiculous to the outside observer, that conditions in Great Britain, for example, are still much as they are described in the pages of Dickens, helps to heighten this sense of achievement.

The sense of danger may operate to much the same effect. The 'capitalist menace' is probably more real to most of the Soviet leaders than it is to most people in the world deemed by them to be capitalist. Whatever its reality, to them it has the practical utility of keeping up the tension. The Russian people after the revolution and civil war, after the violence of Stalin's march to power, and especially after the Second World War, has had enough of disorder, and the suggestion of the leaders that they are the sole pillars of peace against the threat of aggression from without may be supposed to be a strong inducement to their subjects to submit to and support their authority. There can be little doubt that the support which the government receives for its successive peace campaigns is substantially genuine. That the government itself may be one of the forces militating against peace is not brought to the attention of the people, and, as in most other countries, it probably does not occur to them spontaneously.

[1] Kulski, op. cit., pp. 650–9.

It must also be a support to the present regime and an element in Russia's political process that under its present management the country's influence in the world has been greatly enhanced. This is partly due to the external circumstance that there are now fewer great powers in consequence of the decline of possible rivals. There is, however, a more positive side to Russia's achievements. By all reliable indices of influence—industrial capacity, possession in quantity of the more destructive weapons of war, powerful presumptive allies, client states and friendly neutrals and sympathisers among the subjects of its potential enemies who can be expected to prefer its cause to that of their own countries, widespread interest in its ways of settling social and other problems and a conviction among leading people of some at least of the world's more considerable countries that they have much to learn from it—it is a country to which others must pay some attention in framing their policies, and more securely so than it was even in the years following the fall of Napoleon. It has a hold over central Europe and an influence in Asia such as the Tsars long sought but never achieved. In any case, whatever the cause of the increased influence, the regime in power gets the credit, as usually happens in such situations. Moreover, this rise in influence accords well with an official mythology which gives a pleasant sense of being on the side of humanity and inevitability.

In this system a large place belongs to fictions. Since the possession of an infallible key to the understanding and management of social processes forms the basis of the claim of communists to wield authority, error in the party itself or in the system of government which it has established can never be admitted. Consequently anything which goes wrong has to be imputed to the ill-will or selfishness of some form of rival influence explicable in terms of Marxist theory. The external menace is convenient, but cannot be stretched to explain everything; internal resistance, which in other countries could be ascribed merely to the tendency of all human beings to prefer their own interests to those of others, can in a society allegedly both Marxian socialist in its analysis and classless in its structure be accounted for only by supposing the existence of 'survivals of bourgeois mentality'. It may be necessary to keep this fiction in being after the extinction of the last of the generation which could possibly have belonged to any bourgeoisie other than that of the communists' own making. Even as it is, it is not applicable to all situations; it may be possible to explain the misdeeds of Beria by a fiction of contact with foreign influences and a desire to restore capitalism, but the misdeeds of Stalin can hardly be explained by anything other than defects of personal character unmotivated by any social forces, however deeply this may perturb foreign communists.

The elimination of all opposition of a party-political nature has been achieved at the cost of the loss of those services which a rival party normally performs for the one in power, in keeping its members up to the mark, pointing the finger of scorn at weak men and weak policies, finding a place as critics for the difficult men, thinking out alternative aims and methods which the ruling party can at a favourable opportunity discreetly purloin, and providing an identifiable enemy which can be blamed for shortcomings without poisoning the whole of social relations. In this and in the elimination of independent opinion generally the Marxist believers in the dialectic process have so sterilised their system that there is no dialectic operating, no mechanism to warn them when they are going too far on any tack of policy and to slow down and reverse trends before they degenerate from productive insight into destructive fanaticism. In consequence, it has been suggested, they have been obliged themselves to create an artificial dialectic. This is probably not an entirely conscious process, but it has a distinguishable function in the system. It shows itself in the repeated sudden reversals of policy in all fields of the national life: on the rights of the peasant in collectivised agriculture, on managerial methods, on literary and architectural styles or the theory of language or otherwise. It is manifested, too, in the dropping of leaders, with or without violence, and the successive disowning of the past as represented by the elaborately constructed prestige of the late Mr. Stalin of the less fully developed cult of the personality of his ingenious demolisher.

BIBLIOGRAPHY

The following list contains no Soviet-published material. The Soviet Union produces neither political scientists nor such factual analyses of the system as political scientists sometimes write and use. Since, however, most Soviet publications—books, periodicals and newspapers, especially those intended for lawyers and practitioners in management and administration, but even general newspapers and works of fiction—are largely devoted to indicating how for the time being authority wants the system operated and denouncing failures to operate it properly, the serious student of Soviet politics can with advantage, though not without suffering, read anything written by Russians for Russians which comes his way, and hope for glimpses of the way in which things work.

Much sifting has already been done in books published outside the Soviet world—less exclusively in America than a few years ago, though still predominantly so. A few of these we list below:

TEXTBOOKS ON POLITICAL INSTITUTIONS

Frederick C. Barghoorn, *Politics in the USSR*, Boston: Little Brown, 1966.

L. G. Churchward, *Contemporary Soviet Government*, London: Routledge and Kegan Paul, 1968.

Robert Conquest (ed.), *The Soviet Political System*, London: Bodley Head, 1968 (a volume in the Soviet Studies series which already contains several other studies on special aspects of Soviet politics, written by unspecified authors and all edited by Mr. Conquest).

Merle Fainsod, *How Russia is Ruled*, Cambridge, Mass.: Harvard U.P., revised edition, 1963.

Richard C. Crisp, *Patterns of Soviet Politics*, Homewood, Illinois: The Dorsey Press, revised edition, 1967.

Alfred G. Meyer, *The Soviet Political System, an Introduction*, New York: Random House, 1965.

SPECIAL ASPECTS OF POLITICS

Personalities and their Interaction

Isaac Deutscher, *Stalin, a Political Biography*, Oxford: O.U.P., 1949 (Apart from its biographical merits provides one of the best shorter histories of the period).

R. Conquest, *Power and Policy in the U.S.S.R.: the Study of Soviet Dynastics*, London: Macmillan; New York: St. Martin's Press, 1962. (The politics of personalities in the last phase of Stalin and the first seven years of his successors.)

Carl A. Linden, *Khrushchev and the Soviet Leadership 1957-64*, London: O.U.P., 1967.

Michel Tartu, *Power in the Kremlin: From Khruschov's Decline to Collective Leadership* (translation from the French), London: Collins, 1969 (Good journalism).

Some of the main processes in operation

John N. Hazard, *The Soviet System of Government*, Chicago and London: U. of Chicago Press, 4th edition, 1968.

Law

Peter Archer, *Communisim and the Law*, London: Bodley Head, 1963.

H. J. Berman, *Justice in Russia*, New York: Vintage Books, 1963.

John N. Hazard, *Law and Social Change in the U.S.S.R.*, London: Stevens, 1953.

Ivo Lapenna, *Soviet Penal Policy*, London: Bodley Head, 1968.

The Economy

Alec Nove, *The Soviet Economy: An Introduction*, London: Allen and Unwin; New York: Praeger, 3rd edition, 1969.

Abram Bergson, *The Economics of Soviet Planning*, New Haven and London: Yale U.P., 1964.

Joseph S. Berliner, *Factory and Manager in the U.S.S.R.*, Cambridge, Mass.: Harvard U.P., 1957.

H. S. Dinerstein, 'Communism and the Russian Peasant', in H. S. Dinerstein and Leon Gouré, *Two Studies of Soviet Controls*, Glencoe, Ill.: Free Press, 1955.

D. Granick, *The Red Executive*, London: Macmillan, 1960. (The world of the Soviet manager.)

Barry M. Richman, *Soviet Management with Significant American Comparisons*, Englewood Cliffs, N.J.: Prentice Hall, 1965.

Barry M. Richman, *Management Education and Development in the Soviet Union*, East Lansing, Michigan: Michigan State University, 1967.

Trade Unions

Emily Clark Brown, *Soviet Trade Unions and Labour Relations*, Cambridge, Mass.: Harvard U.P., 1966.

Ideology and Propaganda

Barrington Moore, Jr., *Soviet politics, the Dilemma of Power*, Cambridge, Mass.: Harvard U.P., 1951.

Alex Inkeles, *Public Opinion in Soviet Russia: a Study in Mass Persuasion*, Cambridge, Mass.: Harvard U.P., 1950.

Education

Nigel Grant, *Soviet Education*, London: Penguin Books, 2nd edition, 1968.
N. DeWitt, *Education and Professional Employment in the U.S.S.R.*, Washington D.C.: Government Printing Office, 1961.
See also the second book of Barry M. Richman, mentioned above.

Coercion

Barrington Moore, Jr., *Terror and Progress, U.S.S.R.*, Cambridge Mass.: Harvard U.P., 1954 (in fact broader in scope than this category or its title suggest).
And book on the Soviet police system in Soviet Studies series (ed. Robert Conquest) mentioned above.

Armed Forces

Harold J. Berman and Miroslav Kerner, *Soviet Military Law and Administration*, Cambridge, Mass.: Harvard U.P., 1955.
Zbignieiv Brzezinski (ed.), *Political Controls in the Soviet Army: a Study Based on Reports by Former Soviet Officers*, New York: Praeger, for Research Program on the U.S.S.R., 1954. (The officers are named and individually contribute sections.)

BACKGROUND

Geography

Georges Jorré, *The Soviet Union, the Land and its People* (translation by E. D. Laborde from the French), London: Longmans, 1967 (revised edition).

Post-revolutionary History

E. H. Carr, *A History of Soviet Russia*, London: Macmillan, 1950. (A multi-volume work, still growing; invaluable.)
Leonard Schapiro, *The Communist Party of the Soviet Union*, London: Eyre and Spottiswoode; New York: Random House, 1960.

Pre-revolutionary History

Almost any of the general histories of Russia. Two of the more recent publications are very useful:

Michael T. Florinsky, *Russia, a History and an Interpretation*, New York: Macmillan, 1955. (Two volumes, extending up to and including the revolution.)
Richard Charques, *A Short History of Russia*, London: Phoenix House, 1956. (Sketches in briefly the post-revolutionary period, and is generally directed towards an understanding of the present.)

Also, with a more limited period:

Hugh Seton-Watson, *The Decline of Imperial Russia, 1855–1914*, London: Methuen; New York: Praeger, 1952. (Of great assistance in the understanding of the conditions which the revolution inherited.)

Three specialised histories deserve the attention even of those not specialists in history:

M. Kovalevsky, *Russian Political Institutions*, Chicago: U. of Chicago Press, 1902. (Partial in both senses, but accurate, illuminating and as a specialised history in its field effectively alone.)
Nicholas Berdyaev, *The Origins of Russian Communism*, London: Bles, 1937. (An account of pre-revolutionary thought.)
G. T. Robinson, *Rural Russia under the Old Regime*, New York: Longmans, 1932. (An account of the principal discontent which destroyed imperial Russia in both its economic and its political aspects.)

JOURNALS

Current Digest of the Soviet Press, weekly, New York: Joint Committee on Slavic Studies appointed by the American Council of Learned Societies and the Social Science Research Council. (Translations, without comment, of selected articles from the Soviet daily and periodical press.)
Soviet Studies, a Quarterly Journal on the U.S.S.R. and Eastern Europe, quarterly, Glasgow: University of Glasgow. (Also, published with it, but separately available, its Information Supplement, briefly noting some of the more significant recent indications in the Soviet press of economic and social conditions.)
Survey, a Journal of Soviet and East European Studies, quarterly, London: Information Bulletin Ltd., on behalf of the Congress for Cultural Freedom.
Problems of Communism, bimonthly, Washington, D.C.: United States Information Service.
Osteuropa, monthly, Stuttgart: Deutsche Gesellschaft für Osteuropakunde. Also the associated specialised quarterlies *Osteuropa-Recht* and *Osteuropa-Wirtschaft*.

Index

Abhazian autonomous republic, 70
Academies, 228–9
'activists'
  and the party, 53, 184
  and soviets, 102–3, 110–11
  and trade unions, 218
Adjarian autonomous republic, 70
administration
  'acts of', by Supreme Soviet, 105
  areas of, 72–7
  collective, 77–9
  complication of, 45, 184
  the party as organisation for, 50, 153–4, 176–84
  pre-revolutionary tradition of, 23–29
Adygei autonomous region, 76
Agricultural Deliveries, State Committee for, 128, 197
Agricultural Machinery Association (sel'hoztehnika), 128
Agricultural Sciences, Academy of, 101, 228
agriculture
  collectivisation of, 49, 51, 61–2, 73, 163
  conditions for, 21, 29
  Khrushchov and, 75, 79, 174, 199–200, 236
  management in, 79, 196–9, 201–3
  Ministry of, 126, 179–80, 193, 197
  the party and, 153–4, 179–83
  see also farms
Andreev, A. A., 145
animal husbandry, see livestock
appeals, legal, 210–13
appointments
  by Council of Ministers, 133
  by heads of units, 221
  by the party, 114–15, 133, 153–4, 180–2, 188

by Praesidia of Supreme Soviets, 120–1, 133
arbitration tribunals, 208–9
area or circuit (okrug), 72, 73, 74
areas, national, 64, 66, 71
armed forces, 231–3
  of Ministry of Internal Affairs, 231
  officers of, 50, 98, 142, 166, 172, 232–3
  the party and, 142, 154, 156, 166, 172, 232, 233
  in the revolution, 41, 57, 58
  and soviets, 90, 98
  of union republics, 84
Armenia, 66, 71, 74, 110
  the party in, 165
  Supreme Soviet of, 90, 97, 121
arrest, constitution on power of, 83, 207
Artists, Union of Soviet, 229
Arts, Academy of, 229
Asia, central, Russian expansion into, 23, 44
assessors, judicial, 210
audit, 105, 203
autocracy, 49, 52; Tsarist, 23, 24
autonomous regions and republics, see regions, republics
autonomy, 64, 67, 69
Azerbaidjan, 65, 66, 70, 71, 74
  autonomous regions and republics in, 70, 71, 79
  Supreme Soviet of, 90
Azerbaidjanis, 23

Bagirov, M. D., 145
ballot, for election of party officials, 173; of Soviets, 93, 95
Baltic republics, 63, 70, 91
  see also Esthonia, Latvia, Lithuania

banks, 205; *see also* State Bank
Bashkir autonomous republic, 70, 74, 90
Belorussia, 63, 66, 74
    the party in, 165
    Supreme Soviet of, 90
Belorussians, 23
Beria, L. P., 110
    member of Praesidium of Council of Ministers, 118
    member of Praesidium of party Central Committee, 146
    Minister for Internal Affairs, 249
'Black Hundreds', 64
Bolsheviks, faction of Social Democrat Party, 35, 40, 137, 158
    and Congresses of Soviets, 59
    and Constituent Assembly, 46
    'Old', 163
    and Social Revolutionaries, 58, 61
    and trade unions, 216
Bonaparte, danger of a, 42, 233
    quoted by Lenin, 38
bonuses in industry, 194, 195, 196
book-keepers of collective farms, 198–9
bourgeoisie
    Lenin and, 35
    pre-revolution, 29, 33
Brezhnev, L. I.
    chairman of Praesidium of Supreme Soviet, 106, 113; member, 107
    first secretary (General Secretary) of party, 149
Bubnov, 144
budget, 67, 110, 239–41
    debates on, 104
    standing commissions of soviets on, 102, 103, 240
    see also planning
Budjonni, Marshal, 113
Buharin, 48
Building Matters, State Council for (*Gosstroi*), 127, 129
Building, Ministry of, 178
Bulganin, N. A.
    on education, 227n, 230n
    on managers' powers, 195
    member of Praesidium of Supreme Soviet, 149
    on planning, 195, 237
    on supervision, 246

vice-chairman and chairman of Council of Ministers, 118, 149
bureaucracy, efforts to combat, 53, 123, 135, 155, 184
bureaux, within party committees, 71, 140; within party primary organisations, 138; within republican Councils of Ministers, 119; within 'sections', 102; within soviet executive committees, 112
Burjat (Burjat-Mongol) autonomous republic, 70, 90
Burjat national areas, 71
by-elections, 89, 95, 115

cadres, *see* staffing
cadres secretaries (party officials), 173
campaigns, government for discussion of 1936 constitution, 82, 242
    Komsomol and, 157–8
    village soviets and, 107
    voluntary work in, 54, 103, 170–1, 175
candidate, academic title equivalent to master's degree, 155, 226
candidates for election to soviets, 94–5
candidates or probationary members of party, 141, 158, 160, 164, 165
    of party, Central Committee, 142
capital, foreign
    admitted during N.E.P., 47
    in industrialisation under Tsars, 29
capital punishment, 247–8
Caucasus, Russian expansion into, 23
'cells' of the party, 138
centralism, democratic, 40, 137, 169
chairmen
    of collective farms, 79, 172, 174, 181, 182, 198, 222
    of Councils of Ministers, 118, 149, 151
    of soviets and executive committees, 98, 100, 102, 114–16, 222
    of Supreme Soviet, 101; of Praesidium of, 77, 112–13
Chechen-Ingush autonomous republic, 70, 71

checking commissions
Central, of party, 141, 143, 150–1, 233
of collective farms, 198
of party organisations, 139
of trade unions, 218
Che-ka or Special Commission (secret police of revolution), 47, 205
churches, 220
Chuvash autonomous republic, 70, 90
coercion, machinery of, 246–9
tradition of, 43
collectivisation of agriculture, 49, 51, 62, 160
in Baltic republics, 74
collegia
assisting and limiting commissars (ministers), 78, 134
of Supreme Court, 211
'collegiality', 77, 112, 116
Cominform (Informburo), 190
Comintern (Third International), 137, 190
Commissariats, 60, 67, 78; *see further under* Ministries
Commissars, 60, 78; *see further under* Ministers
Councils of, 60, 65, 116; *see further under* Ministers, Councils of
political, in the armed forces, 156
commissions, party, 139, 151
commissions, standing (of soviets), 102–3, 105
communications, 21–2
Ministries for, 67, 78, 126
communism
Stalin and, 38, 41, 50, 81
of war period, 45–6
Communist Manifesto, 64
Composers, Union of Soviet, 229
congresses
of *Komsomol*, 157
of party, *see* party congresses
of soviets, *see* Soviets, Congresses of
of trade unions, 218
constituency conferences (to select candidates for election), 94–5
Constituent Assembly (1918), 46, 59, 60, 80
constitutionality, no means of passing judgment on, 68, 86

constitutions, 79–80, 88; (1918), 80; (1923–4), 66, 67, 81; (1936), 68, 70, 71, 81–7, 99, 104, 242
new, under preparation, 82
of republics, 65, 80, 84, 86–7, 100
'consultation, special', cases dealt with in private by, 214–15
Control, Party, Committee of, 151
co-operative organisations, 94, 142, 204
collective farms as, 79, 198, 238
taxation of, 241
correspondence, education by, 224
Councils of Ministers, *see* Ministers
Councils of State, 24, 32
Counter-Intelligence in the Armed Forces, Chief administration for, 232
Courts of Justice, 209–14, 215–16; *see also* People's Courts, Supreme Court
credits, from State and other banks, 205
Crimea, 21, 23, 71
criticism
of executive committees by soviets, 109
and self-criticism, in the party, 40, 168, 169–70, 178
see also press
culture, Ministries of, 126, 219, 221, 226, 229–30
cyrillic alphabet, 68

Dagestan autonomous republic, 70, 90
debt, foreign, under Tsars, 29, 43
decision-making
central, location of, 234–6
initiative from below, 242–4
decisions (*reshenie*) of local soviet executive committees, 123
decrees (*postanovlenie*), of Councils of Ministers, 119–20; of Supreme Soviet, 105
Defence, Ministries of, 84, 130
degrees, academic, 155, 226
democracy, Lenin on, 92
deputies
to soviets, 96–9, 109–11; executive committees not always chosen from, 115; on standing commissions, 102, 103

'deviation', 46
dialectic, artificial, 232
dialectical materialism, 33, 36–7, 170
dictatorship, of the party, 39; of the proletariat, 33, 36, 56, 80, 81
directors
  of factories and other enterprises, 194–6, 215–16, 244
  of machine-tractor stations, 202
  of state farms, 174
dispositions (rasporjazhenie), of councils of Ministers, 119–20; of local soviet executive committees, 123–5
districts
  economic, 71, 76, 179; divided into industrial and agricultural, 75
  (raion), 72, 75, 76; party committees of, 139, 174–5, 180, 181, 183
  soviets of, 72, 75–6, 90, 91, 108
  within cities, 73, 76, 91
  (uezd), 27, 72
divorce, 212
doctorate, 155, 226
doctrine, 33–41; see also ideology
Duma, of boyars, 24; State (1905), 32; town, 28

Economic commission, of Soviet of Nationalities, 102
economics, primary concern with, 16, 43, 69, 191
  in education, 227, 237, 242
  in judicial system, 208
  in party work, 138, 153, 176, 183, 189
Economy
  Councils of the,
  central (1920–32), 67, 78; (1950's–1960's), 79, 129
  local, 78, 91–2, 179, 193
editors of journals, party appointment and training of, 155, 188, 229
education, 221, 223–8
  fees for higher (1940–56), 86, 225
  Ministries for, 67, 126, 127, 128, 130–1, 221
  political, 154–5, 156–7, 186, 228, 231–2
  pre-revolution, 27

and social position, 249
standard of, among army officers, 233; among party members, 163, 166; among party officials, 175
Ehrenberg, Ilja, The Storm, by, 170
elections, procedure and administration, 92–6; of judges, 209–10; to party organisations, 139, 172–173; to local soviets, 91; to Supreme Soviets, 89–90; of trade union committees, 218
Electoral Commissions (to conduct elections), 93, 96
Engels, Friedrich, 33, 38, 64
'enterprise fund', 244
Esthonia, 70, 74, 95
  the party in, 165
  Supreme Soviet of, 90, 95, 97
examinations, for entry to higher education, 221, 224; at party schools, 155
exile, for offender, 22, 215, 247

Factories
  management of, 79, 193–6
  party organisation in, 138, 179
  see also industry
family legislation, vested in federal authorities, 84
'familyness', sin of, 44, 183
Far Eastern territory, 73
farm production administrations, 75
farms
  collective, 61, 197–200; chairmen of, 79, 172, 181, 198, 222; industries run by, 192; local soviets and, 75, 107–8; management of, 79, 198; the party and, 166, 181–2, 183, 198; taxation of, 241
  state, 71, 75, 79, 199; Ministry of, 197
federalism, 67, 68, 69, 137–8
federation, 63–4, 80, 84–5
finance
  of the economy, budgetary responsibility, 242
  Ministries of, 203, 204, 205, 221, 240
  of party organisations, 138
  see also pay
Finland, 63
fisheries, Ministries of, 191

Five-Year Plans, 48, 49, 104, 237, 238; *see also* planning
food
supply problem 43, 46–7, 61, 108, 123
taxation on, 241
foreign affairs
Ministries for, 67, 118
standing commission of Supreme Soviet on, 103
union republics and, 84–6
foreign trade, Commissariat for, 67
'fractionalism', 46
franchise 32, 92–3
Furtseva, E. A., 147, 186

Gazettes, official, 18, 87–8, 125
Georgadze, M., 113
Georgia, 66, 70, 74, 110
autonomous republics and autonomous and administrative regions in, 70, 71, 74
the party in, 136, 165
Supreme Soviet of, 90, 114
Glavlit (censorship), 219, 230
Gorny Altai autonomous region, 10
Gorny Badahshan autonomous region, 71
Gosplan (State Planning Committee), 127, 129, 131, 239, 240
discontinuities in function of, 129
Gossnab (State Committee for material and Technical Supply, 127
Gosstroi (State Committee for Building Matters), 127, 129, 131
governorships (*gubernija*), 25, 27, 72
G.P.U. (State Political Administration), 205
Grishin, V. V., 217
Gromyko, A. A., 118

Hakass autonomous region, 70
health services
Ministries for, 67, 127, 131
pre-revolution, 27
Hegel, dialectic of, 33, 36, 37
Hitler, rise to power of, 50, 81
honours and awards, 120, 121, 176
hospitals, 242
housing, 123, 193, 244

Ideology, 33–41, 184–90; constitutions as, 88

illiteracy, 27, 125
income tax, 105, 241
Industrial Bank, 195
industrialisation, 237, 250
pre-revolution, 28–9
revolution and, 37–8, 43, 48
industry
Khruschchov reforms in management of, 78–9, 129, 130
organisation of, 191–6
the party in, 79, 179
taxation of, 241
young people in, 224
Informburo (Cominform), 190
inspections, 246; by party officials, 178–9; by press, 219; by procurator service, 207; by standing commissions, 103
inspectorates, 203–4; trade union, 218
instructions (*instruktsia*), of Ministers, 133–4
instruments (*polozhenie*), of Council of Ministers, 120, 133
intelligentsia
effect of party ideology on, 185
members of soviets from, 97–8
party members from, 159, 163
pre-revolution, 27–8, 30, 41
Internal Affairs
Commissariats for, 60, 67, 205–6
Ministry of, 206, 214, 247; armed forces of, 231; budget of, 249
International, Third (Comintern), 137, 190
Internationale, the, 143
internationalism, 44, 51, 190
Izvestia, 219

Japan, 31, 43
Jewish autonomous region, 70
Jews, 220
judges, 86, 209–10, 215
judicial system, 86, 206, 207–8, 209–216; pre-revolution, 28, 30
Juridical Sciences, Academy of, 228–229
Justice, Ministry of, 208, 216, 247; republican commissariats for, 67

Kabarda-Balkar autonomous republic, 70, 90
Kaganovitch, L. M., 118, 146

Kalmyk autonomous republic, 70, 71
Kamchatka, 71, 73, 76
Kamenev, 50
Karachai-Cherkess autonomous region, 70, 71
Kara-Kalpak autonomous republic, 70
Karelo-Finnish union (later Karelian autonomous) republic, 70, 74, 90
Kazahs, 23
Kazahstan, 70, 71, 73, 74
soviets of, 90
virgin lands of, 157–8, 199
Kerenski, 36
Khabarovsk territory, 72, 74, 76, 109
Khrushchov, N. S.
and agriculture, 75, 76, 199, 236
Chairman of Council of Ministers, 106, 117
and constitution, 82, 106
and education, 225, 231
and elections, 94
fall of, 146
first secretary of party, 149
and Kazahstan, 199
member of politburo of party, 144–5
and party Central Committee, 144, 146
on party decision making, 144–5
member of Praesidium of Supreme Soviet, 149
reforms of, 71–2, 75, 76, 79, 91–2, 129, 225; retreat from, 126, 127, 129
rise of, 52, 55
on Stalin, 50, 51, 83, 144, 236
at Supreme Soviet, 105, 106
Kiev, 22, 222
Kirgizia, 69, 71, 74, 90, 165
Kirilenko, A. P., 146
Kirov, Sergei, murder of, 48, 49, 162
Komi autonomous republic, 70, 90
Kommunist, party journal, 186
Komsomol (All-Union Lenin Communist League of Youth), 142, 156–8, 164; in armed forces, 232; in boarding schools, 225
Kosygin, A. N., 106, 117, 145, 146, 149
Kozlov, F. R., 146, 149

Krasnodar territory, 76
Krasnojarsk territory, 109
Kremlin, 103–4
Kronstadt revolt (1921), 47
Kropotkin, Prince, 28
Kuibyshev, V. V., 148
kulaks, 61, 81
Kuusinen, O. V., 146
Kuznetsov, V. V., 217

Labour
Commissariat for, 78, 217
forced, 247
soviet departments for recruitment and transfer of, 221
labour books, 221–2
labour camps, 247, 249
labour-days (on collective farms), 200
labour disputes, Commissions on, 212–13
labour offences, legislation on, 248
Labour and Pay Questions, State Committee of Council of Ministers on, 128
Labour Reserves, 221
Lacis, V. T., 101
languages, of nationalities, 44, 65, 68
Latvia, 70, 74
Council of Ministers of, 101, 120
Supreme Soviet of, 90, 99
law, citizens and, 248–9; Civil Code of, 209, 212; Criminal code of, 213
teaching of, 210
Laws (zakon), Acts of Legislation of Supreme Soviet, 85, 105
legislation
activity of Supreme Soviet, 105–7
Council of Ministers as chief source of, 120
signing of, 78
standing commissions of Supreme Soviet on, 102
superfluity of means for, 85
Lenin (V. I. Uljanov)
death of, 47
and economic structure, 45, 47
and factory management, 79
and federation, 63, 64
and N.E.P., 47
and Marxism, 35, 38

and party, 39, 40, 158
on party decision making, 144
and peasants, 35
and politburo, 144
and propaganda, 187
in 1917 revolution, 36, 41, 45, 46,
  58, 144
and soviets, 57, 62n, 91, 92
and Stalin, 48
and Trotski, 48, 57
Lenin Draft, for party, 160
Leningrad
  city, 77; Soviet of, 112, 123
  region, 77; Soviet of, 99, 109
  see also St. Petersburg, Petrograd
Leninism, 153; see also Marxism-
  Leninism
Liberman, Professor E. G., of Kharkov, 194
Lihachov, I. A., 117
Literature, Chief Administration of
  the Ministry of Culture for (Glavlit), 219, 230
Lithuania, 70, 79
  Supreme Soviet of, 90
livestock
  collectivisation and, 49
  three-year plan for improvement
    of output of, 237–8
Lobanov, P. P., 101
localism, sin of, 193
Lvov, Prince, 36
Lvov, university of, 226
Lysenko, 229

Machine-building, Ministries of, 127
machine-tractor stations, 201–2
  the party and, 174, 179–80
  revenue from, 241
Magadan region, 76
Malenkov, G. M., 52, 165
  chairman of Council of Ministers,
    118
  fall of, 146
  Secretary of Party Central Com-
    mittee, 148
  and Stalin, 52
management boards (pravlenie), of
  collective farms, 198
managers, 43, 54–5, 166
  difficulties encountered by, 194–7,
    244–5
  as party members, 166, 172

mandates, commissions of soviets,
  101
Mari autonomous republic, 70, 90
market tax, 241
Marx, Karl, 33, 38, 56
Marx-Engels-Lenin Institute, 153
Marxism, 33–41, 237
  and federation, 64, 68
  indoctrination with, 19, 54, 184–5,
    231, 247
  party as link with ideals of, 190
Marxism-Leninism, 139, 177, 184–
  185, 228
Medical Sciences, Academy of, 228
meetings, of party organisations,
  138, 139, 140, 141, 143, 186; of
  soviets, 99–100
Meljnikov, L. G., 145
Mensheviks, faction of Social Democrat Party, 36, 39–40, 59, 158–
  159, 216
Mikojan, A. I., 110
  vice-chairman of Council of
    Ministers, 118; chairman of
    Praesidium of Supreme Soviet,
    106, 107, 113
  member of Praesidium of party
    Central Committee (retired
    1966), 145
military collegium of federal Supreme Court, 211
Military Procurator, Chief, 206, 212
military service, 123, 154, 231, 232;
  see also armed forces
militia 132, 206
Ministers (previously People's Commissars), 85–6, 98, 117–18, 119,
  133, 148, 151
  Committee of (1802), 24
  Council of (1861), 25; (1905),
    32
  Council of (federal), and Aca-
    demy of Science, 228; agencies
    subordinate to, 127–9, 205; ap-
    pointments by, 133; and budget,
    240; composition of, 116, 126–8;
    decrees and dispositions of, 83,
    117–20; as 'Government', 86,
    116; and Ministry establish-
    ments and powers, 133, 221; the
    party and, 118; Praesidium of,
    118, 120, 121, 122; published
    Acts of, 18–19, 87–8; and rates

of pay, 221; and State Arbitration, 209; and State Bank, 205; and Stroibank, 205
Councils of (republican), 68, 116, 119, 120, 121–2, 130–1, 209
Ministries (previously People's Commissariats), 60, 65, 85, 133
All-Union, 126
published Acts of, 87–8, 133–134
the party and, 178
in republics, 65, 130, 135
mir (village assembly), 26, 30, 34
mobility
of labour, 246
of party officials, 176
social, 249
Moldavia, 70, 74, 228
language of, 68
the party in, 165
Supreme Soviet of, 90, 91, 97
Molotov
fall of, 41, 52, 55, 146
first vice-chairman of Council of Ministers, 118; chairman (in 1936), 82
member of Praesidium of party Central Committee, 146
Secretary of party, 148
Mordovian autonomous republic, 70, 90
Moscow 22, 32, 56, 76
city, soviet of, 58, 91, 99, 112; State Arbitration in, 209; Ten-Year Plan for reconstruction of, 238
region, 73, 76–7, 222; soviet of, 101, 109, 115; internal passports required in, 222

Nagorny Karabah autonomous region, 71
Nahichevan autonomous republic, 70
national areas, 60, 71
nationalisation, decree of general (1918), 45
nationalities, 42, 44, 50
Commissariat for, 65; Commissar for, 66
languages of, 44, 65, 68
Soviet of, *see* Soviet of Nationalities

New Economic Policy (N.E.P.), 38, 46–7, 81
nobility, in Tsarist Rusia, 25, 26, 27–8, 30
nomenklatura (party schedule of appointments), 181–2, 188
Norms and Conflict Commissions (R.K.K.), 212–13
North Ossetian autonomous republic, 70, 90, 114
Nosenko, I. I., 117
Novgorod, 109

oblastj (regions), 25, 72, 73, 74
officials
recruitment in N.E.P. period, 47
of the party, 136, 138, 140, 153–5, 172, 174–6
professional interests of, 44–5, 53
O.G.P.U. (Unified State Political Administration), 204
okrug (area or circuit), 72, 73, 74
opposition, elimination of, 50, 51, 252
orders (*prikaz*), of Ministers, 133
organisers, party officials as, 175
orgburo, of party Central Committee, 144, 145, 148
Orlov, G. M., 117
Orthodox Church, 220

Paleckis, Ju. I., 101
Paris, Commune, 56, 57, 58
Partijnaja Zhizn, party journal, 186
party, the Communist, 34–5, 39, 47–48, 84, 111, 136–90
appointments by, 113, 114–15, 133, 148, 180–2, 188
committees of, *see* party Committees
congresses of, *see* party Congresses
in constitution of 1936, 84
groups, 138
membership of, 158–68
obligations and rights, 168–76
organisation for administration, 50, 153–4, 174, 176–84
as organised faith, 186–90
primary organisations, 138
publications of, 19, 186–7
purges of, *see* purges
staff of, 140, 153–5, 173–6

structure of, 136–40
as symbol, 190
Party Commision, *see* Control,
  Party, Committee of
party committees, 139–40
  Central (federal), 141–50; appoint-
    ments by, 153–72; army repre-
    sentation on, 142, 233; con-
    ferences advisory to, 141; and
    constitution of 1936, 81–2; and
    Gosplan, 239; Praesidium of,
    145, *see also* politburo; and
    purges, 162–3; and religion, 230
  Central (republican), 139, 140,
    148
  in factories, 138
  in Ministries, 178
  see also Checking Commission,
    Control, Party
party Conferences, 141; 8th (1919),
    160; 12th (1922), 141, 161; 16th
    (1929), 162, 238
party Congresses, 139, 140–1; 6th
    (1917), 58, 141, 159; 7th (1918),
    137–41; 8th (1919), 59, 62n, 136,
    137, 144, 160; 9th (1920), 144,
    148; 10th (1921), 46, 159, 160;
    12th (1923), 72; 14th (1925),
    161; 15th (1927), 48, 49, 141;
    17th (1934), 78, 140, 161; 18th
    (1939), 48, 50, 163; 19th (1952),
    139, 142, 145, 165; 20th (1956),
    136, 152, 156, 165, 166, 169,
    186, 202, 225; 21st (1959), 140;
    22nd (1961), 137; 23rd (1966),
    140
Party Secretariat, 148
'partyness', 183
passports, internal, 124, 222
pay
  of collective farm workers, 197,
    199–200, 202
  in factories, 194–5
  grades of, 221
  of party officials, 138, 174, 176,
    178
  of research students, 226
peasants, 249–50
  alliance of, with proletariat, 35,
    57, 61
  committees of poor, 61, 62
  Marxist doctrine and, 33, 34, 35
  members of soviets from, 97–8

party members from, 160–2, 163,
    166
  pre-revolution, 25, 26, 27, 30, 31
  in revolution, 41, 57
Pedagogical Sciences, academy of,
    229
Peive, J. A., 101
Pelshe, A. Ja., 147
penal system, 246–9; of party, 171;
    pre-revolution, 28
People's Courts, 93–4, 209–10, 212,
    215
Perm region, 76
Pervuhin, M. G., 145
Petrograd, soviet of, 58, 59; *see also*
    St. Petersburg, Leningrad
Pioneers (children's organisation),
    157
planning and budgeting, 67–8, 217,
    236–9
  in industry, 193–6
  rigidities of, 110, 194–6
  State Committee for, *see* Gosplan
Plekhanov, 187
plots of land, personal, of collective
    farmers, 200; taxation of, 106,
    241
Podgorny, N. V., 107
Poland, 63
police, 205–6; secret of revolution
    (*Che-ka*), 47, 205; Tsarist, 25,
    28
political education, *see* education
politics, defined, 21
politburo, 144–5, 235
Ponomarenko, P. K., 145
poor committees of the, 61, 62
population, figures for, 23, 76–7; and
    representation, 89–90
populists, (*narodnik*), supported by
    Marx, 34
Pravda, 57, 186–7, 219
predictability, desire for, 53, 184
press the 186–7, 219–20
  criticisms in, of illegal practices,
    196; of judges, 216; of party
    officials, 173, 179, 219; of plan-
    ning rigidities, 194–5; of re-
    search subjects, 227; of soviets,
    124–5, 219
  letters to, 219, 243
  the party and, 139, 142, 155, 186,
    188–9, 229

as source of information about
Russia, 19, 53
see also Izvestia, Pravda
Primorski (Litoral) territory, 73, 177–178
printing, 83, 230
prisons, 28, 208, 247
Procurator-General (Soviet), 142, 207, 211–12
(of Tsars), 25
procurator service, 83, 206, 207–8, 247
and collective farms, 198, 199
and courts, 211, 213
and local soviets, 125
military and transport, 207, 208
production administrations, collective-state farm, 75, 180, 202
Production Committees, State, 129
profit, linking of managers' bonuses to, 194
proletariat
alliance of, with peasants, 35, 57, 61
dictatorship of, 33, 36, 56, 81
Lenin on, 35; Marx and Engels on, 33
pre-revolution, 29
representation of, in soviets, 92
propaganda and agitation
Lenin on, 187
party departments for, 140, 153–4, 187, 188
property, state and private, 248
provisional government (1917), 36, 58
Public Order, Ministry for Preservation of, *see* Internal Affairs, Ministry of
purges
of party (1921), 46, 160; (1930s), 49, 81, 144, 162–3 (1950s), 165
of trade union leaders (1929), 217
violent phase, 49–50

questions to ministers or government, 119
quotas, of produce from collective farms, 200

railways, building of, 23; ministerial responsibility for, 126
rank, in armed forces, 232–3

regions (*oblastji*)
administrative, 25, 72, 73
autonomous, 65–7, 70
deputies of, in Soviet of Nationalities, 66, 69
religion, party members and, 170
reprimand as penalty, 171, 248
republics, autonomous and union, 65–7, 69–71, 116n
constitutions of, 65, 80, 86–7
deputies of, in Soviet of Nationalities, 66, 89
Ministries of, 65, 130–1
the party in, 136–7
Supreme Soviets of, 90
research, 226, 228, 230n
responsibility
of chairmen of soviets, 116, 124, 125n
of Ministers, 134
of party officials, 173
personal, in collective administration, 77, 78, 79
revenue, 102, 241–2
revolution
(of 1905), 31–2, 35
(of 1917, 'February'), 35–6
(of 1917, 'October'), 36, 41–5; the party as embodiment of tradition of, 190
rights of citizens under constitution, and circumvention of, 83–84
roads, building and repair of, 103, 242
rural locality (*selo*), 73–4
Russian Soviet Federated Socialist Republic (R.S.F.S.R.), 64, 65, 66, 70–1, 130–1, 136–7
Academy of Sciences in, 228
autonomous regions and republics in, 70–1, 87
constitution of, 80
Ministries of, 130–1
the party in, 136–7, 154, 166
soviets of, local, 100; Supreme, 90, 101, 103–4, 114
Russians, 23, 44; dominance of, 51, 68, 166
Russo-Japanese war (1905), 31
Ryzhov, N. S., 117

Saburov, M. Z., 145

St. Petersburg, 22, 32, 56; *see also* Petrograd, Leningrad
schools
  boarding, 225, 228
  elementary and middle, 223, 224, 228
  fees at higher (1940–56), 86, 225
  local soviets and, 108, 131–3
  ministry control, 126–7, 220–1
  party political, 154–5
  'of rural and working youth', 224
sciences
  Academy of, 228
  natural, 227
  social, 155, 227
Science and Technology
  State Committee for, 128
scientists, 227, 229, 230
secession, right of, 64, 70, 84
secretaries
  of local soviet executive committees, 115, 116
  of party organisations, 138, 140, 154, 174
  (first), 114–15, 140, 167, 172, 183; (General), 149
  of Praesidium of Supreme Soviet, 104, 113, 121
'sections' (precursors of standing commissions), 102
security, national, preoccupation with, 43–4, 232, 251
  under Tsars, 23; *see also* State Security
serfs, 24, 25–6; emancipation of, 26, 29
settlements (*posjolok*), 74, 76, 77
Shcherbitski, V. V., 148
Shelepin, A. N., 147, 152
Shepilov, D. T., 147
Shvernik, N. M.
  chairman of Central Council of Trade Unions, 217
  member of Praesidium of party Central Committee (*politburo*), 145, 152
Siberia
  autonomous regions and republics in, 70, 71
  as penal colony, 22, 25
  Russian acquisition of, 22, 23
Social Democrat Party, 31, 34, 56, 57, 137, 158–9; *see also* Bolsheviks, Mensheviks
social insurance, 216, 217, 218
Social Revolutionary Party, 34, 36, 46, 57, 59
  in rural areas, 57, 58, 61, 73, 158–159
social sciences, Academy of, 155
  research in, 227
social security
  local soviets and, 75, 131–2
  republican Ministries for, 67, 131
  trade unions and, 216, 217, 218
societies, in the constitution of 1936, 84, 94; licences for formation of, 220
South Ossetian autonomous region, 71
Soviet of Nationalities (one house of Supreme Soviet), 66, 89, 97, 99
  elections to, 82, 89, 93
  Ministers in, 118–19
  standing commissions of, 102
Soviet, Supreme (federal)
  and budget, 102, 240
  business of, 101, 103–7
  chairmanship of, 101
  in constitution of 1936, 82, 85, 86, 99
  meetings of, 99–100
  members of, 98, 104, 111
  military representation in, 89, 98
  and Ministers, 118–19
  Praesidium of, chairman of, 78, 112–13; as 'collective president', 77; in constitution of 1936, 85, 86, 93, 99, 121; and Council of Ministers, 116, 121–2, 133; legislation by, 104, 120–1; and republics, 68; secretary of, 104, 113; and Supreme Soviet, 85, 104, 125
  published Acts of, 18, 87
  two houses of, *see* Soviet of Nationalities, Soviet of the Union
Soviet of the Union (one house of Supreme Soviet), 66, 89, 97
  elections to, 89
  minister in, 118–19
  standing commissions of, 102
Soviets, Congresses of
  All-Russian, 46, 58–9, 61, 62, 72;

Central Executive Committee
of, 59, 65, 66; Praesidium of, 66,
77

All-Union, 66, 81, 82, 87, 238;
Central Executive Committee
of, 66, 82; Praesidium of, 66,
68, 77

at republican and lower levels,
62–3, 68, 72

soviets, local
beginnings of, 32, 41, 56–63
budgets of, 240
business of, 107–8
committees of the poor and, 61, 62
elections to, 93–5
executive committees of, 59, 60–1,
103, 109, 112, 114–16, 122–5,
131, 162, 175
as 'local authorities', 91, 123
meetings of, 100–1, 102, 108, 109
members of, 91, 97, 98–9
the party and, 97, 167, 177, 178
standing commissions of, 102–3
in villages, 73, 75, 76, 103, 107–8,
114

Soviets, Supreme (republican), 63,
65, 90, 93, 100, 101
Praesidia of, 112–14, 116

Special Sections (for Counter-Intelligence), in armed forces, 232

'speculation', 244, 248

Spiridonov, I. V., 101

sponsors, for members of party, 159,
160, 161, 162, 164

sports clubs, taxation of, 241

staffing (cadres)
departments for, in Ministries and
enterprises, 180
education for, 155, 227
party responsibility for, 153–4,
180–2

Stalin, 41–2, 47–52
and agricultural collectivisation,
49
Commissar for Nationalities, 65
and constitution of 1936, 70, 81,
82, 87
decision-taking by, 55
in elections, 94
General Secretary of party, 47–8,
148
Khrushchov on, 50, 51, 84, 144

and machine-tractor stations, 201
on national rights 63
official image of, 252
and old Bolsheviks, 163
on party, 169, 183, 187
and politburo, 144, 145, 174
in revolution, 41–2
rise to power of, 47–50, 141, 160
and scientists, 230
and trade unions, 79, 217
on withering away of state, 36–7,
38

Stalin constitution, see constitution
of 1936

Stalingrad, defence of, 51

State, Councils of (1810), 24; (1905),
32

state, withering away of 33, 36–7, 38

State Arbitration (Gosarbitrazh), 209

State Bank, 128, 204–5, 242

State Committees, 127–8, 129

State Control, Ministry of (1940–57),
204

State Planning Committee, see Gosplan

State   Political   Administration
(G.P.U.), 205

State Production Committees, 129

State Security
Commissariat (Ministry) of, 206
Committee of, attached to Coun-
cil of Ministers, 128, 206, 231

Statistical Administration, Central,
116, 235

'storming', 245

subordination,   (podchinenie),   68,
124, 191–2; dual, 60–1, 203

suffrage, 92–3; (1905–17), 32; (1917–
1936), 92

supervision
Acts of, by Supreme Soviet, 105
of administration under Tsars, by
Procurator-General, 25
of lower by higher organisations
Councils of Ministers, 121;
(party committees), 139; (soviet
executive committees), 73–4, 124
by Ministry collegia, 134
by Party Control Committee, 151
of soviets and enterprises by party,
177–9, 182–3
system of, 203–8, 246; wasteful of
manpower, 184

see also inspection
Supreme Courts, 68, 209–12, 215
Supreme Soviet (federal), *see* Soviets, Supreme
Supreme Soviets (republican), *see* Soviets, Supreme
Suslov, M. A., 149, 152
Sverdlovsk region, 76
sympathisers (with party), groups of, 162, 164

Tadjikistan, 69, 71, 74
Supreme Soviet of, 90
targets of plans, 237, 239
Tatar autonomous republic, 70, 74
Tatars, 22, 23
taxation, 241–2, 244; of collective farms, 200, 241; State Bank and, 204; village soviets and, 108
teachers, training of, 224, 227–8
technical education, strength and weakness, 227, 230
technicums, 224
territories (*krai*), 72, 74
theory, importance attached to, by party, 40–1
towns, population of, 77; pre-revolution, 28–9; soviets in, 72, 73, 74, 76, 108–9, 123
trade unions, 94, 142, 212–13, 216–18
Central Council of, 217, 218
in factory management, 79, 217
taxation of, 241
Transcaucasia, 66, 69
transport, Ministries for, 78, 126, 130–1; courts for, 211
Trotski, 39, 56–7; and Lenin, 47, 57; and Stalin, 55
Turkestan, 69
Turkmenistan, 69, 71, 74
the party in, 137; Supreme Soviet of, 90
turnover tax, 241
Tuva autonomous republic, 70

Udmurt autonomous republic, 70
uezd (districts), 27, 72, 161
Ukraine, 63, 66, 74
the party in, 144, 147–8, 165
soviets of, 90
Ukrainians, 23
Unified State Political Administration (O.G.P.U.), 205

Union of Soviet Socialist Republics, 63–72
universities, 224, 226–7, 228
uprava (administration), of town *duma*, 28; of *zemstvo*, 27
urbanisation, 43, 76, 250
Uzbekistan, 69, 70, 74
Five-Year Plan for development of cotton-growing in, 238
the party in, 137
Supreme Soviet of, 90, 114

vice-chairmen
of collective farms, 181, 198
of Council of Ministers, 116, 118
of Praesidia of Supreme Soviets, 112–13, 114
of soviet executive committees, 114
village soviets, 73, 75, 76, 107–8
committees of the poor and, 61, 62
executive committees of, 114
Volga German autonomous republic, 71
Volkov, A. P., 101
volostj (groupings of villages), 26, 27, 28, 72
Voronezh region, 124
Voroshilov, K. E., 234
voters, absent, 93
voting, age of eligibility for, 92, 93; in soviets, 104

war, of 1914–18, 32; of 1941–5, 50–51
war communism (1917–21), 45–6; return to, in first Five-Year Plan, 48–9
women, in the party, 166
'workers', members of soviets from, 96–8; party members from, 159, 160–1, 163
'workers' settlements', 74, 76, 77
Writers, Union of Soviet, 229

Yakut, autonomous republic, 70
Yezhov, 49
youth organisations, *see Komosol*, Pioneers
Yugoslavia, 65, 167, 184n

zampolit (deputies for political matters to commanding officers), 156, 231–2

Zavenjagin, A. P., 118

Zemski Sobor (Assembly of the Land), 24

zemstvos (land assemblies), 27, 44; leader of Union of, as head of provisional government, 36

Zhdanov, Andrei, 187
  death of, 52, 148; and Stalin, 49, 51

Zhukov, Marshal G. K., 52, 116, 147, 233

Zinoviev, 50, 61

Michael Lewin

RUSSIAN PEASANTS AND SOVIET POWER

Towards the end of 1927, the curious economico-social compromise
known in the U.S.S.R. as N.E.P. entered a period of acute crisis.
The state sector was still small and it faced a vast, though frag-
mented, private sector which dominated agriculture. Lenin had
expected this compromise to last a long time, Bukharin believed
that it could and should continue, but Stalin decided to end it.
However, at the outset he had no alternative policy, and he searched
feverishly for a solution during two critical years of growing tension, finally deciding at the end of 1929 in favour of the policy of
total collectivisation and extremely rapid industrialisation.

It is this dramatic and decisive period that forms the subject of
this book. For the first time in the history of western literature,
these years are examined in depth. The study centres around two
focal points: the Soviet régime and the peasantry. The complex
interrelationship between those two vital factors was a principal
concern of Soviet politics from the first days of the revolution. The
work analyses the social, political, economic and ideological problems of a society in the throes of a great transformation, and every
effort is made to see these questions not only from the urban, or
politician's, point of view, but also from the standpoint of the
peasant. This is not easy since the peasant leaves few written documents behind for historians to study; such works are usually the
work of townsmen and officials. Dr. Lewin, however, was able to
supplement his extensive studies by his own living experience. He
lived in the U.S.S.R. from 1940 to 1946, working in many collective
farms and elsewhere alongside hundreds of peasants, and a mere
dozen or so years after the events described. This adds greatly to
the value of his presentation.

This work should interest not only the Russian specialist, but also
anyone who wants to understand the great events of contemporary
history.

'Dr. Lewin combines mastery of the sources, balanced judgment
and perception in their use, ease and style of exposition, and personal knowledge of Russian peasants, among whom he has lived, to
produce one of the outstanding works of modern history.' *Glasgow
Herald*.

'Mr. Lewin's thorough study is based on a close analysis of contemporary published sources, and he has also utilised the fruits of
Soviet scholarship during the Khrushchev era.' *Economist*.

LONDON: GEORGE ALLEN & UNWIN LTD

GEORGE ALLEN & UNWIN LTD

Head Office
40 Museum Street, London, W.C.1
Telephone: 01-405 8577

Sales, Distribution and Accounts Departments
Park Lane, Hemel Hempstead, Herts.
Telephone: 0442 3244

Athens: 34 Panepistimiou Street
Auckland: P.O. Box 36013, Northcote Central N.4
Barbados: P.O. Box 222, Bridgetown
Bombay: 103–105 Fort Street, Bombay 1
Buenos Aires: Escritorio 454–459, Florida 165
Beirut: Deeb Building, Jeanne d'Arc Street
Calcutta: 285J Bepin Behari Ganguli Street, Calcutta 12
Cape Town: 68 Shortmarket Street
Hong Kong: 105 Wing On Mansion, 26 Hancow Road, Kowloon
Ibadan: P.O. Box 62
Karachi: Karachi Chambers, Mcleod Road
Madras: 2/18 Mount Road, Madras
Mexico: Villalongin 32, Mexico 5, D.F.
Nairobi: P.O. Box 30583
Philippines: P.O. Box 157, Quezon City D-502
Rio de Janeiro: Caixa Postal 2537-Zc-00
Singapore: 36c Prinsep Street, Singapore 7
Sydney N.S.W.: Bradbury House, 55 York Street
Tokyo: C.P.O. Box 1728, Tokyo 100–91
Toronto: 81 Curlew Drive, Don Mills